D0111803

ISBN 978-0-9915285-9-2
Printed and bound in the USA

Library of Congress Catalog
2019907668

Far Out Press
San Francisco, CA

BOOK THREE

BEAUTIFUL

Game of Crones

by Marie D'Abreo

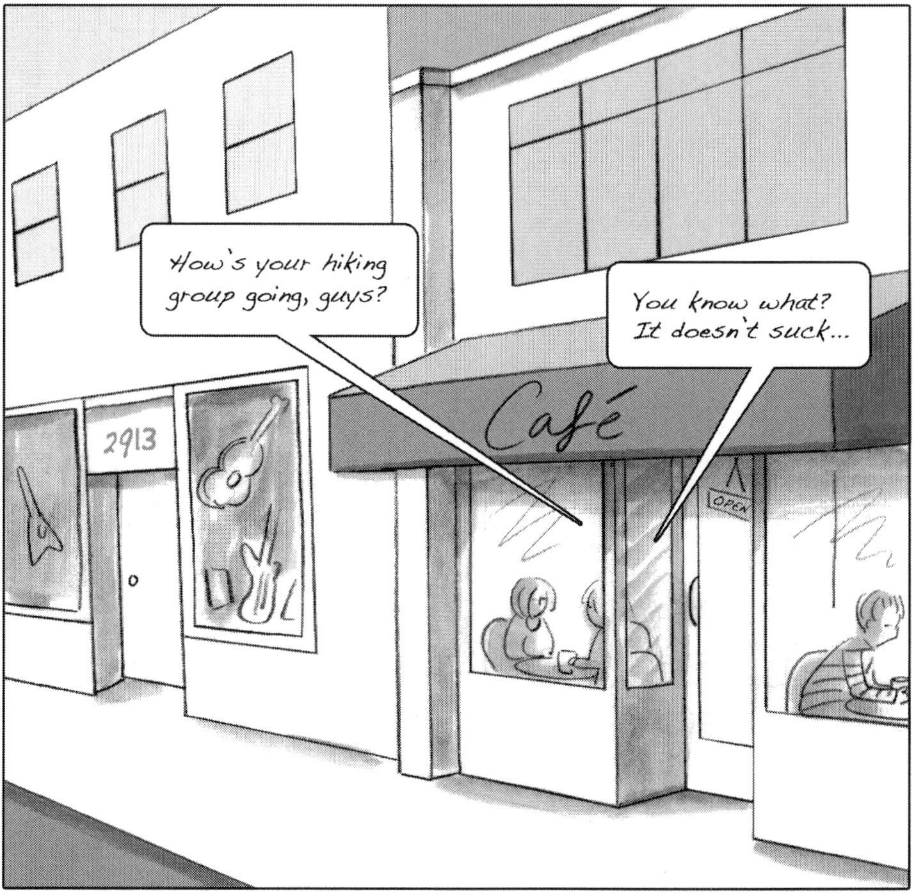
How's your hiking group going, guys?
You know what? It doesn't suck...
Café
2913
OPEN

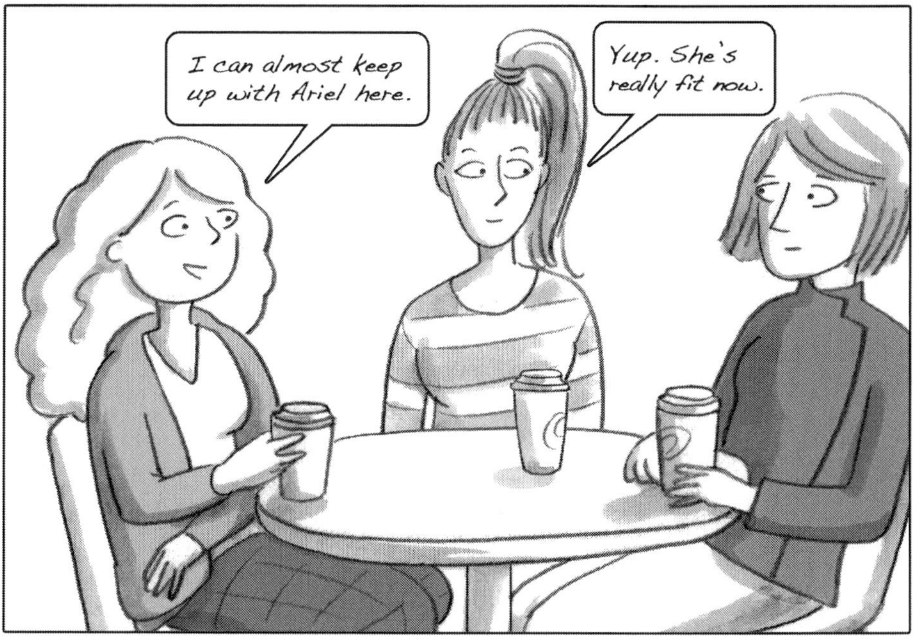
I can almost keep up with Ariel here.
Yup. She's really fit now.

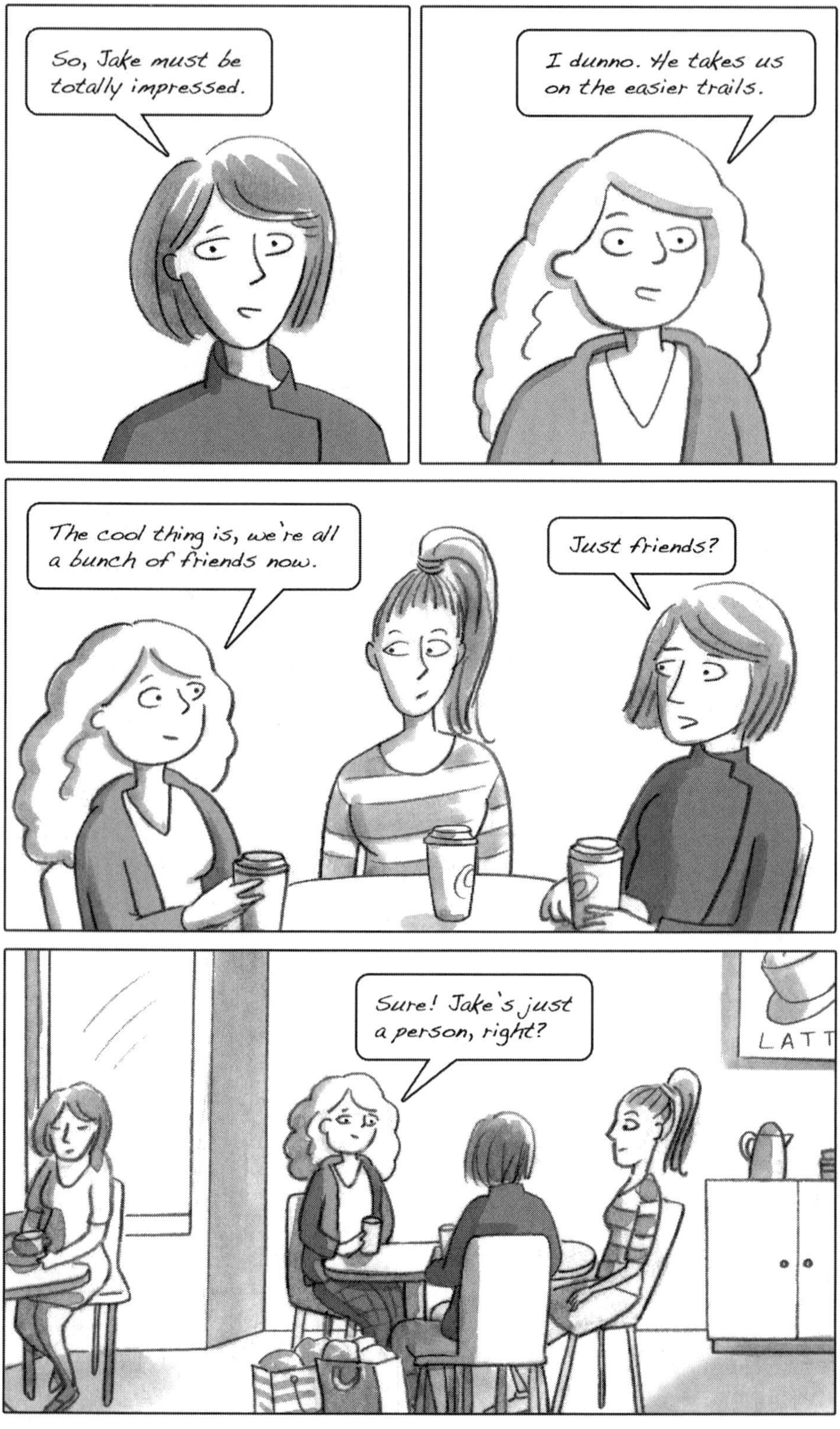
So, Jake must be totally impressed.
I dunno. He takes us on the easier trails.
The cool thing is, we're all a bunch of friends now.
Just friends?
Sure! Jake's just a person, right?
LATT

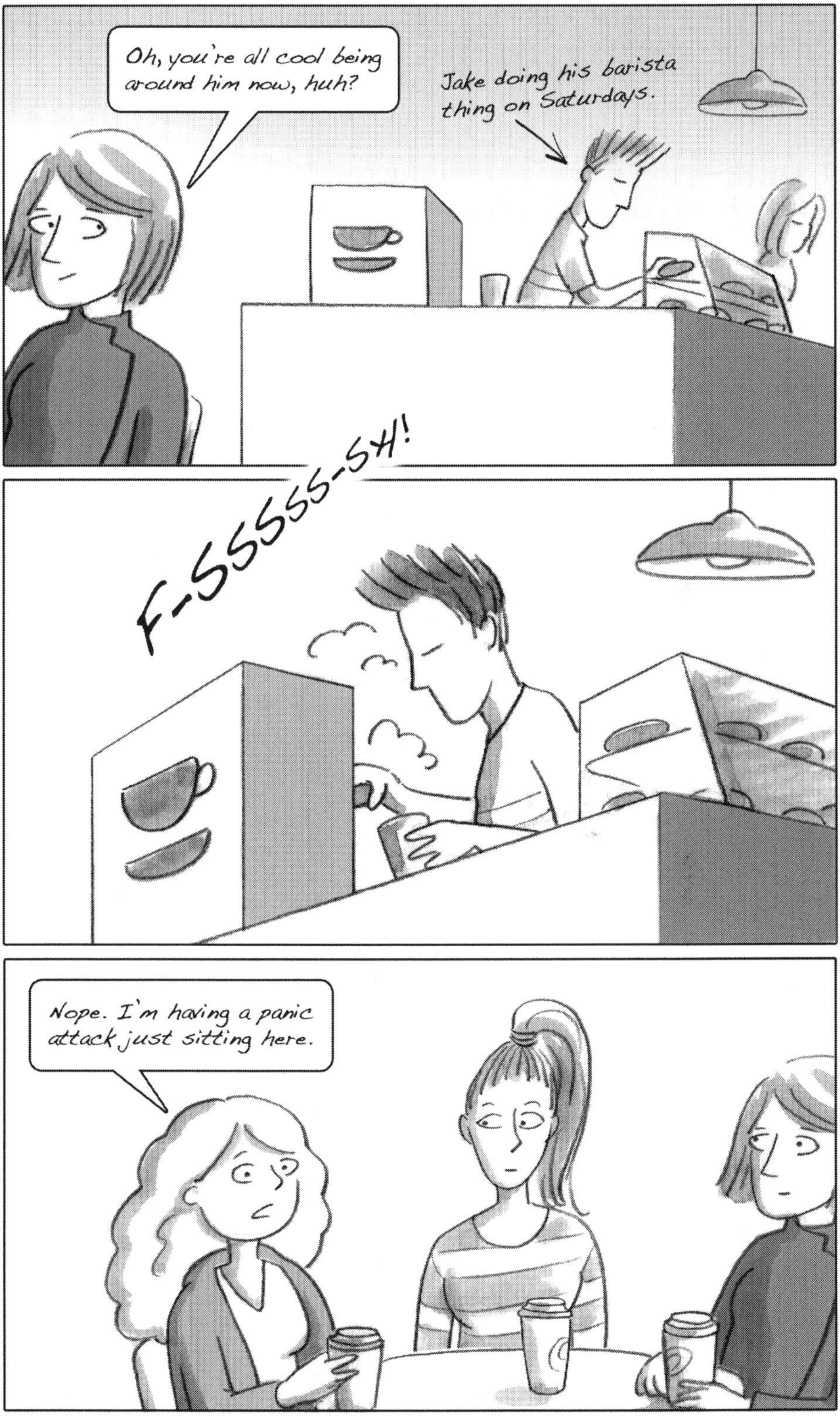
Oh, you're all cool being around him now, huh?
Jake doing his barista thing on Saturdays.
F-SSSSS-SH!
Nope. I'm having a panic attack just sitting here.

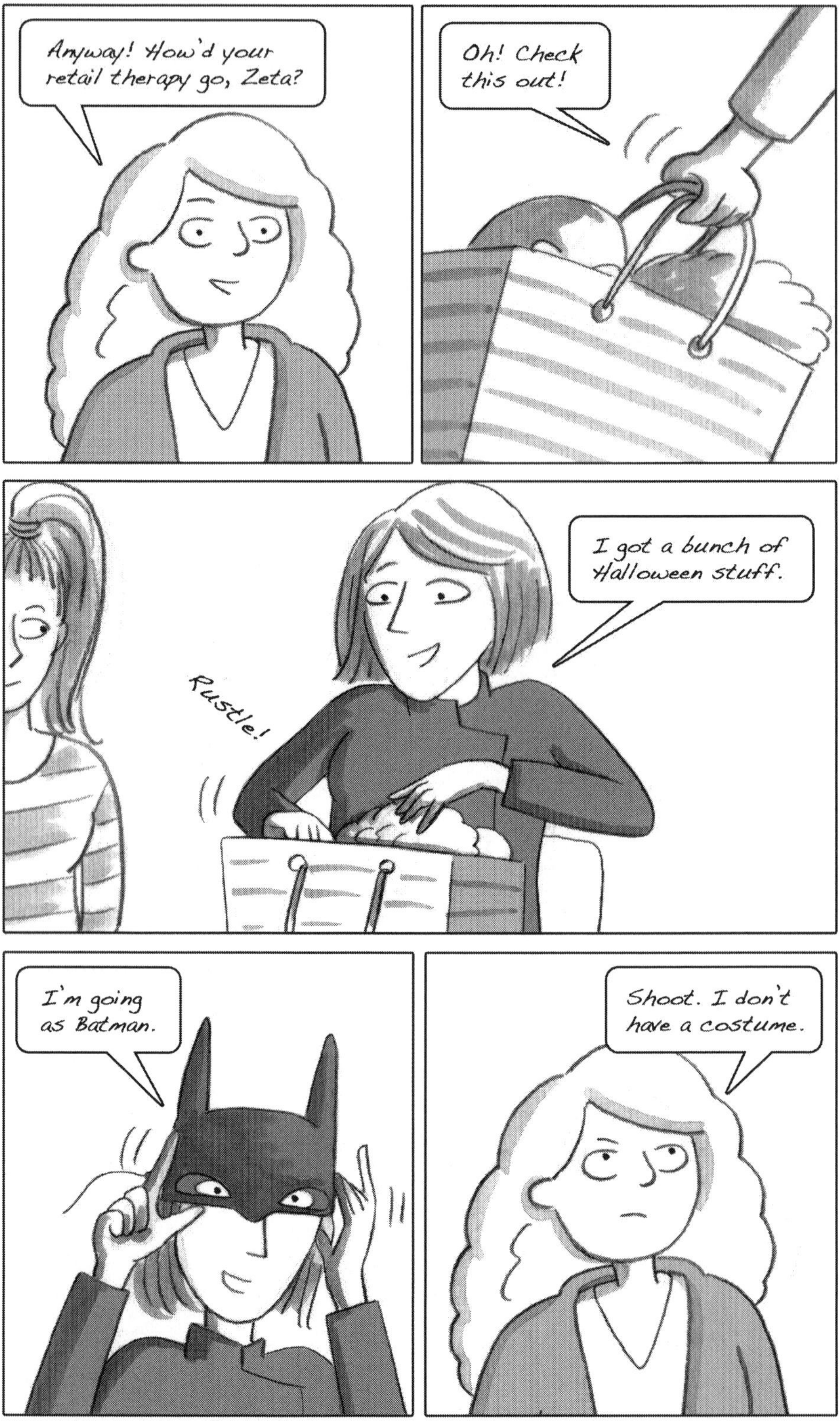
Anyway! How'd your retail therapy go, Zeta?
Oh! Check this out!
I got a bunch of Halloween stuff.
Rustle!
I'm going as Batman.
Shoot. I don't have a costume.

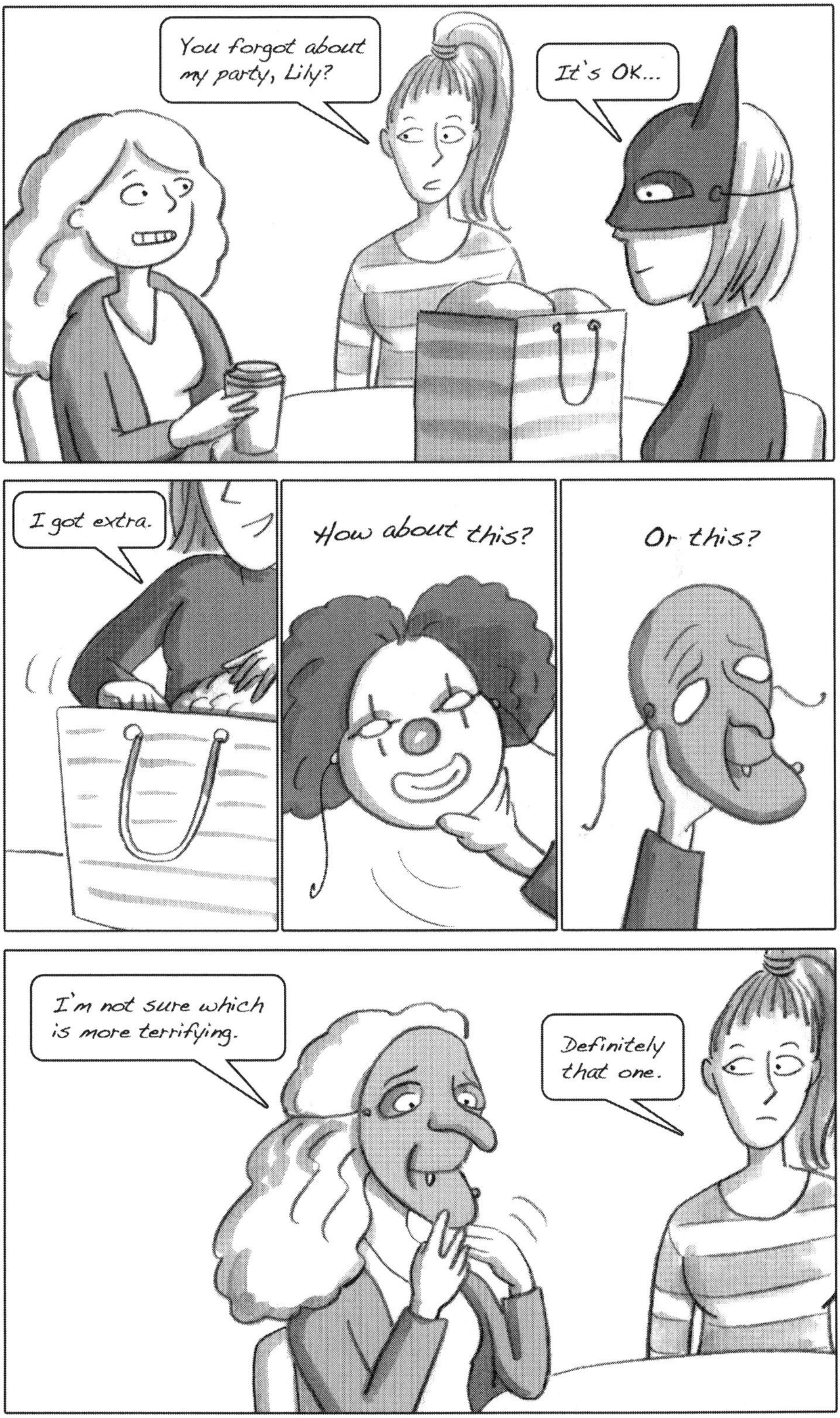
You forgot about my party, Lily?
It's OK...
I got extra.
How about this?
Or this?
I'm not sure which is more terrifying.
Definitely that one.

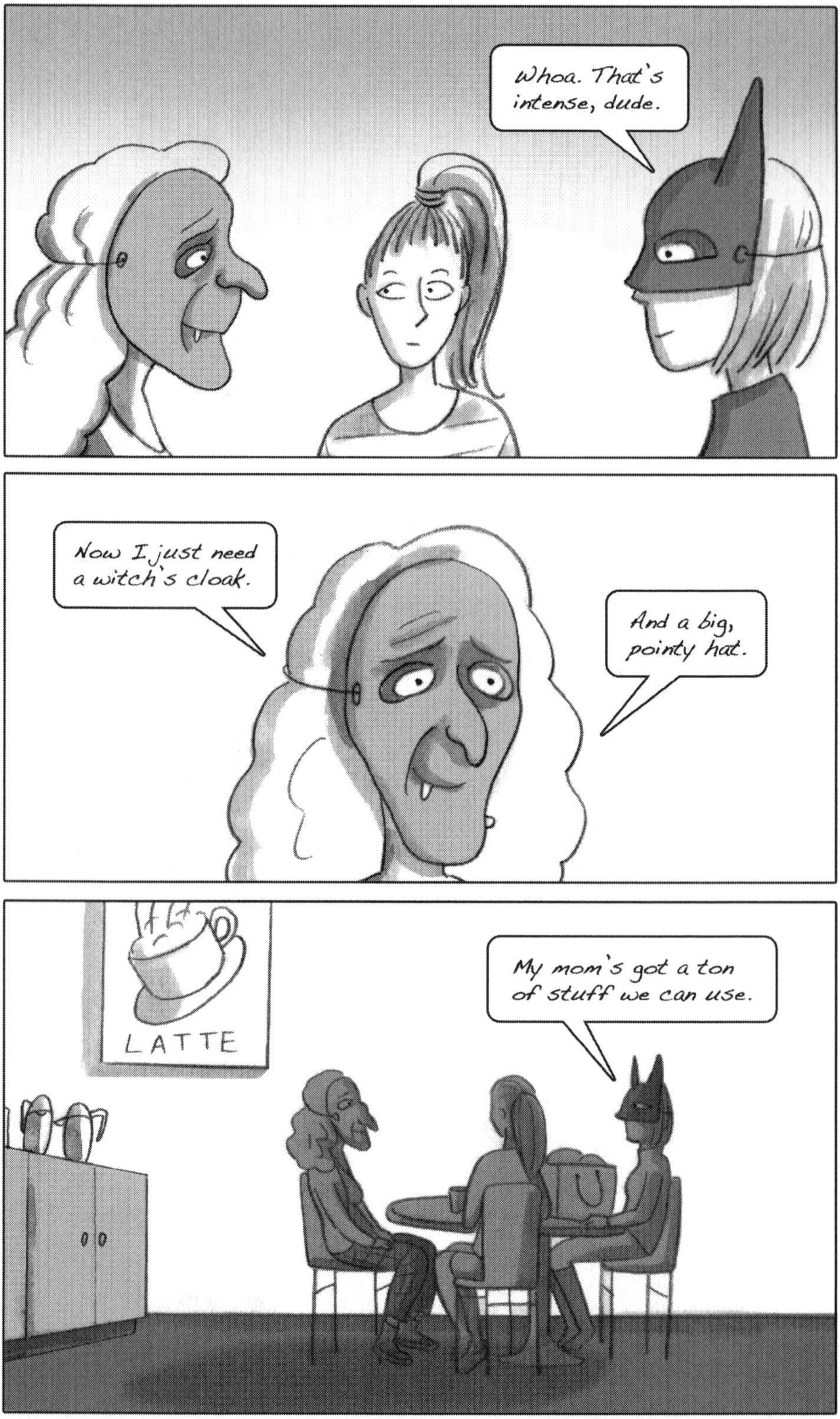
Whoa. That's intense, dude.
Now I just need a witch's cloak.
And a big, pointy hat.
LATTE
My mom's got a ton of stuff we can use.

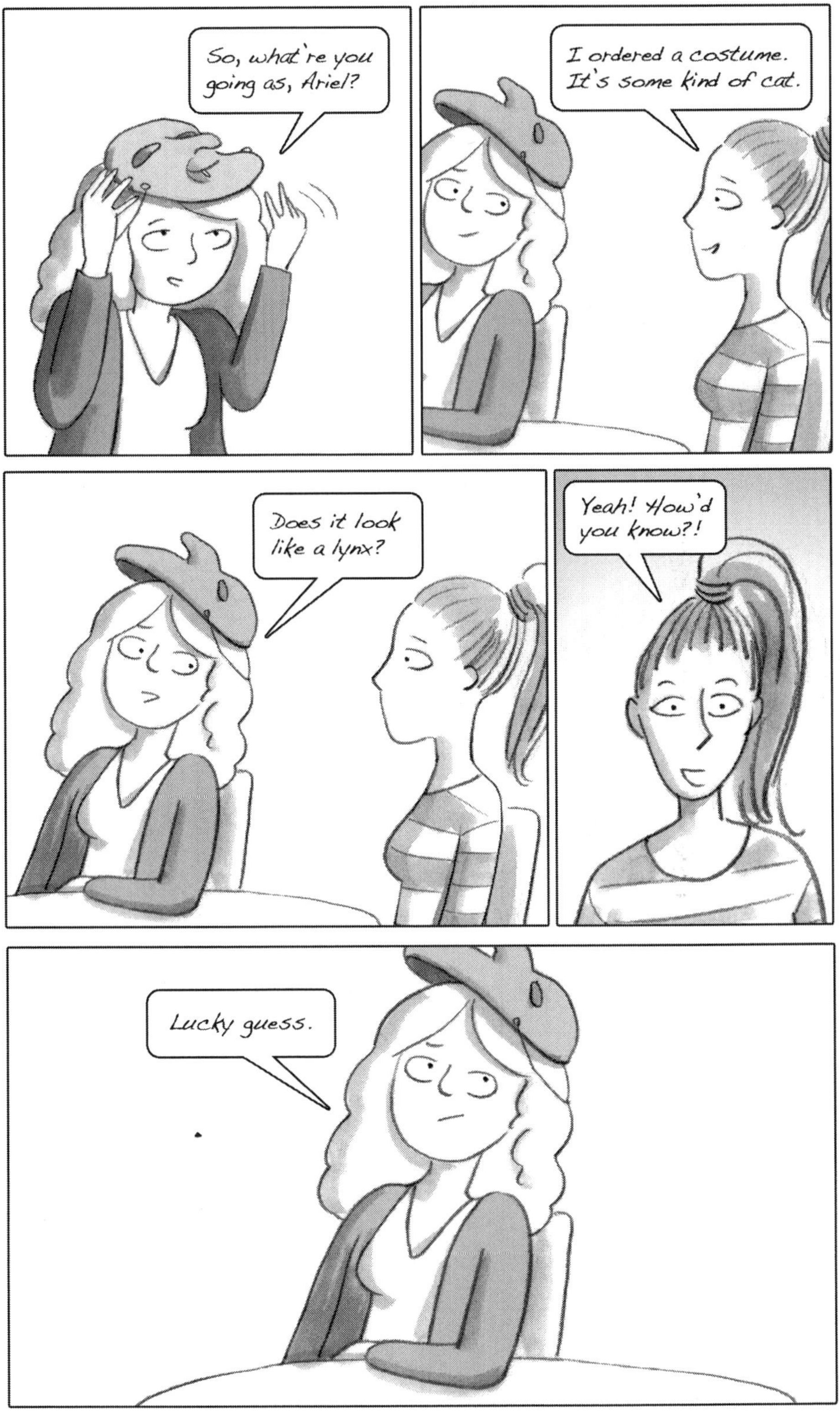
So, what're you going as, Ariel?
I ordered a costume. It's some kind of cat.
Does it look like a lynx?
Yeah! How'd you know?!
Lucky guess.

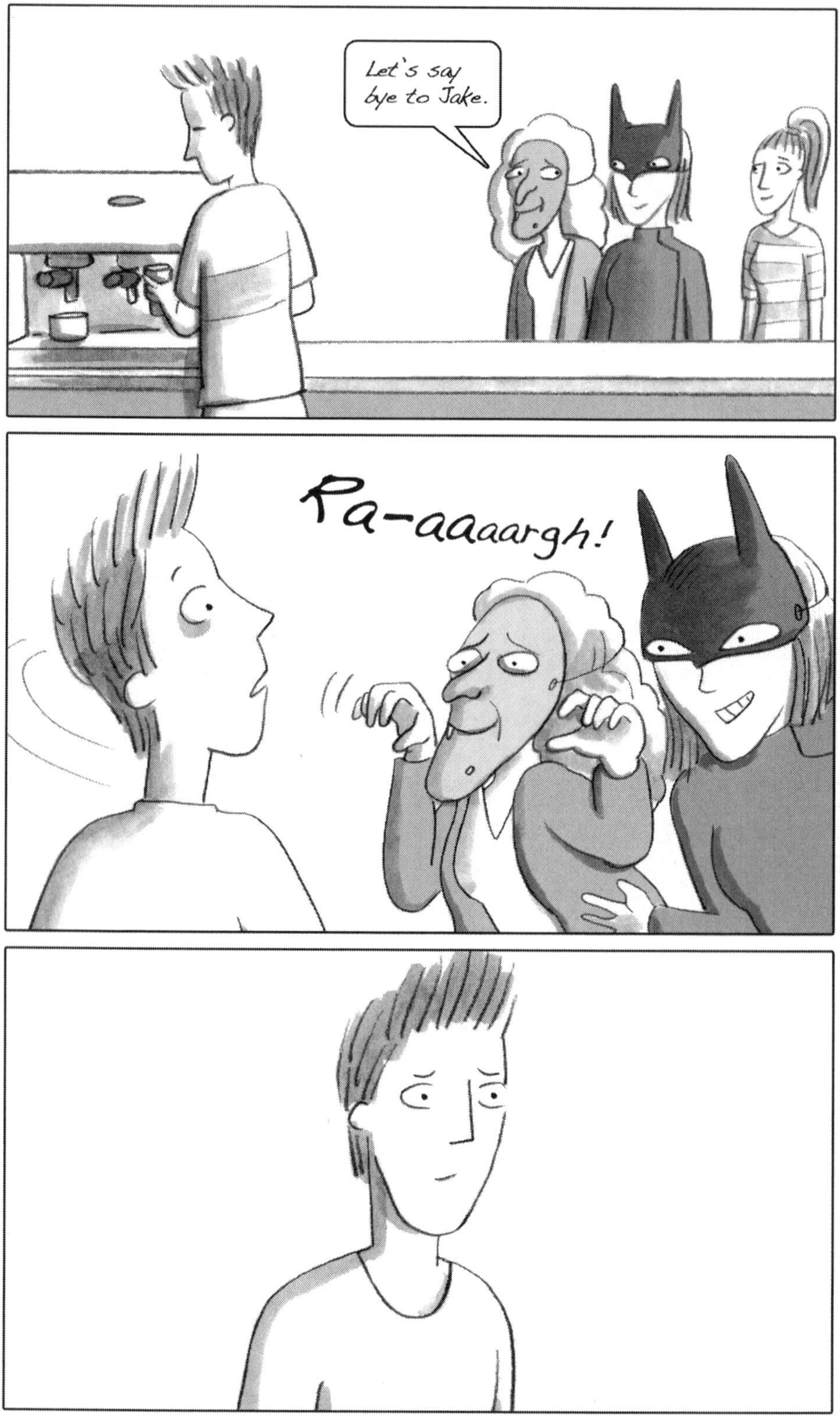
Let's say bye to Jake.
Ra-aaaargh!

Give a man a mask and

he will tell you the truth.

OSCAR WILDE

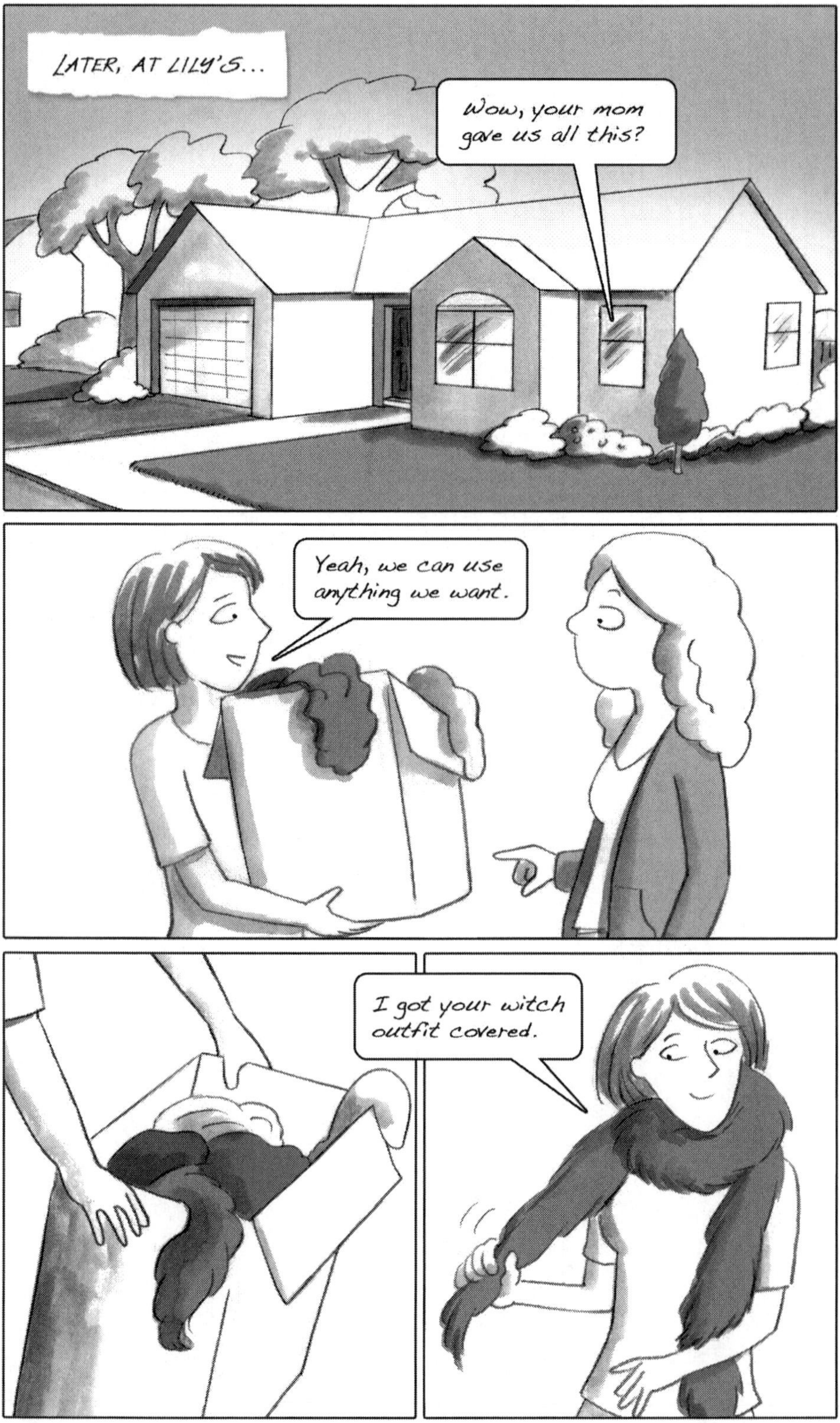
LATER, AT LILY'S...
Wow, your mom gave us all this?
Yeah, we can use anything we want.
I got your witch outfit covered.

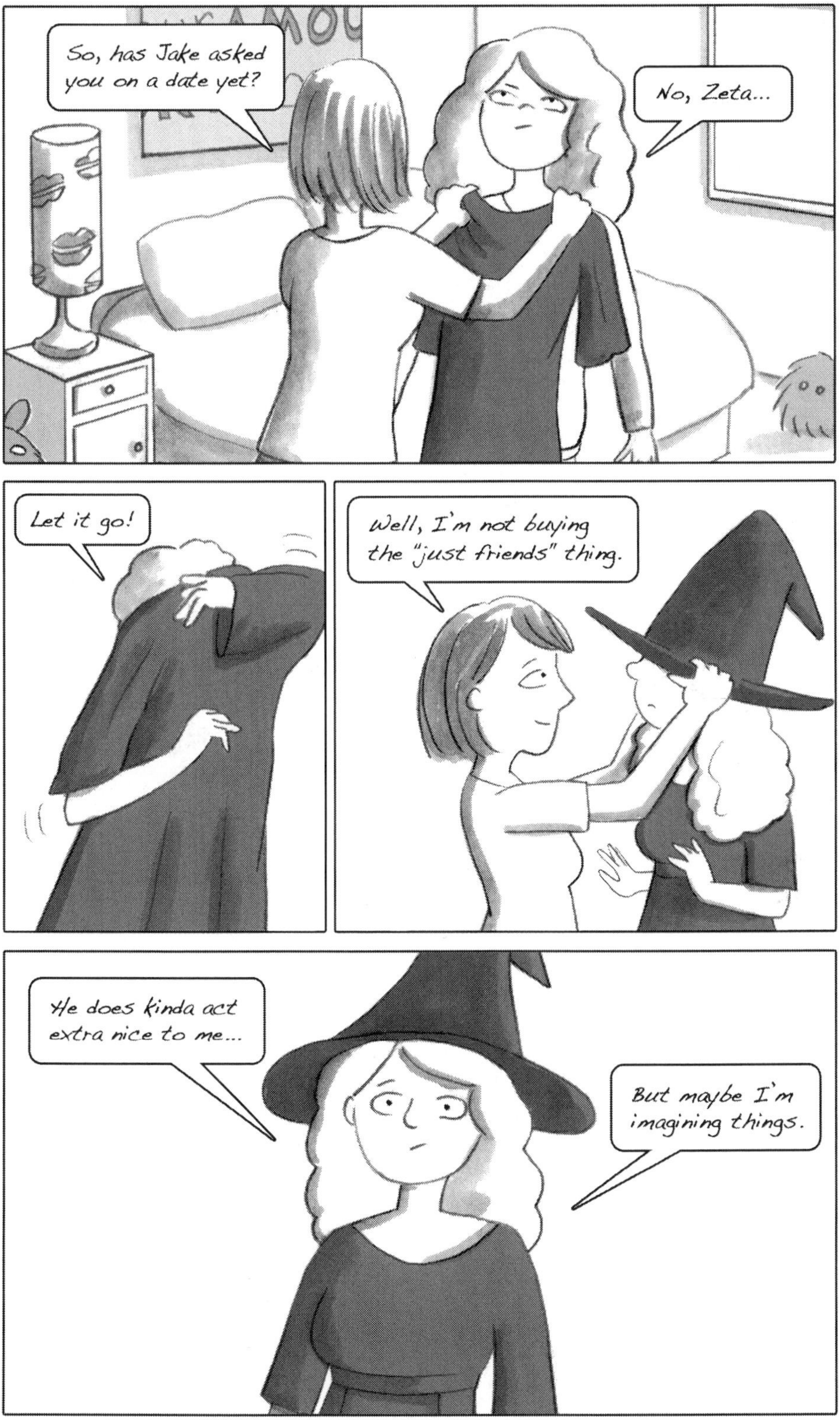
So, has Jake asked you on a date yet?
No, Zeta...
Let it go!
Well, I'm not buying the "just friends" thing.
He does kinda act extra nice to me...
But maybe I'm imagining things.

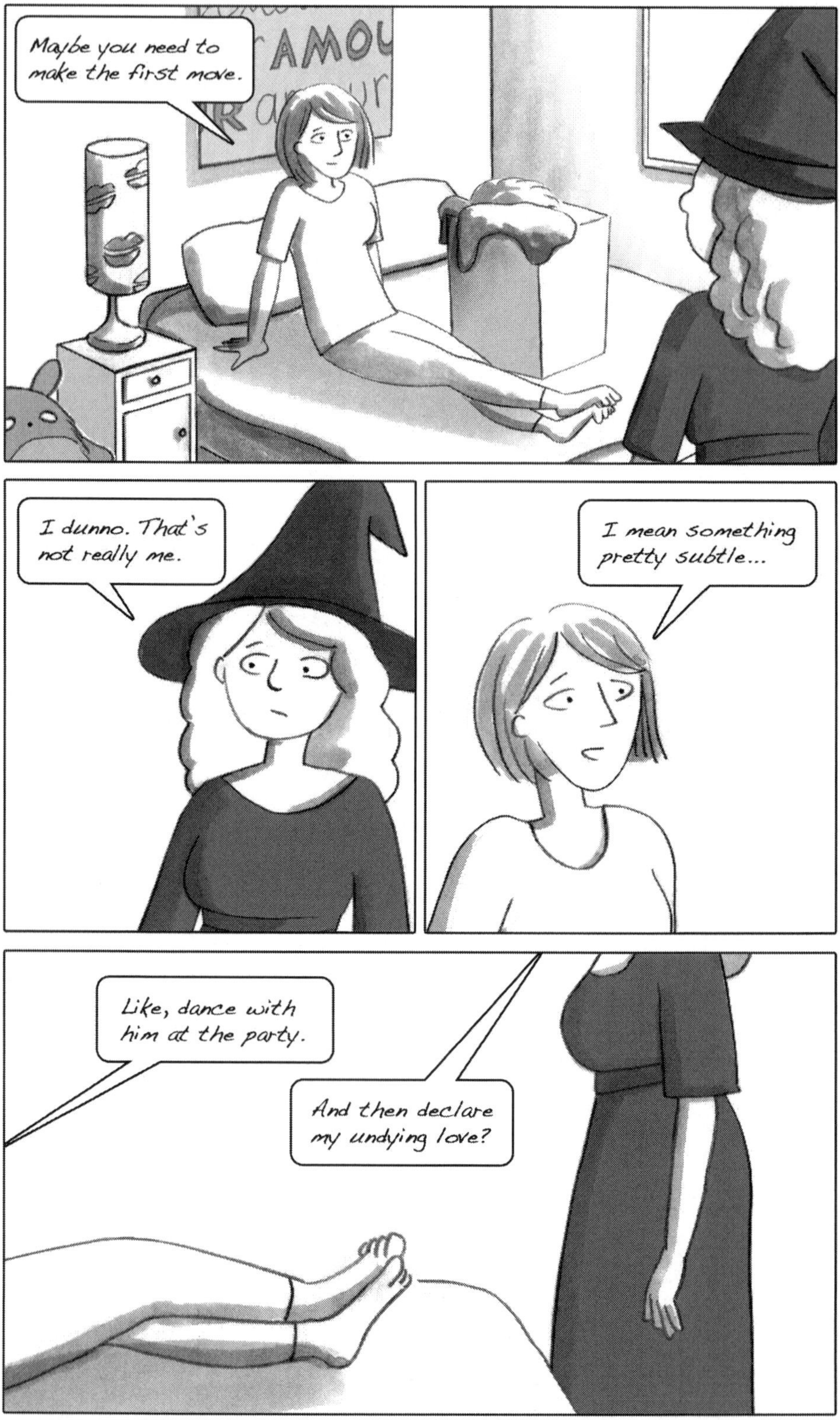
Maybe you need to make the first move.
I dunno. That's not really me.
I mean something pretty subtle...
Like, dance with him at the party.
And then declare my undying love?

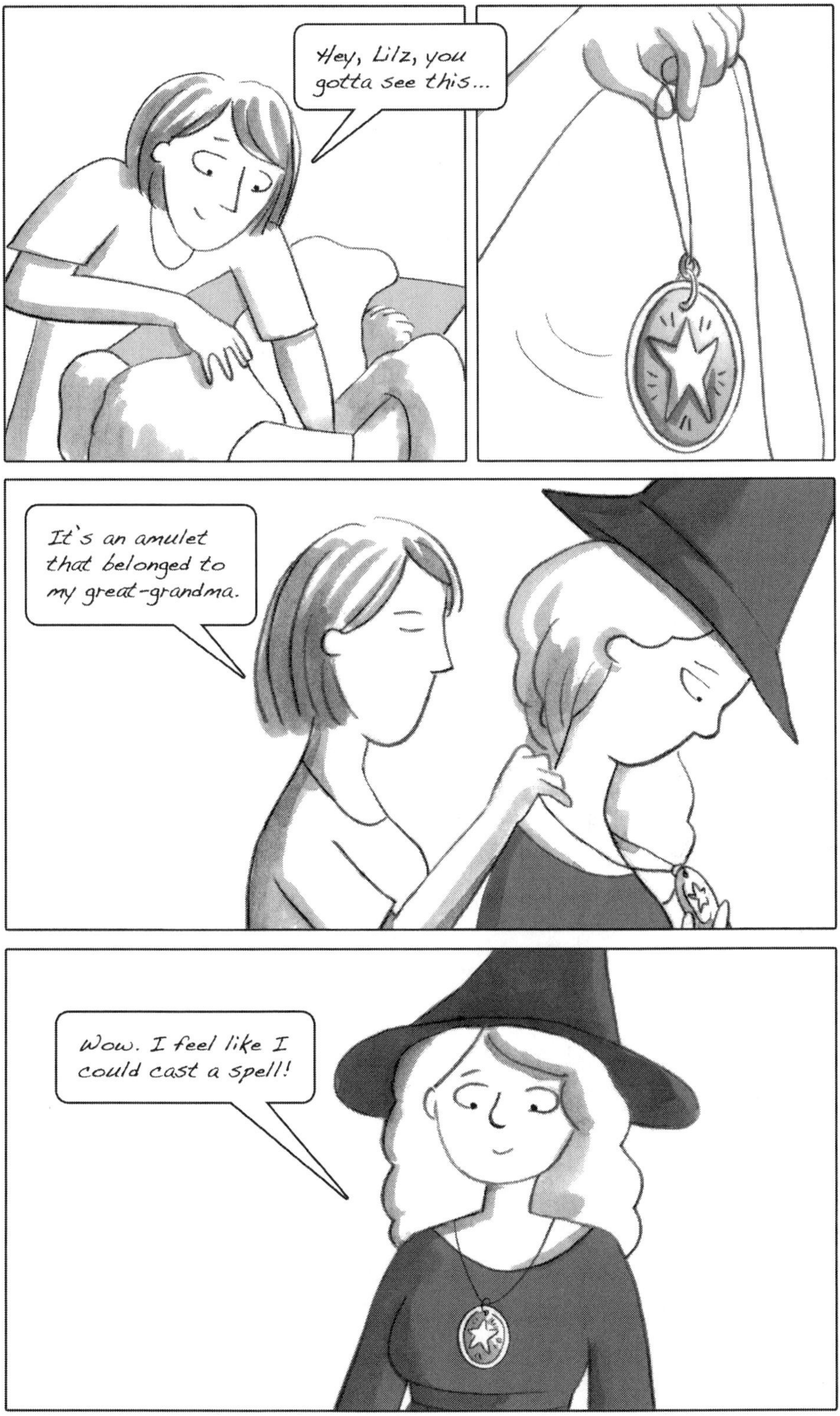
Hey, Lilz, you gotta see this...
It's an amulet that belonged to my great-grandma.
Wow. I feel like I could cast a spell!

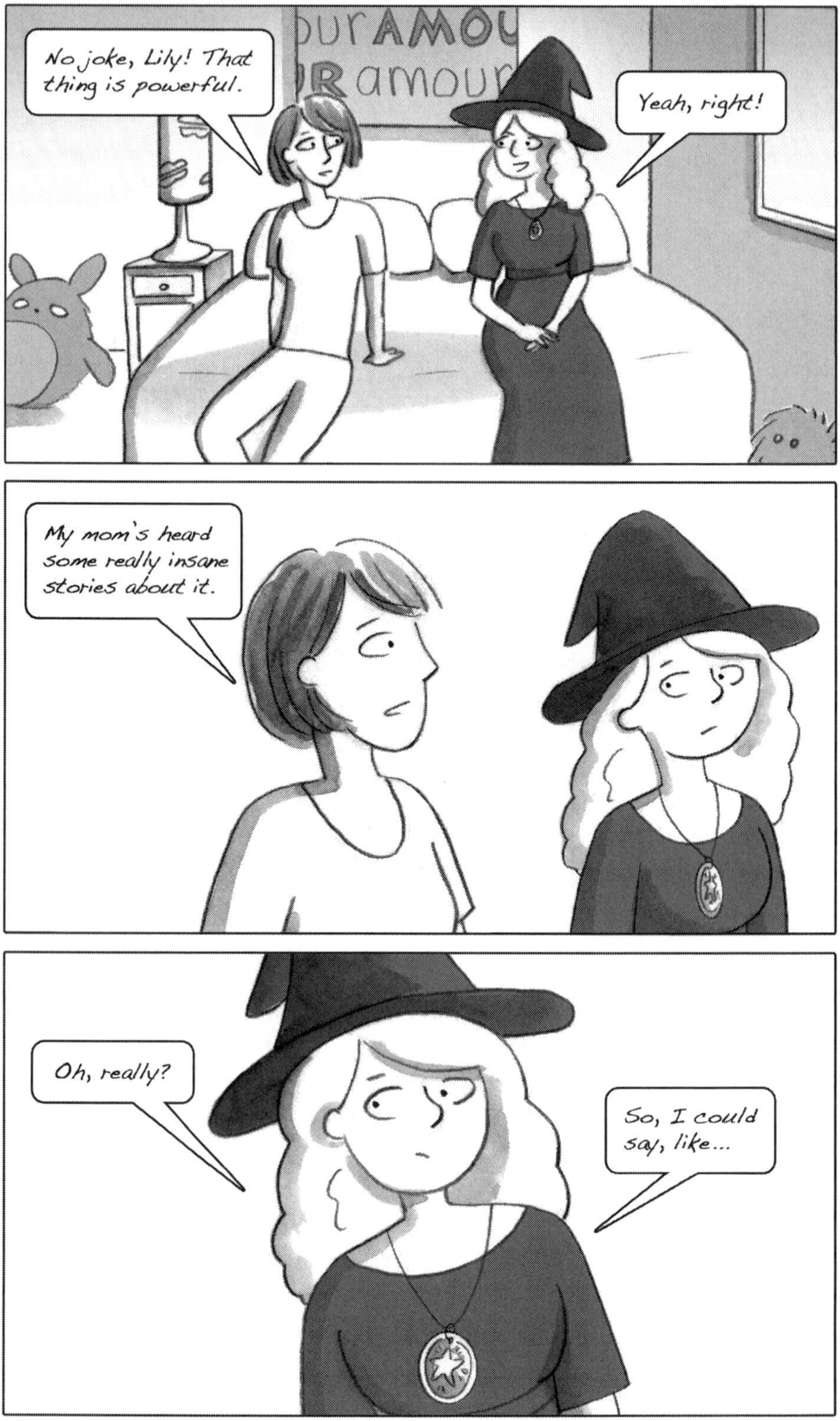
No joke, Lily! That thing is powerful.
Yeah, right!
ourAMOU
Ramour
My mom's heard some really insane stories about it.
Oh, really?
So, I could say, like...

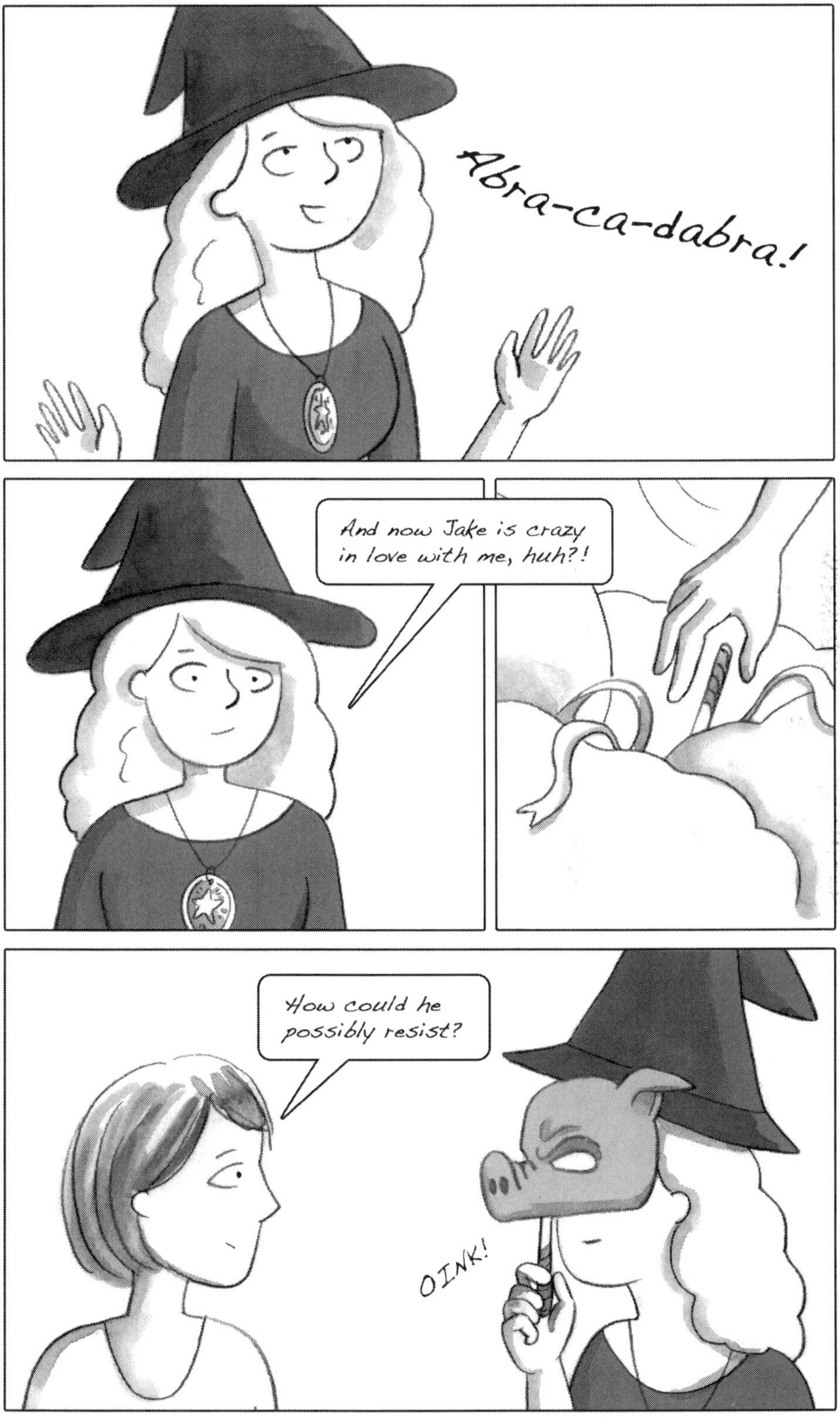
Abra-ca-dabra!
And now Jake is crazy in love with me, huh?!
How could he possibly resist?
OINK!

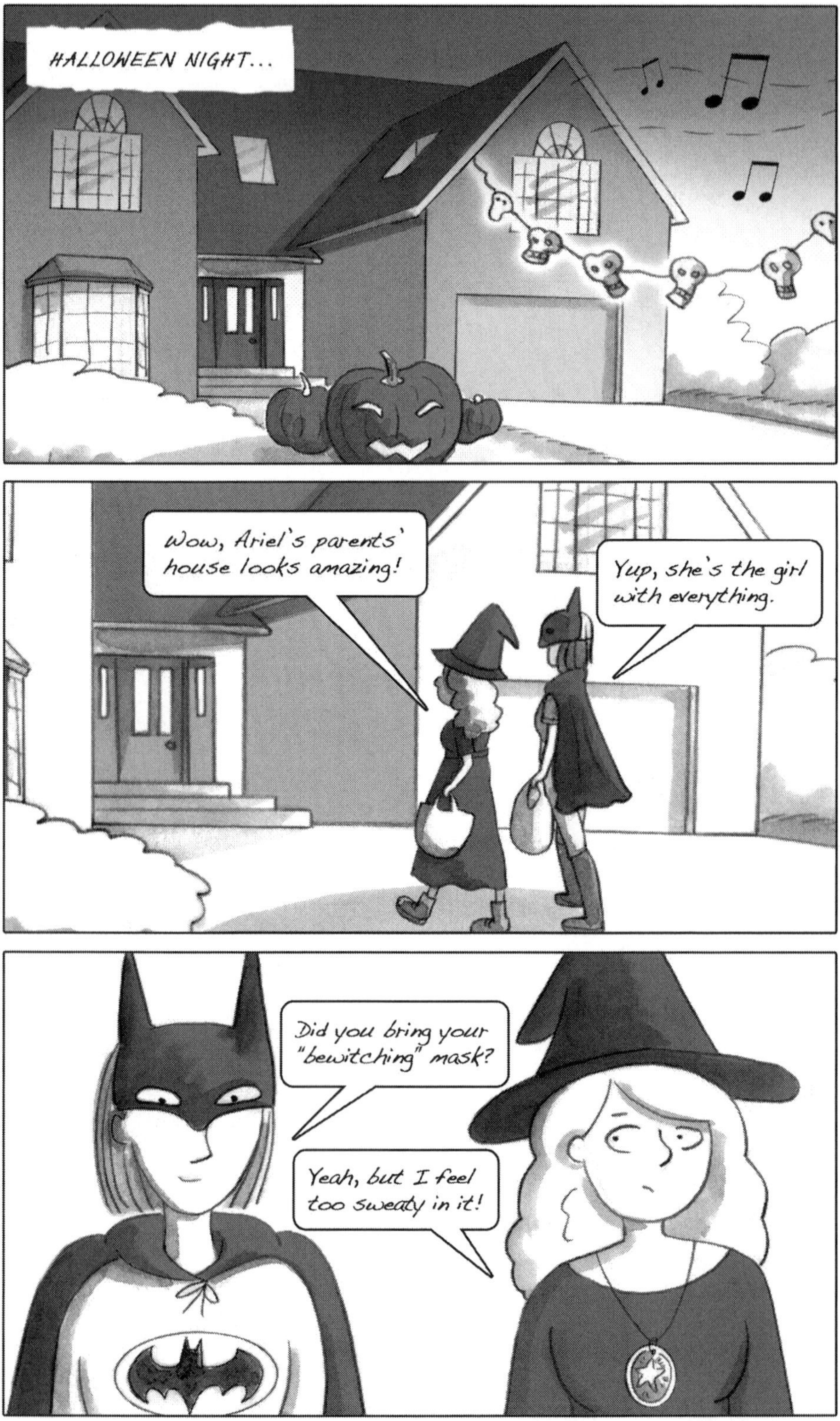
HALLOWEEN NIGHT...
Wow, Ariel's parents' house looks amazing!
Yup, she's the girl with everything.
Did you bring your "bewitching" mask?
Yeah, but I feel too sweaty in it!

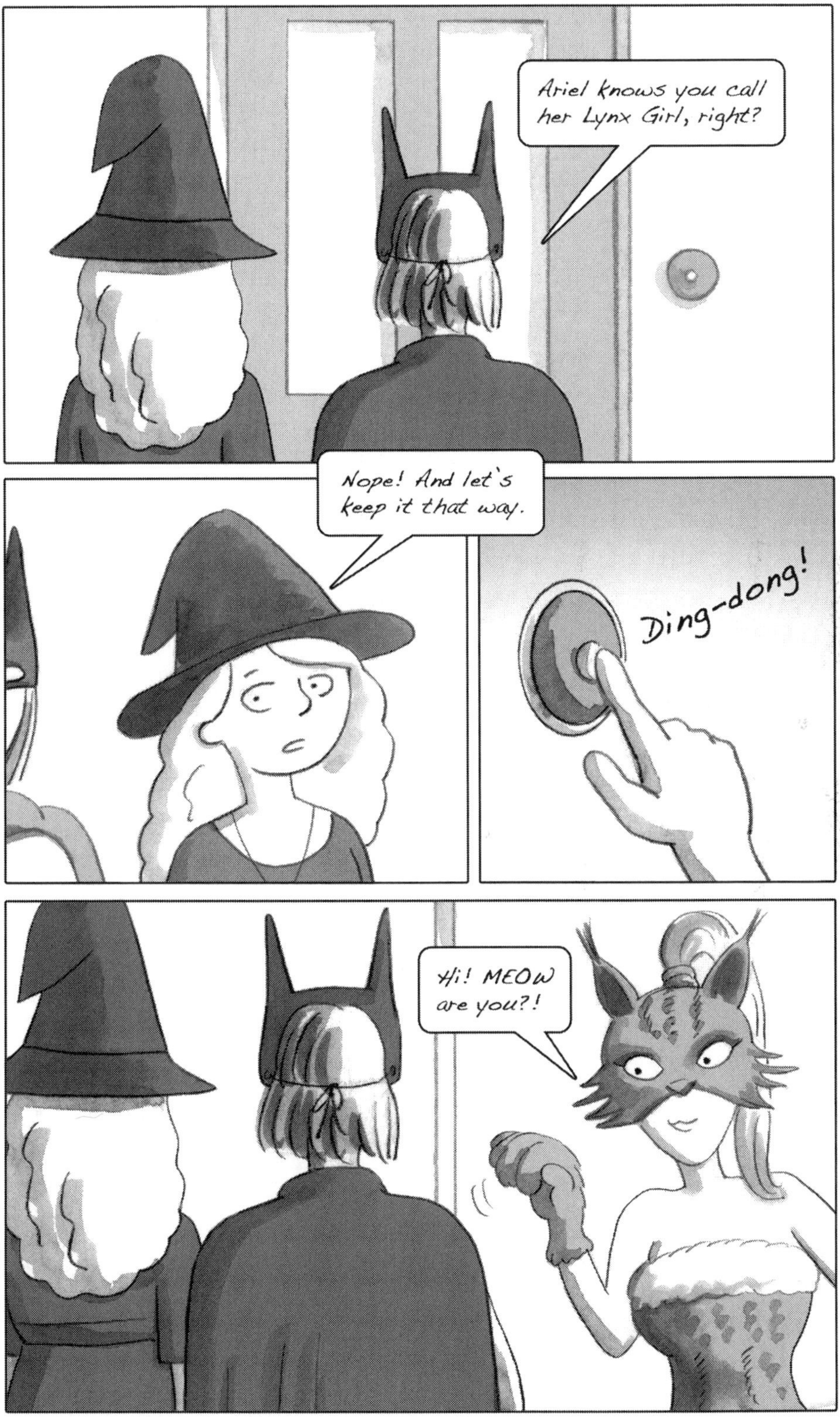
Ariel knows you call her Lynx Girl, right?
Nope! And let's keep it that way.
Ding-dong!
Hi! MEOW are you?!

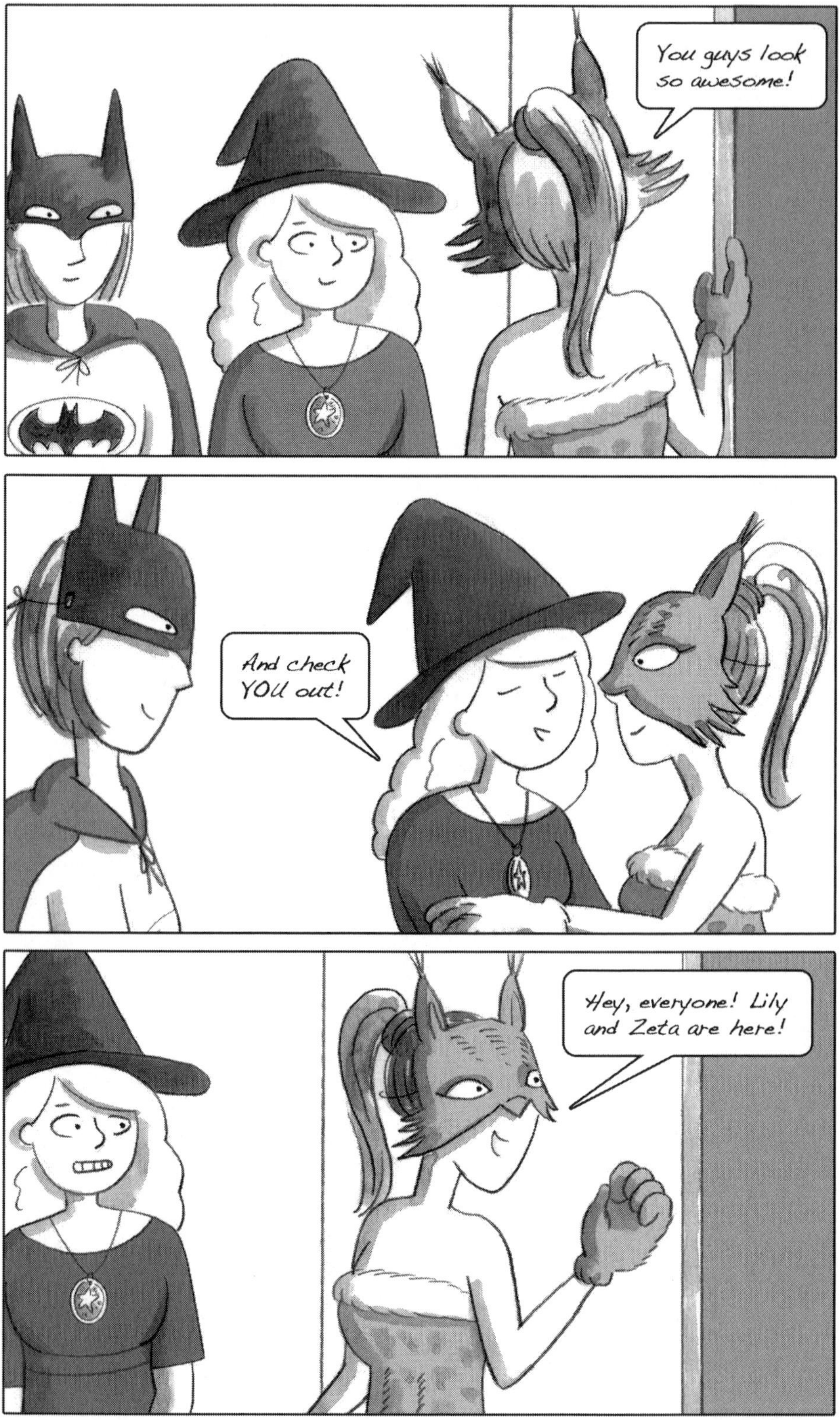
You guys look so awesome!
And check YOU out!
Hey, everyone! Lily and Zeta are here!

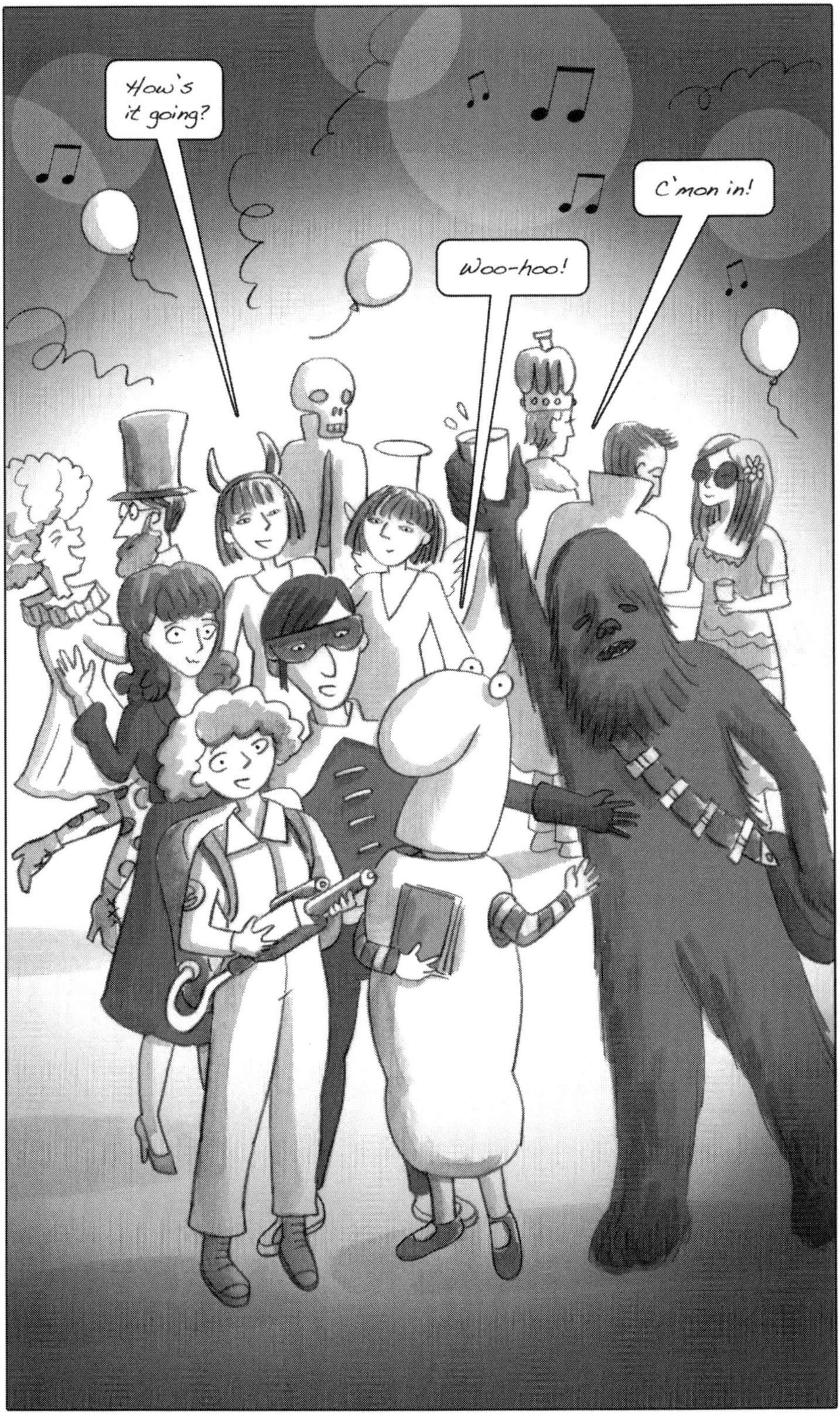
How's it going?
Woo-hoo!
C'mon in!

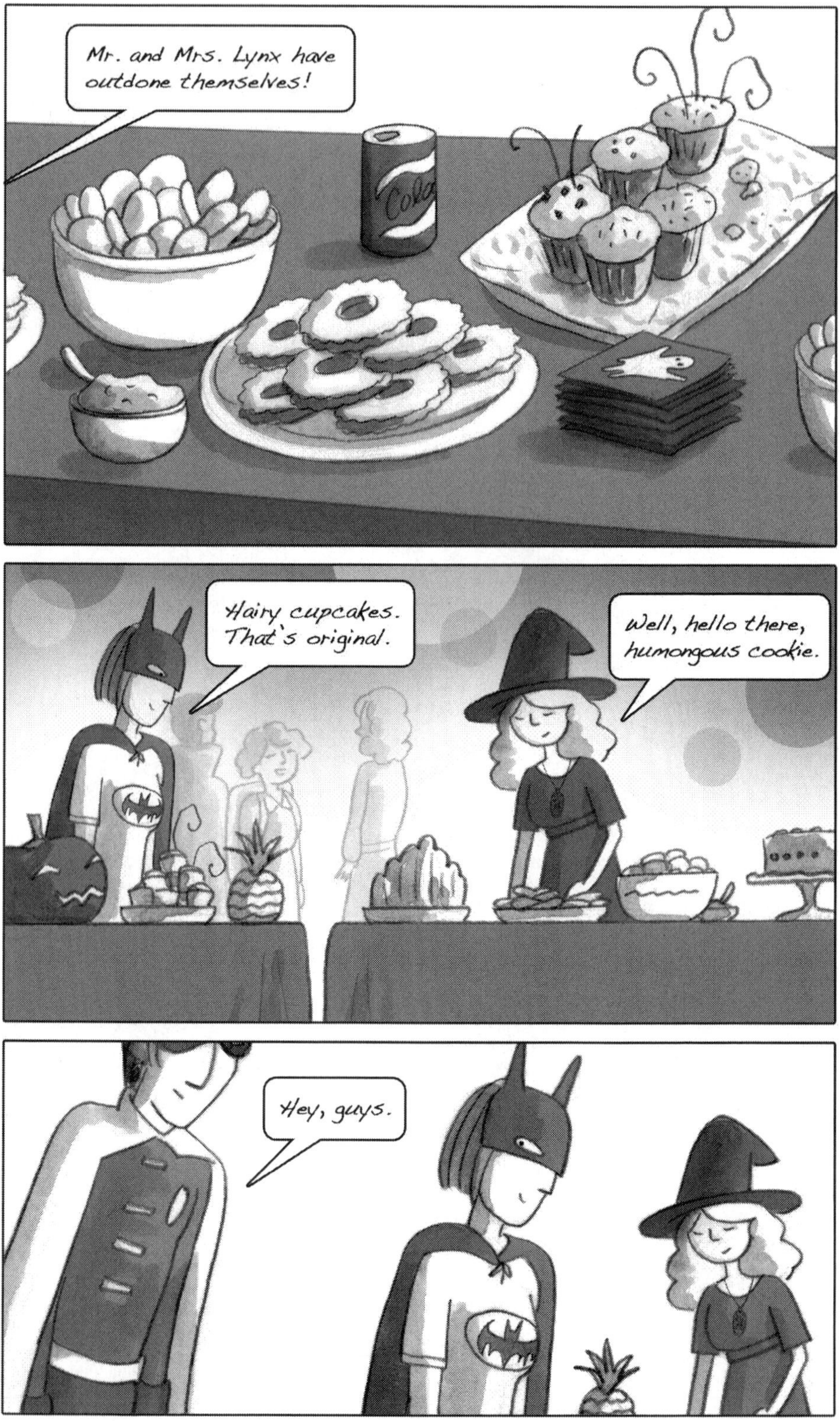
Mr. and Mrs. Lynx have outdone themselves!
Hairy cupcakes. That's original.
Well, hello there, humongous cookie.
Hey, guys.

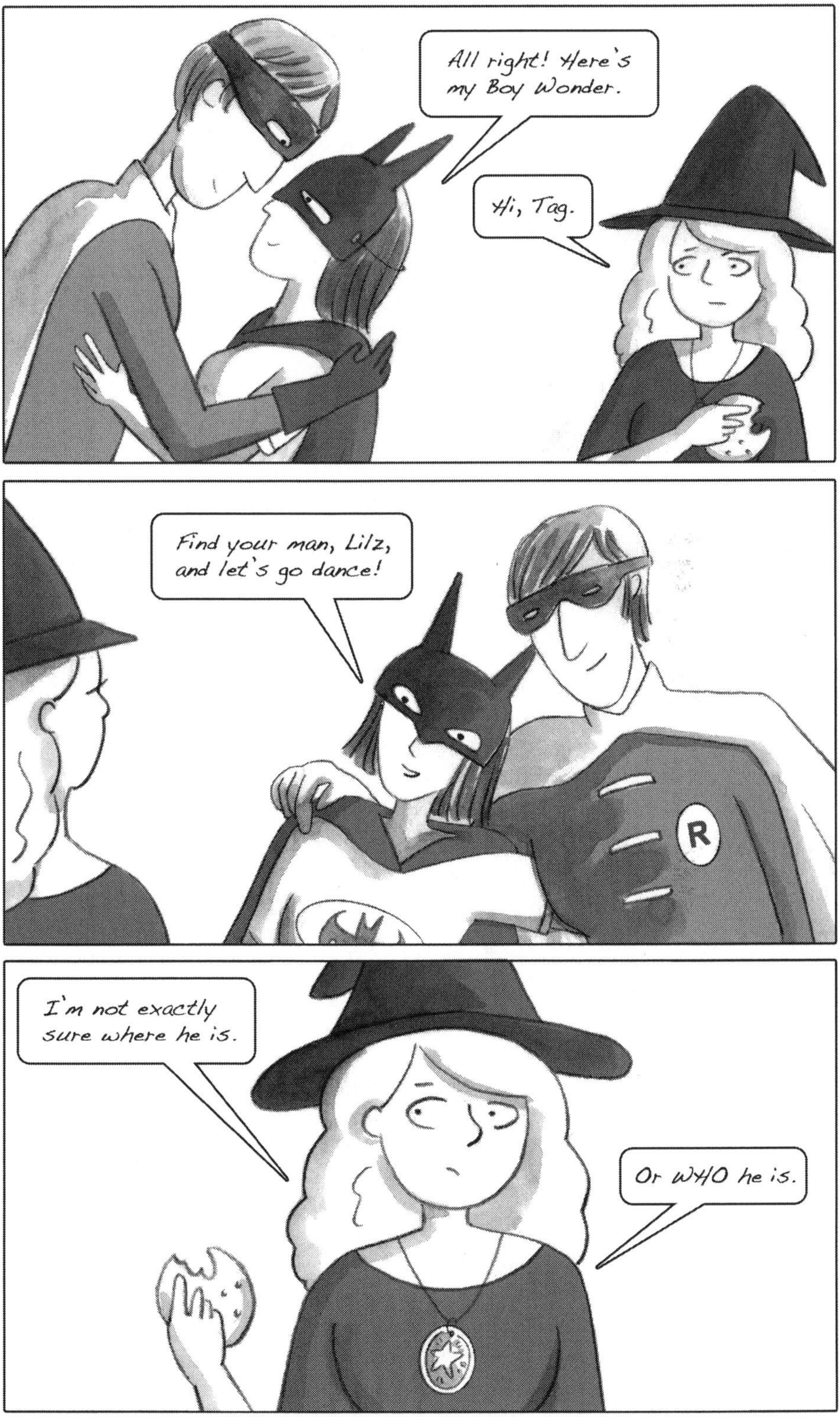
All right! Here's my Boy Wonder.
Hi, Tag.
Find your man, Lilz, and let's go dance!
I'm not exactly sure where he is.
Or WHO he is.

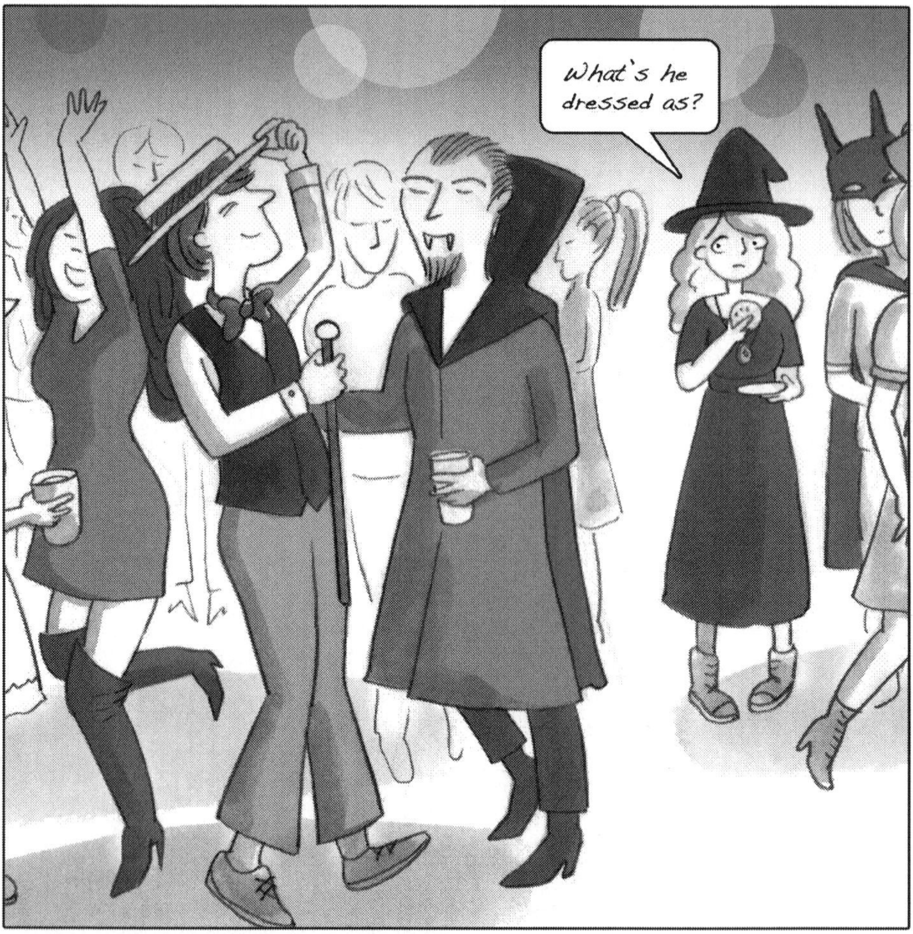
What's he dressed as?

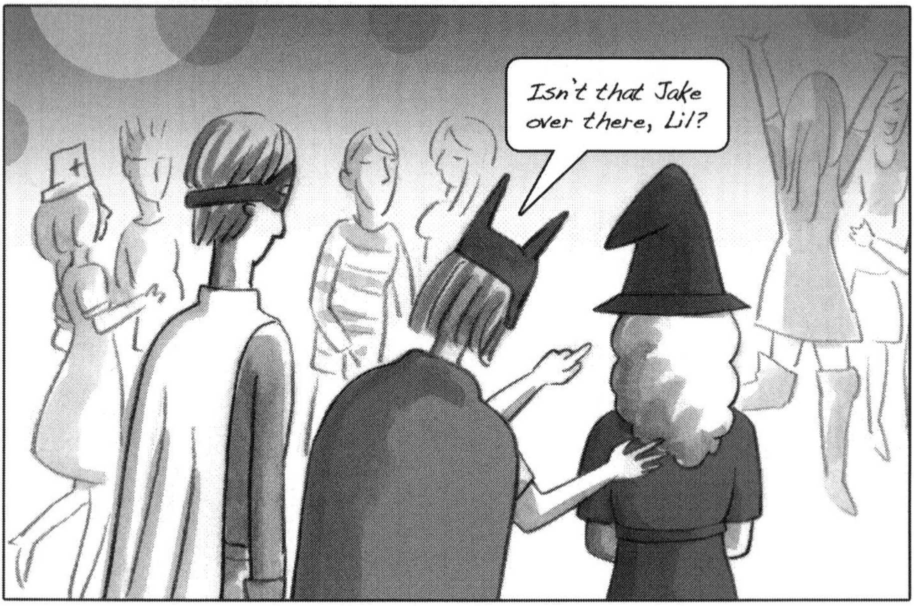
Isn't that Jake over there, Lil?

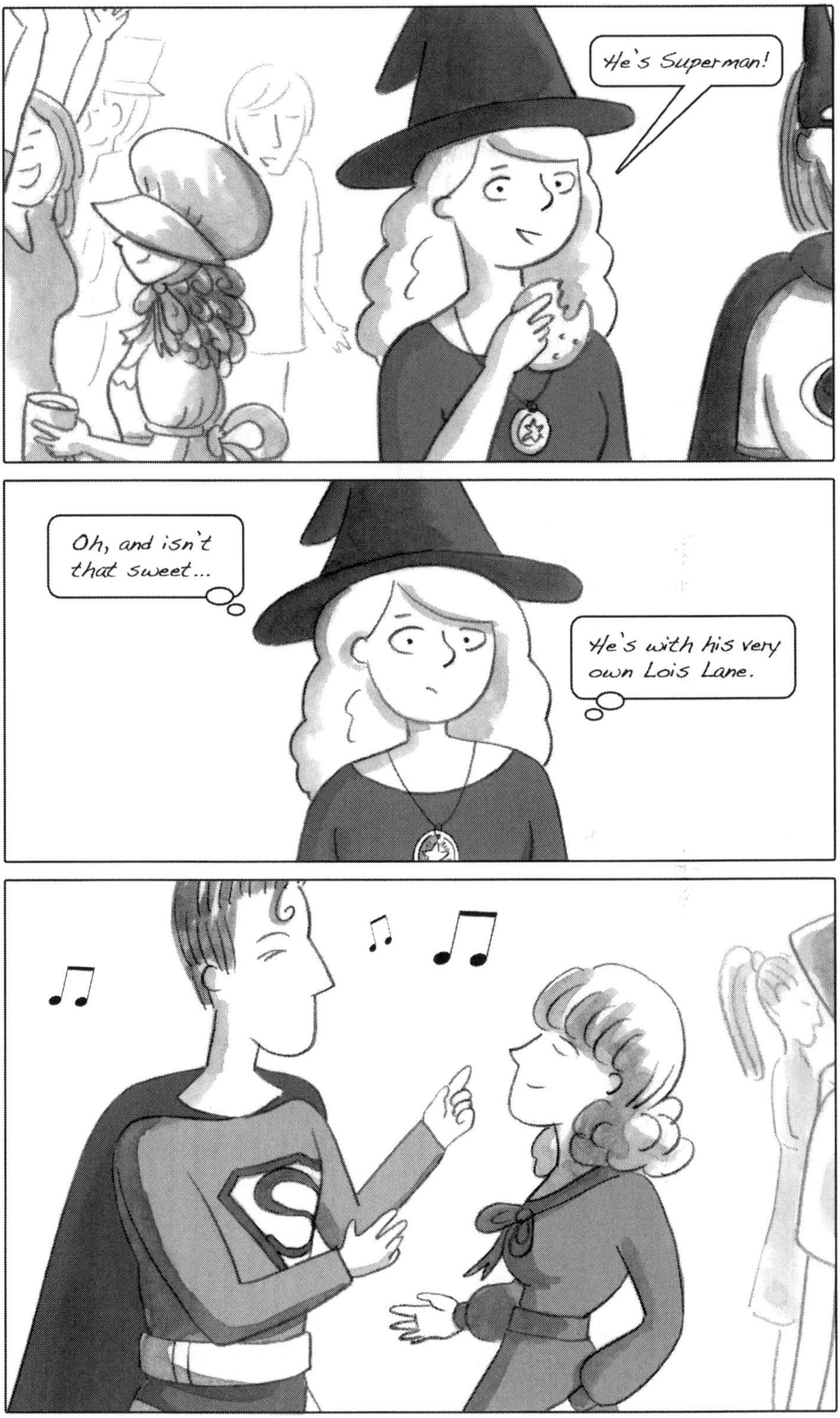
He's Superman!
Oh, and isn't that sweet...
He's with his very own Lois Lane.

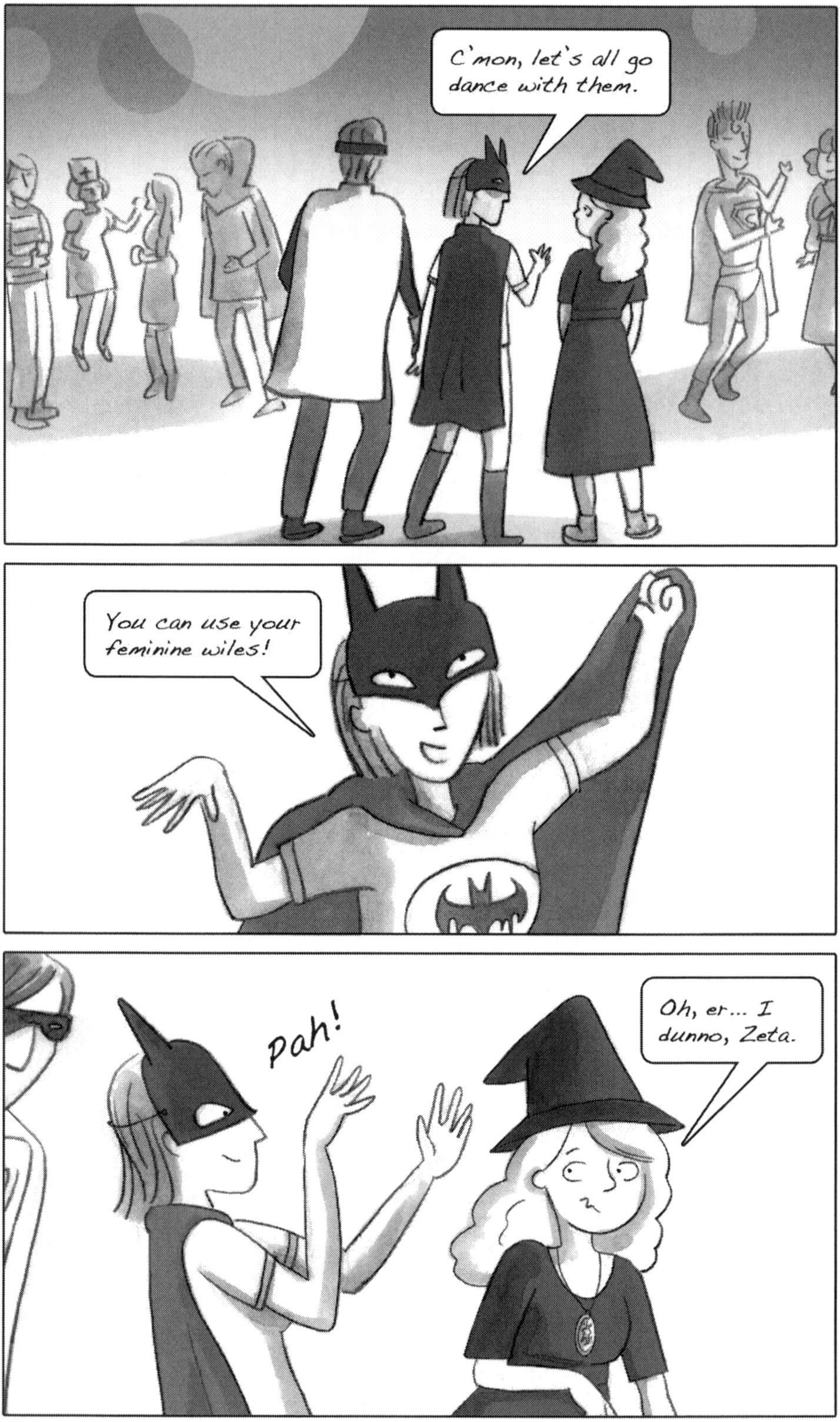
C'mon, let's all go dance with them.
You can use your feminine wiles!
Pah!
Oh, er... I dunno, Zeta.

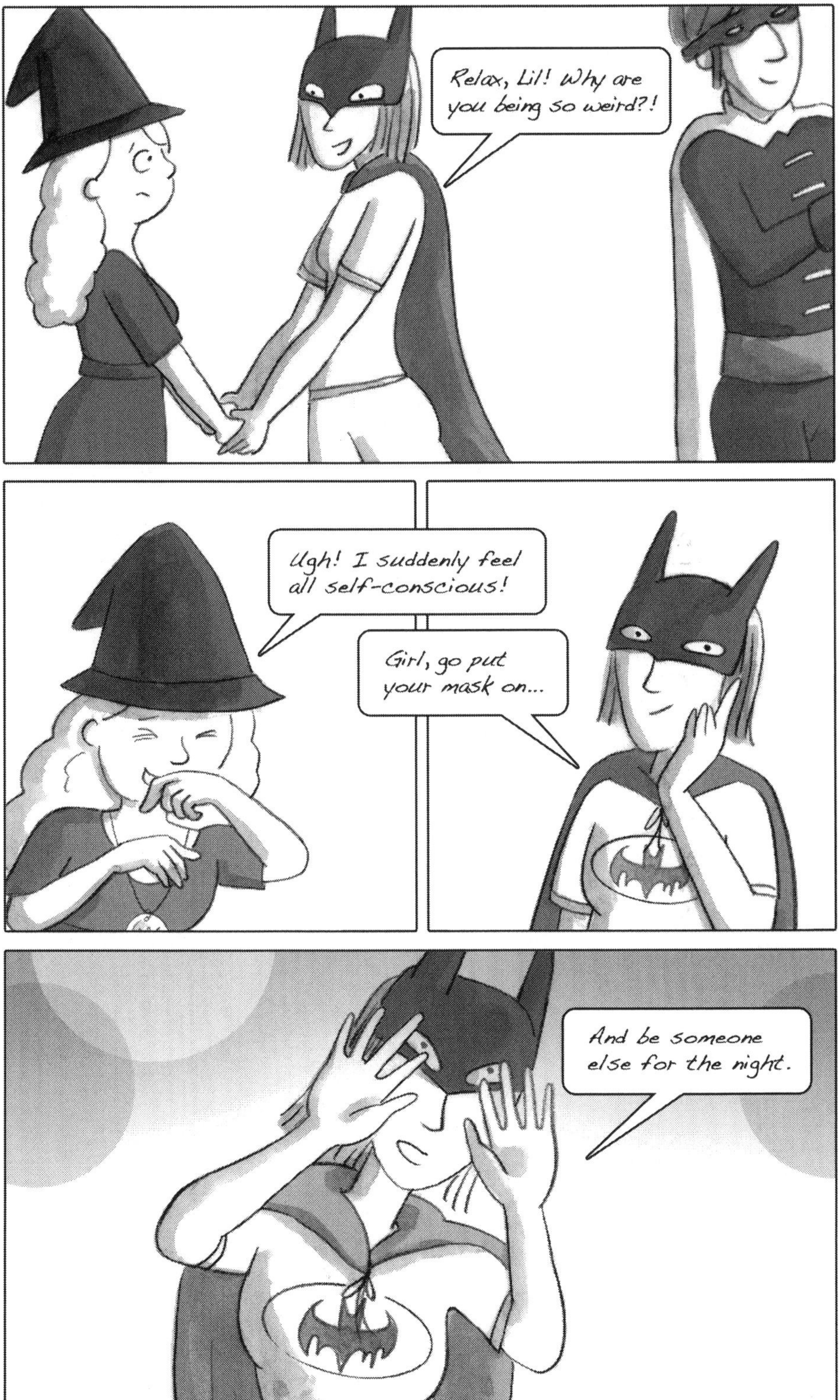
Relax, Lil! Why are you being so weird?!
Ugh! I suddenly feel all self-conscious!
Girl, go put your mask on...
And be someone else for the night.

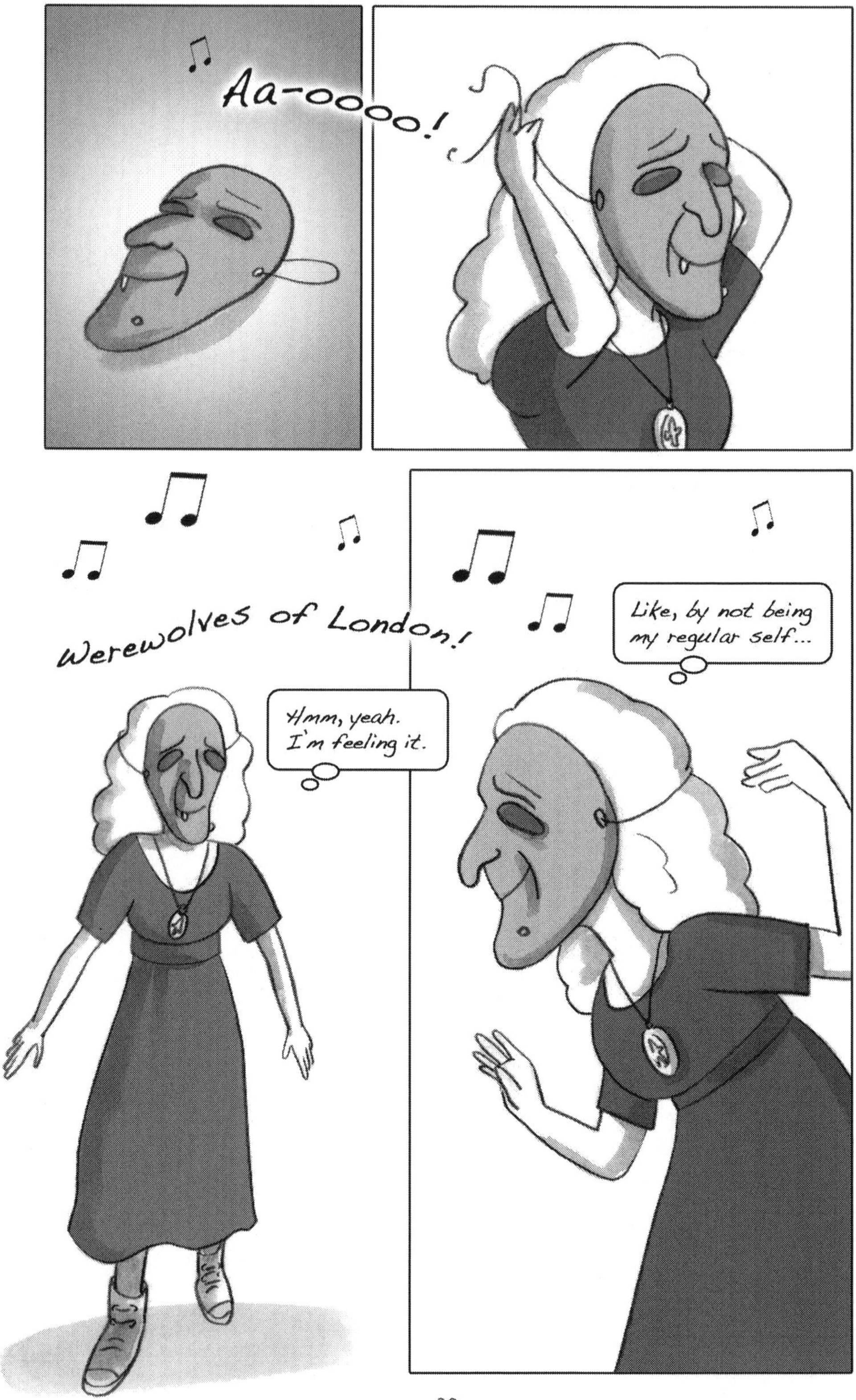
Aa-ooooo!
Werewolves of London!
Hmm, yeah. I'm feeling it.
Like, by not being my regular self...

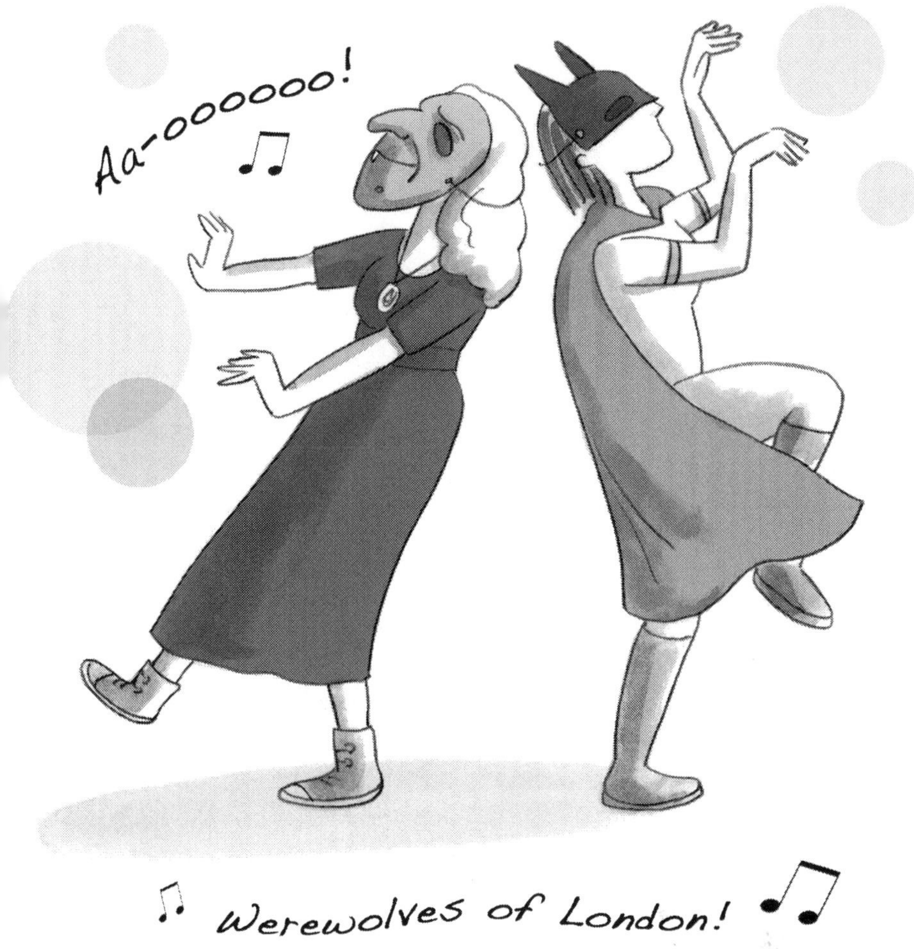
Aa-oooooo!
Werewolves of London!

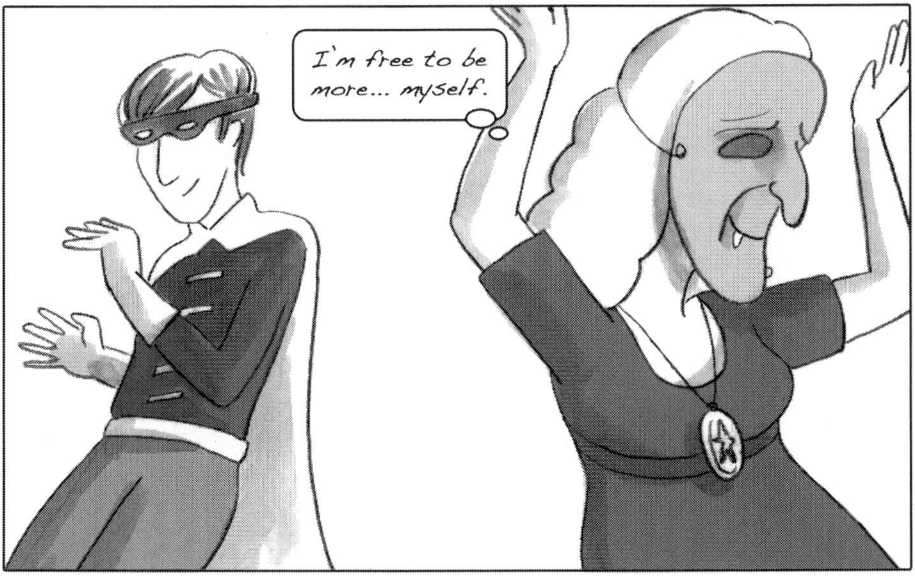
I'm free to be more... myself.

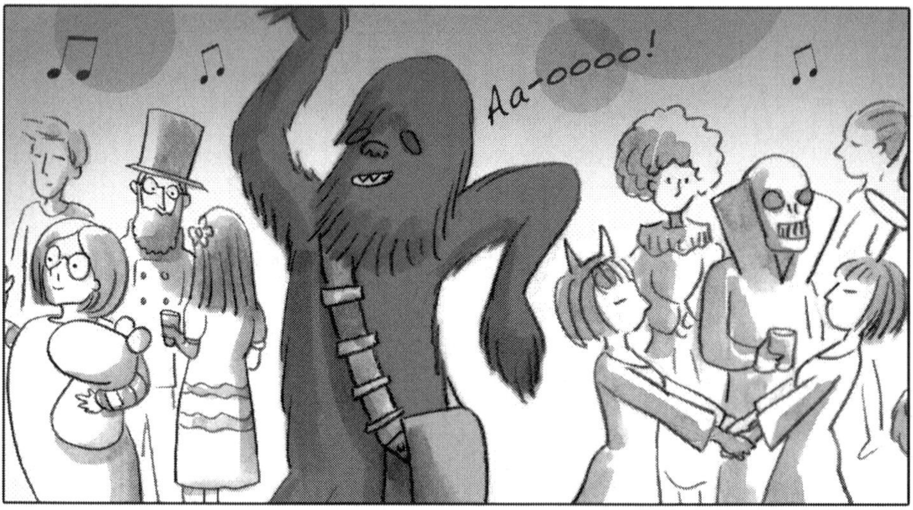
Aa-oooo!

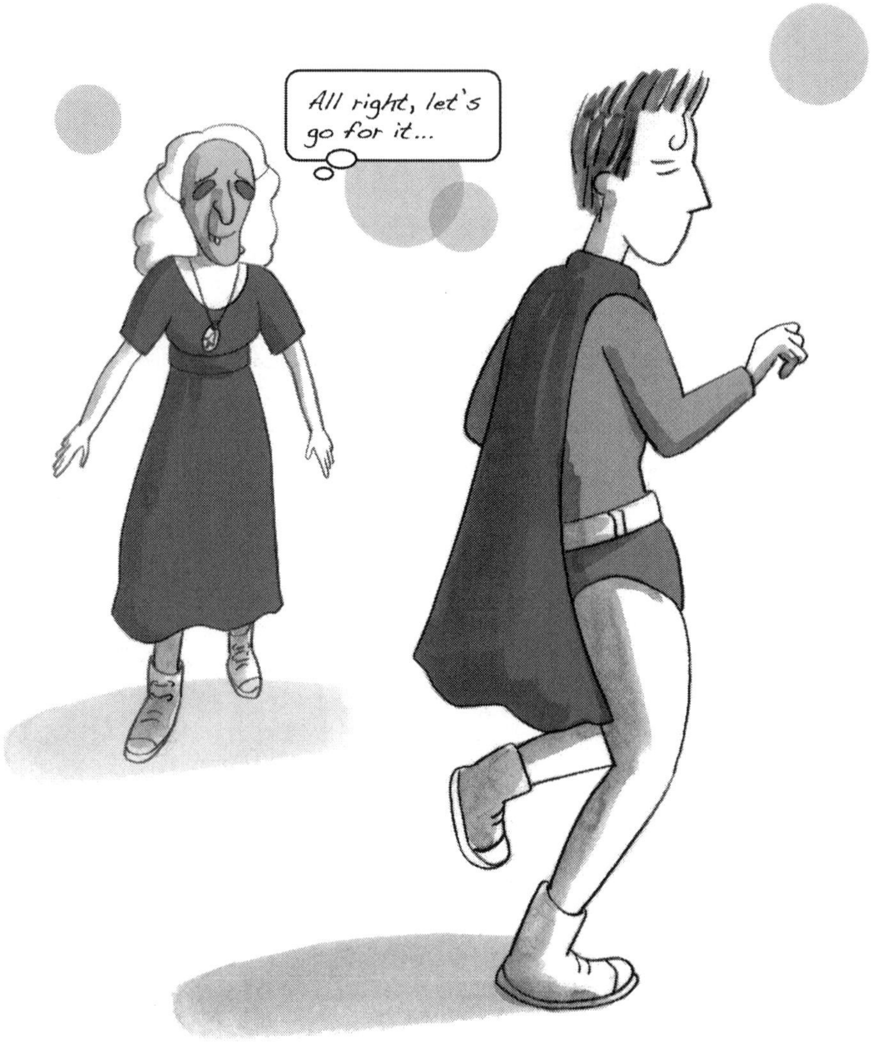
All right, let's go for it...

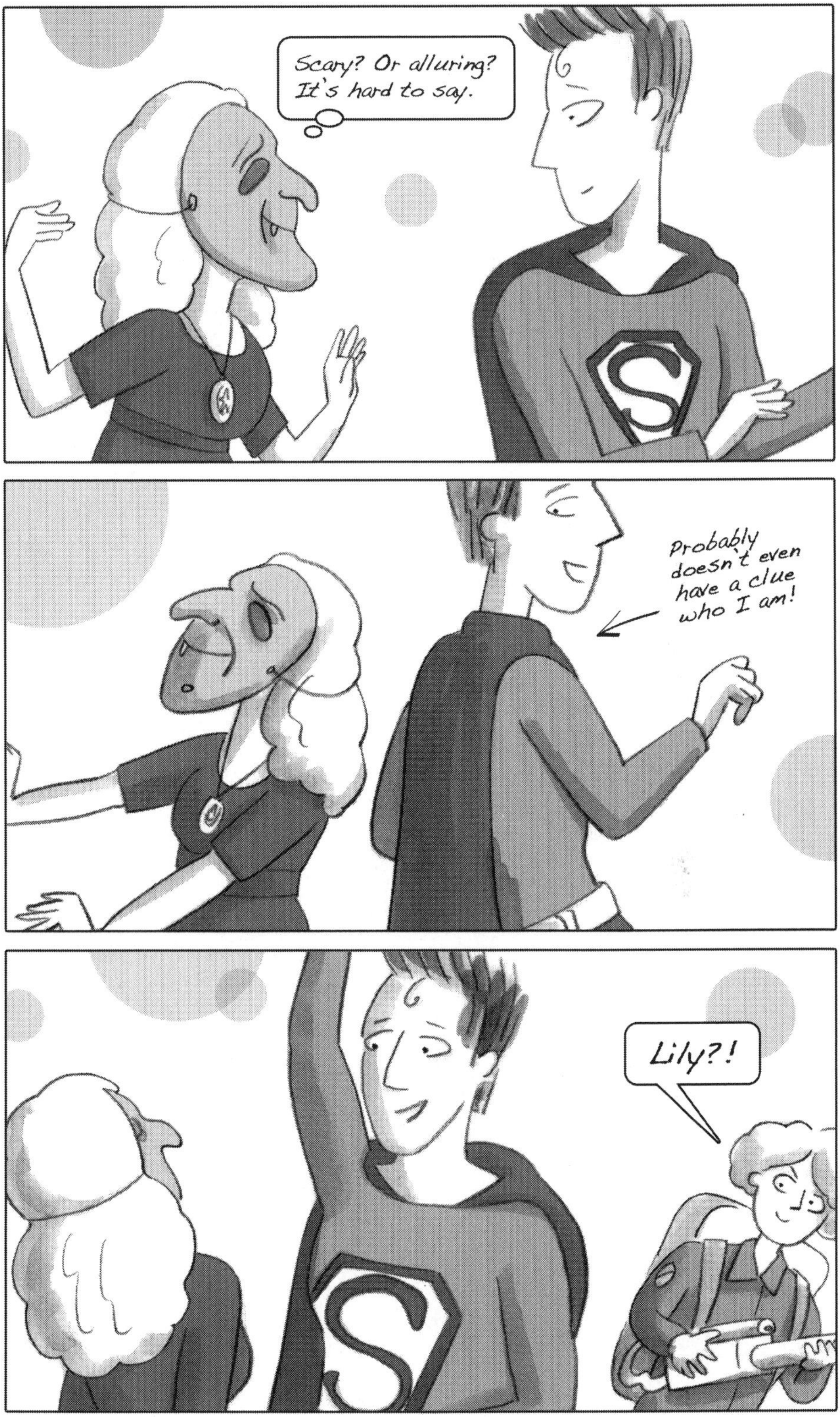
Scary? Or alluring? It's hard to say.
Probably doesn't even have a clue who I am!
Lily?!

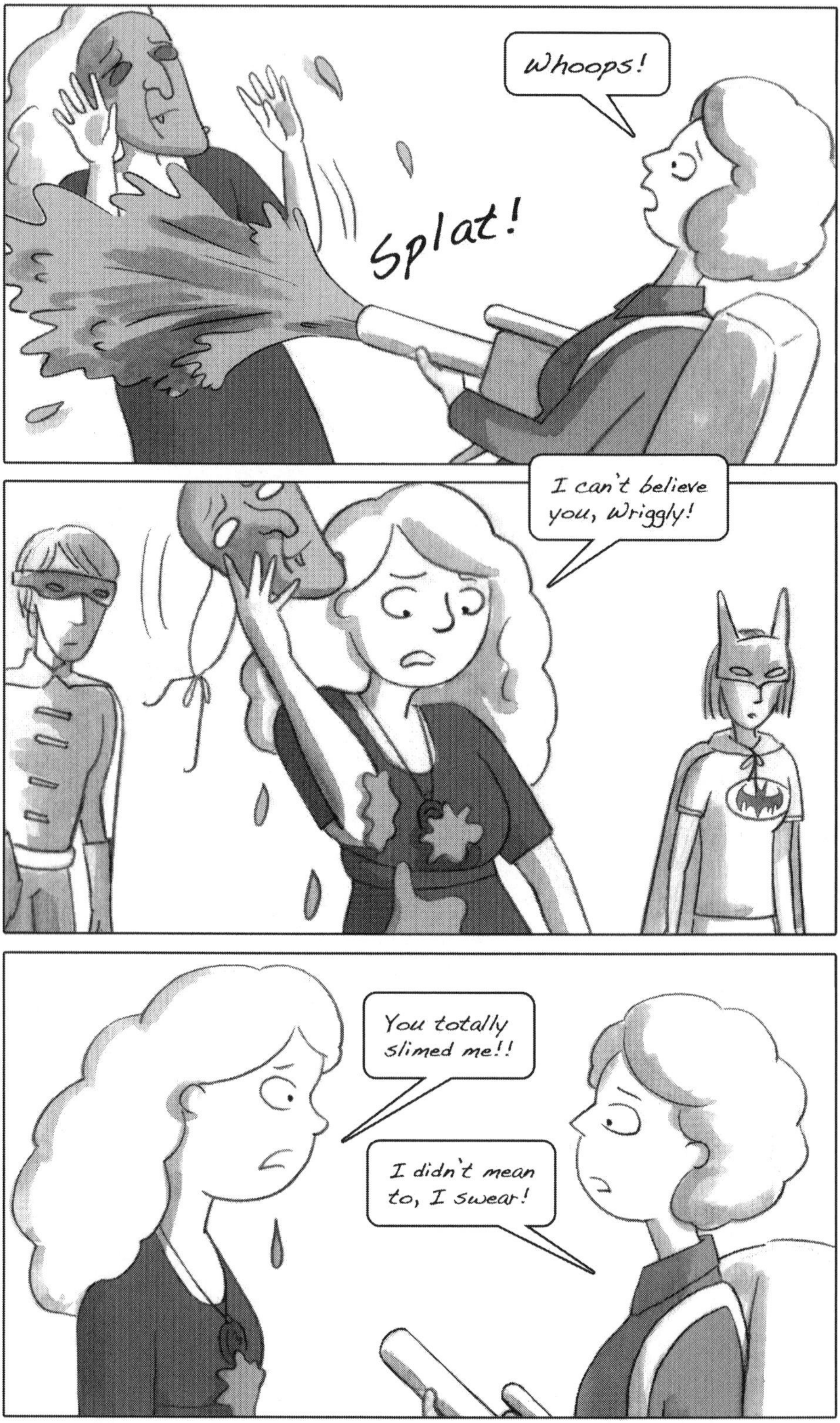
Whoops!
Splat!
I can't believe you, Wriggly!
You totally slimed me!!
I didn't mean to, I swear!

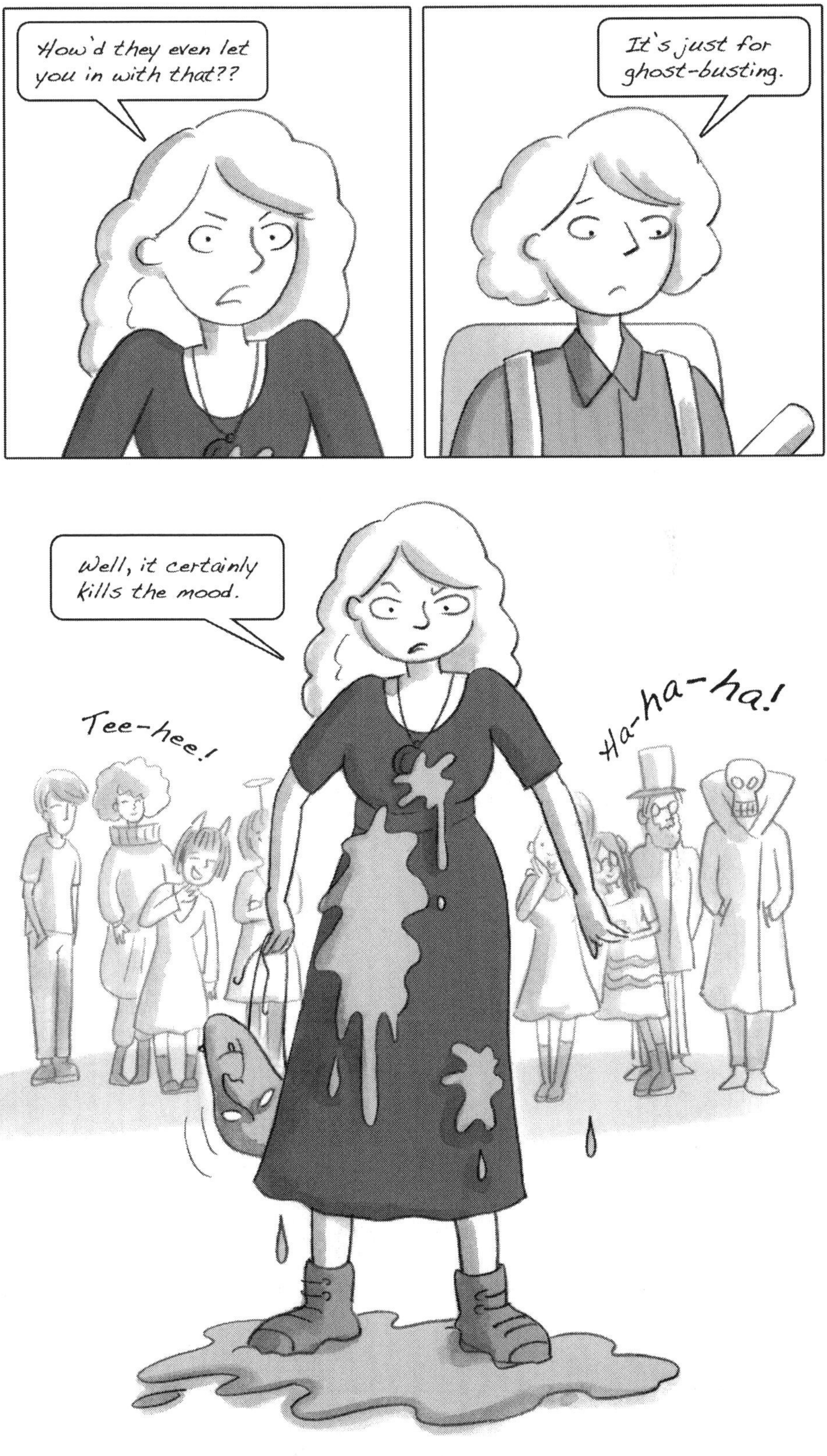
How'd they even let you in with that??
It's just for ghost-busting.
Well, it certainly kills the mood.
Tee-hee!
Ha-ha-ha!

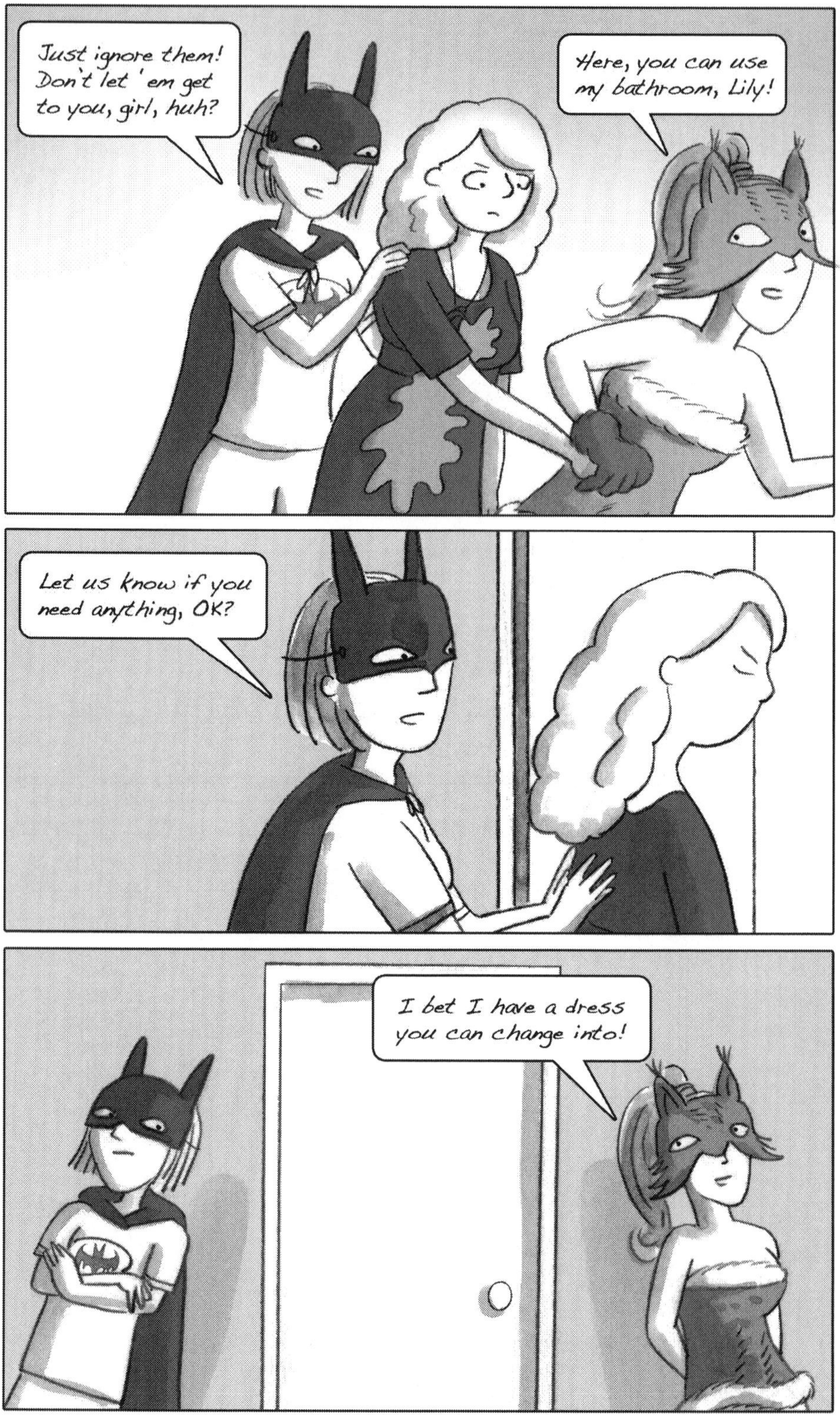
Just ignore them! Don't let 'em get to you, girl, huh?
Here, you can use my bathroom, Lily!
Let us know if you need anything, OK?
I bet I have a dress you can change into!

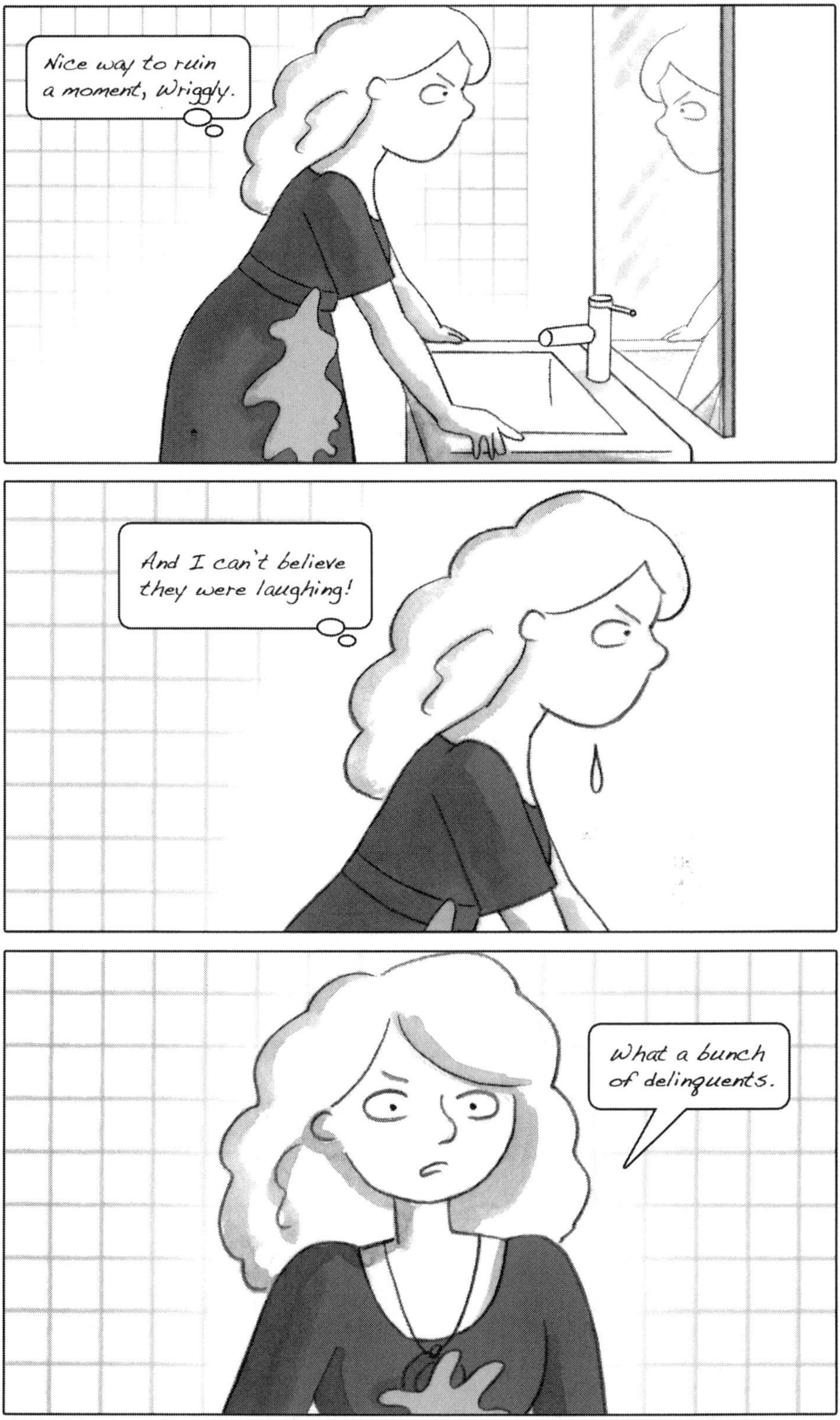
Nice way to ruin a moment, Wriggly.
And I can't believe they were laughing!
What a bunch of delinquents.

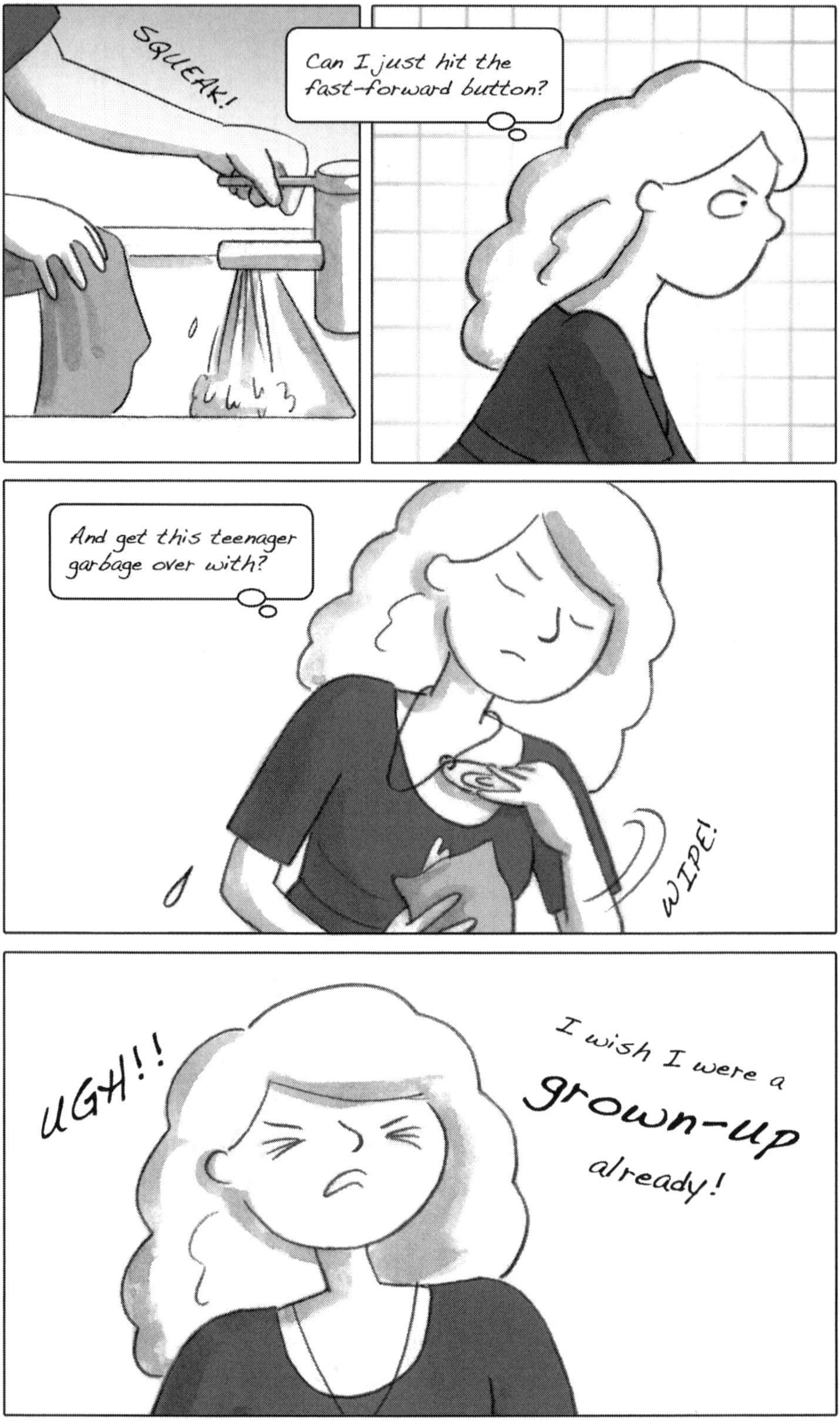
SQUEAK!
Can I just hit the fast-forward button?
And get this teenager garbage over with?
WIPE!
UGH!!
I wish I were a grown-up already!

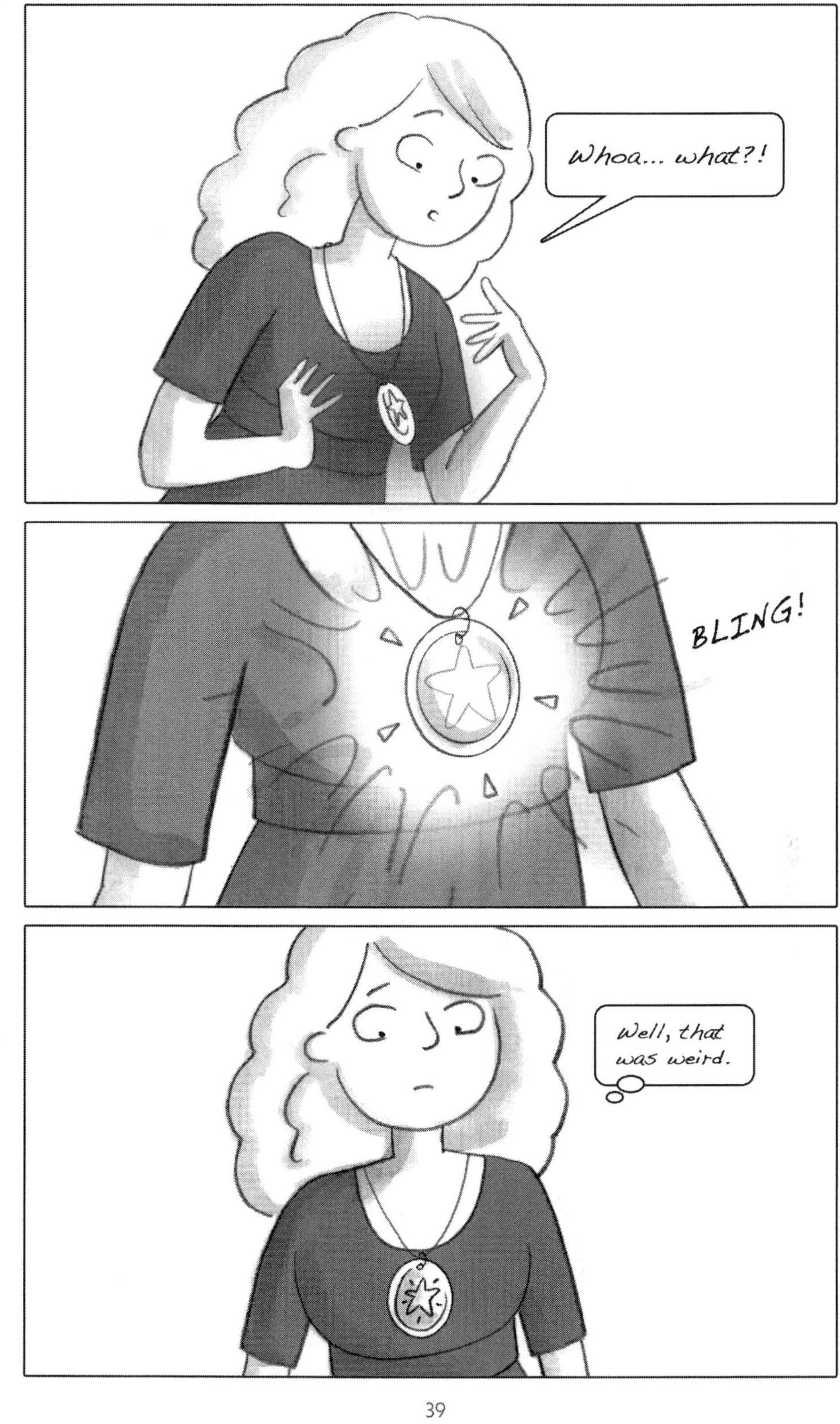
Whoa... what?!
BLING!
Well, that was weird.

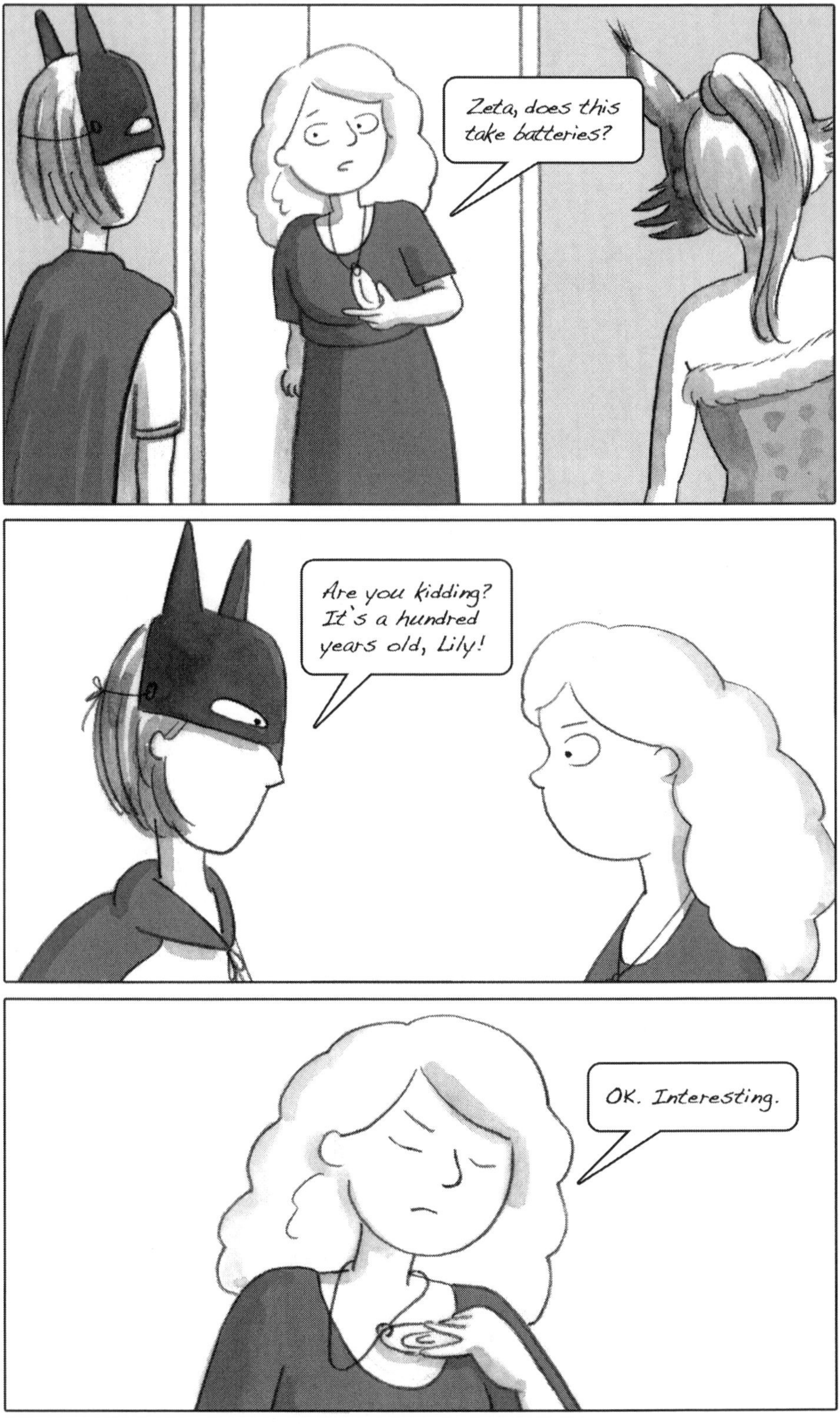
Zeta, does this take batteries?
Are you kidding? It's a hundred years old, Lily!
OK. Interesting.

Be careful what

you wish for.

CHINESE PROVERB

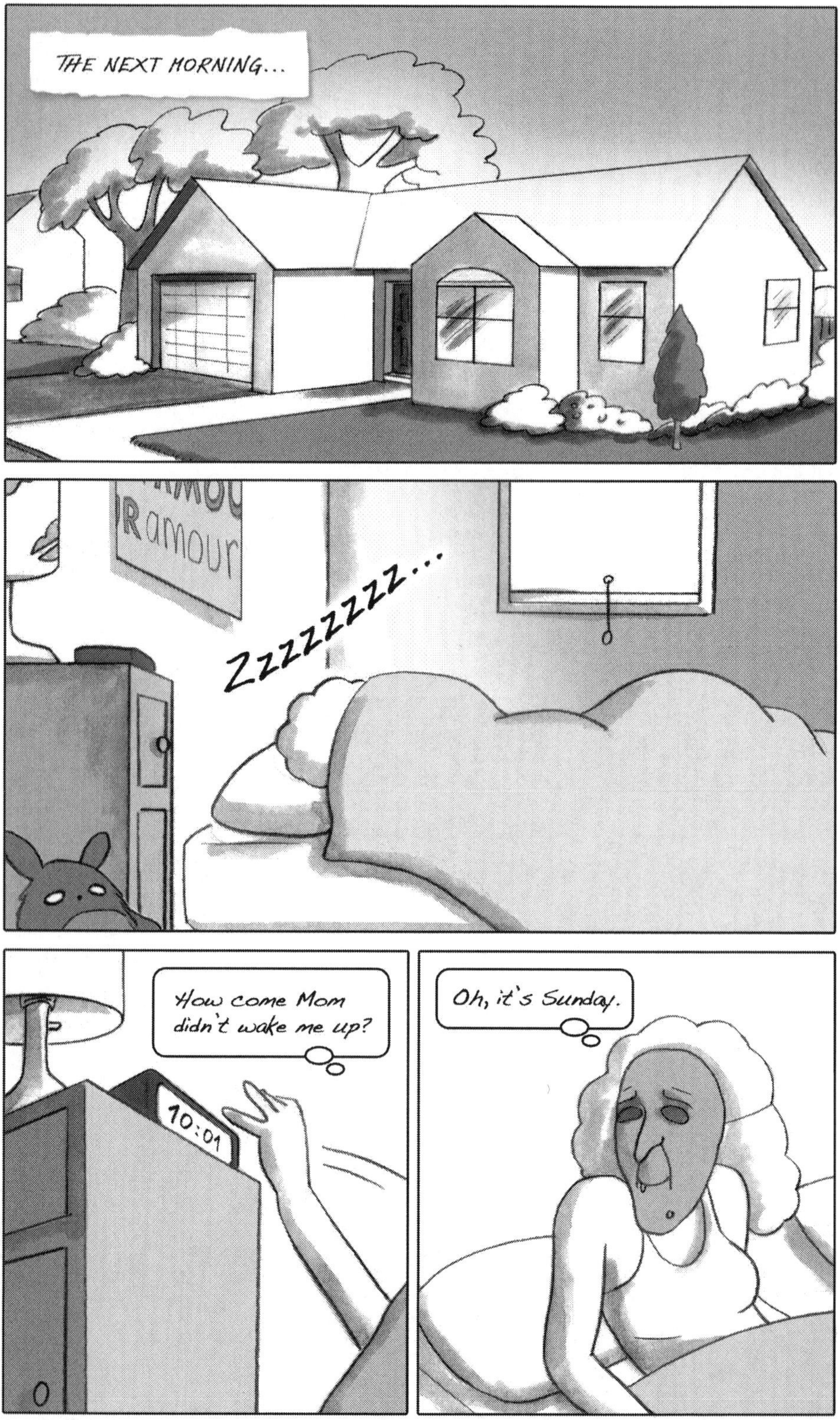
THE NEXT MORNING...
Zzzzzzzz...
10:01
How come Mom didn't wake me up?
Oh, it's Sunday.

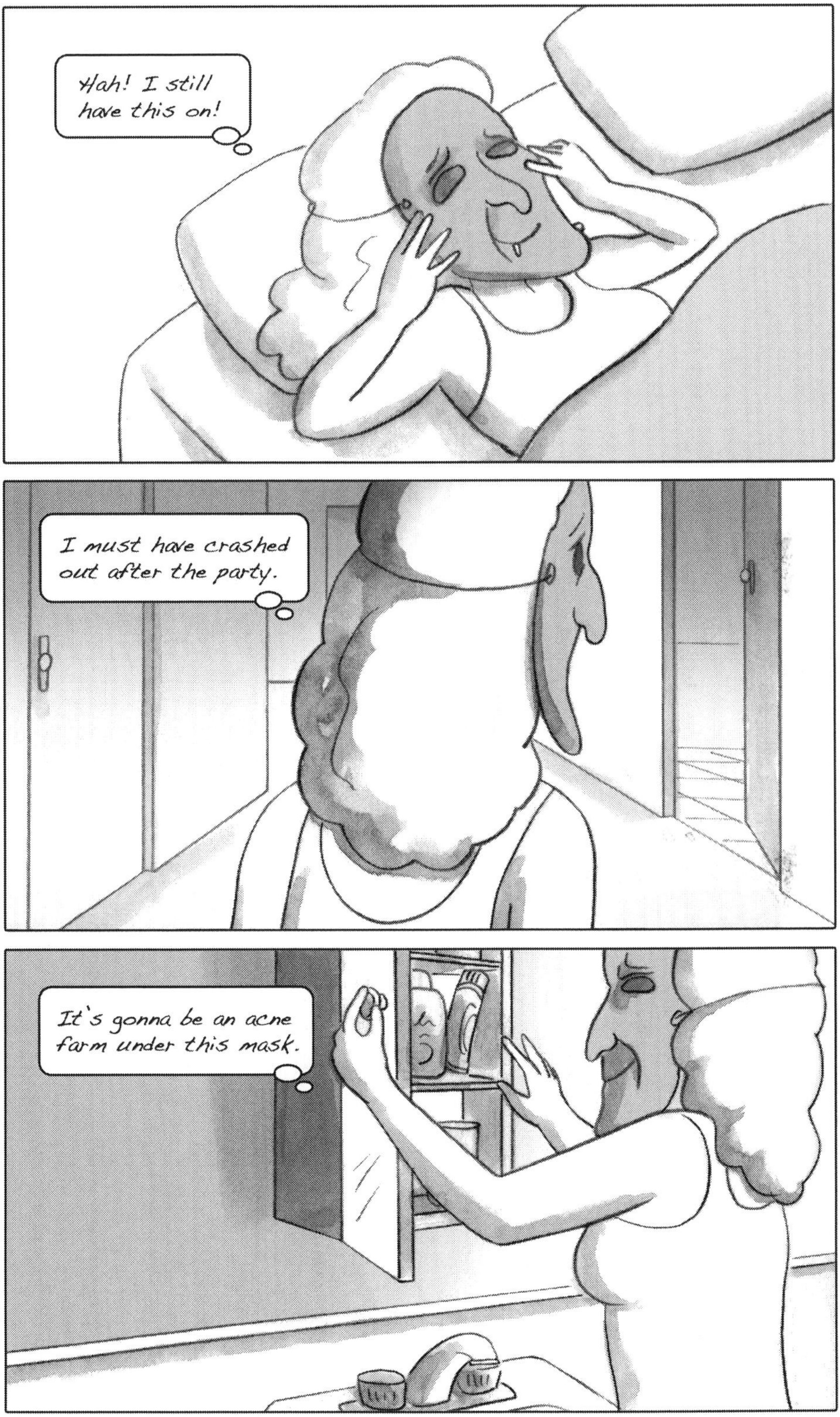
Hah! I still have this on!
I must have crashed out after the party.
It's gonna be an acne farm under this mask.

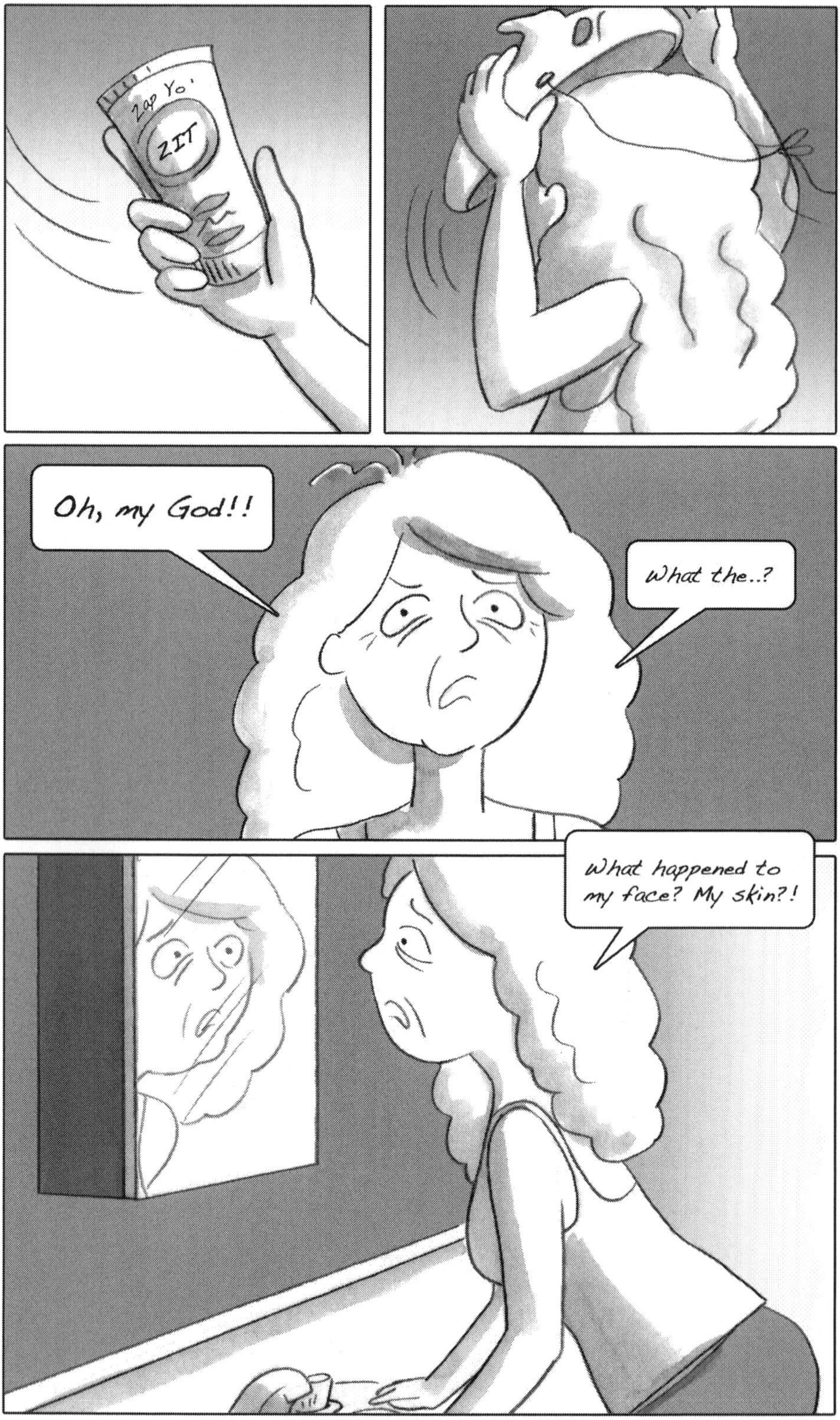
Zap Yo'
ZIT
Oh, my God!!
What the..?
What happened to my face? My skin?!

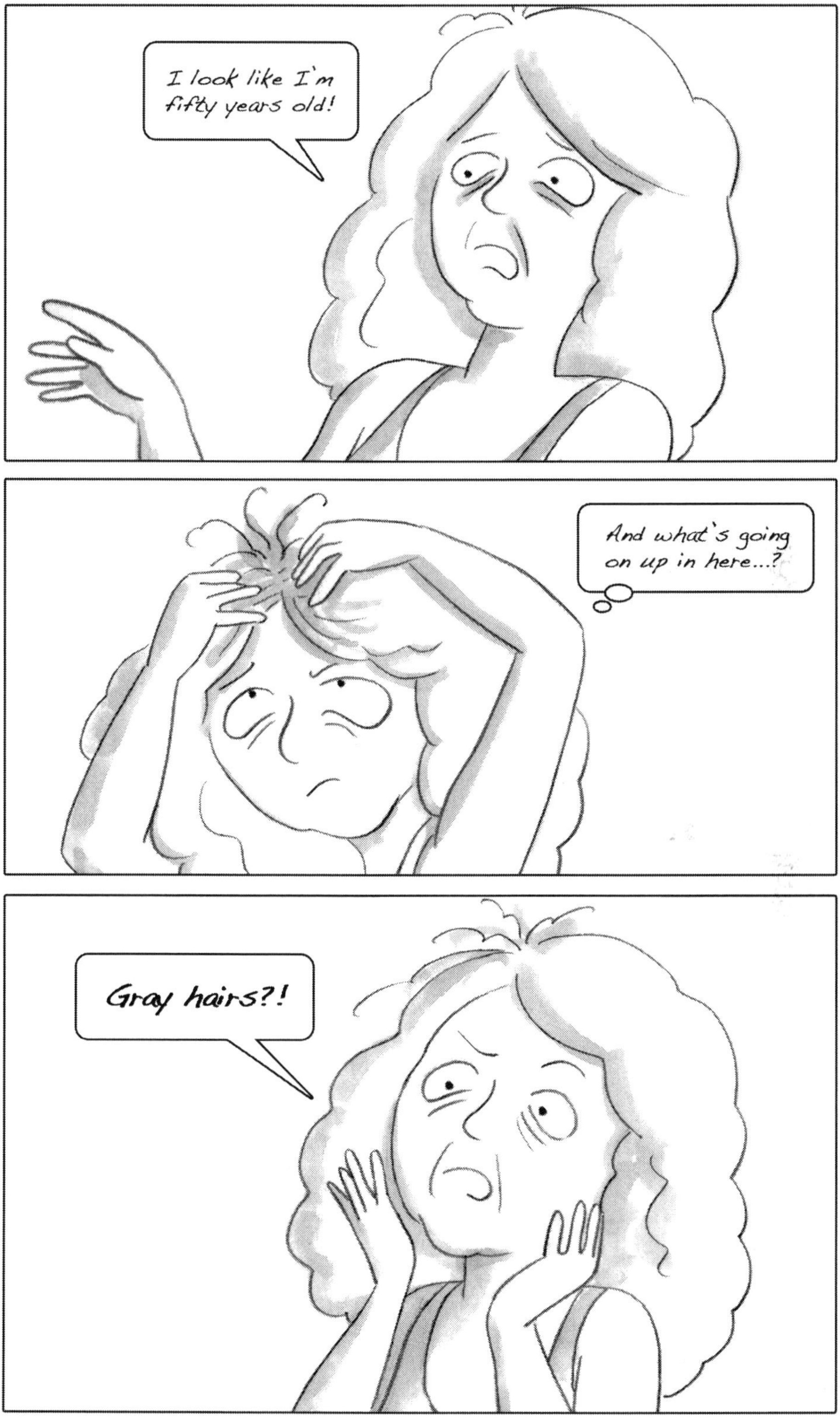
I look like I'm fifty years old!
And what's going on up in here...?
Gray hairs?!

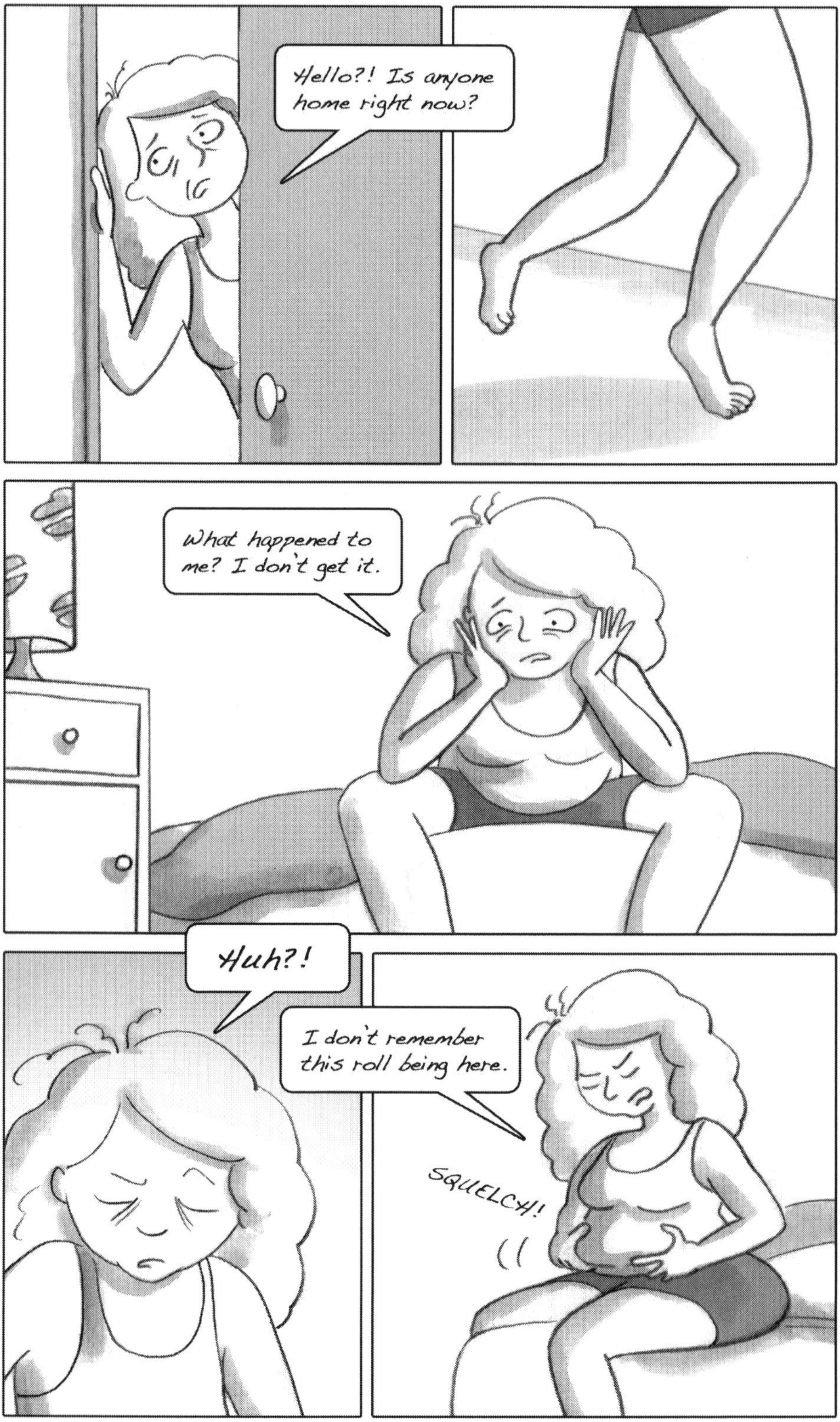
Hello?! Is anyone home right now?
What happened to me? I don't get it.
Huh?!
I don't remember this roll being here.
SQUELCH!

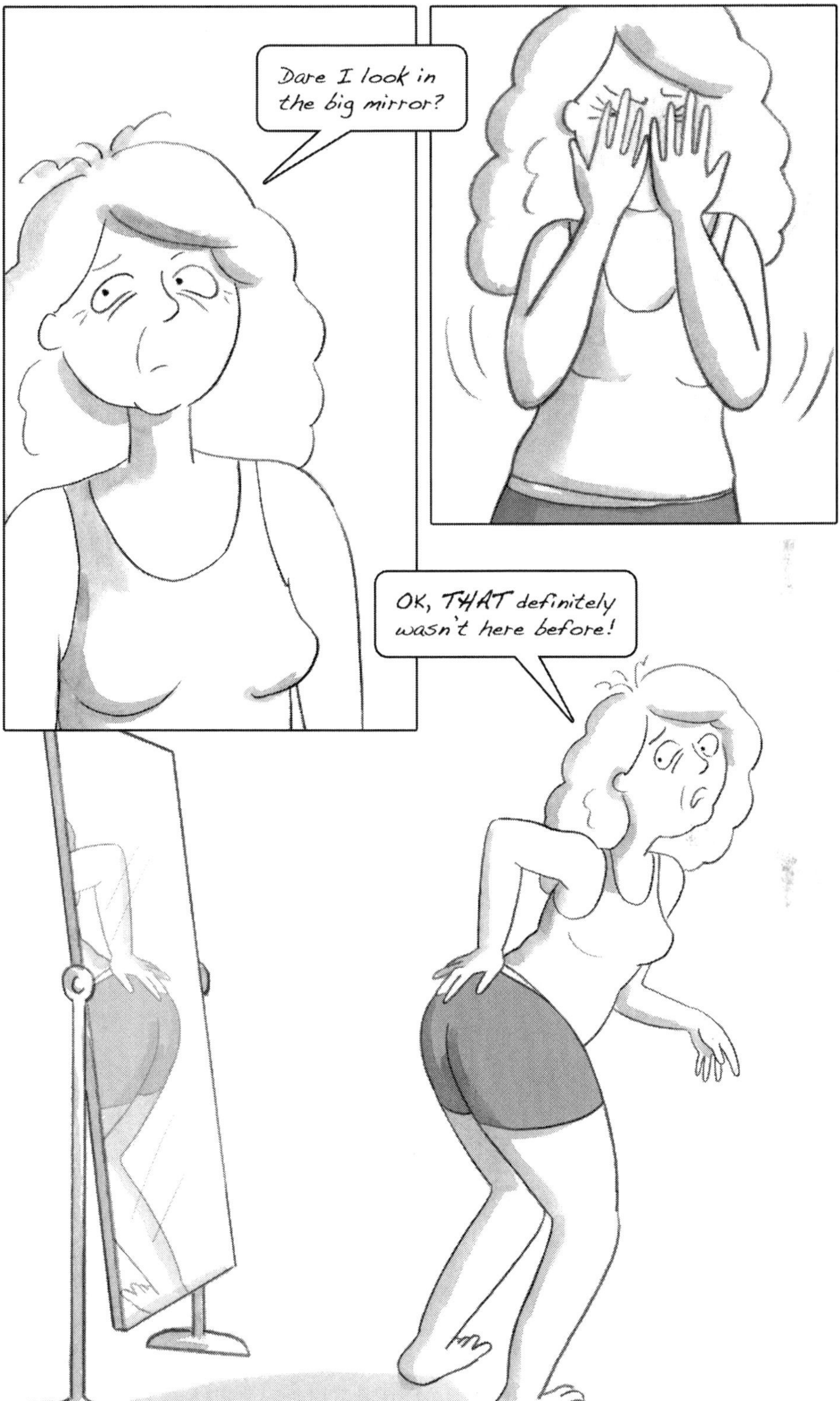
Dare I look in the big mirror?
OK, THAT definitely wasn't here before!

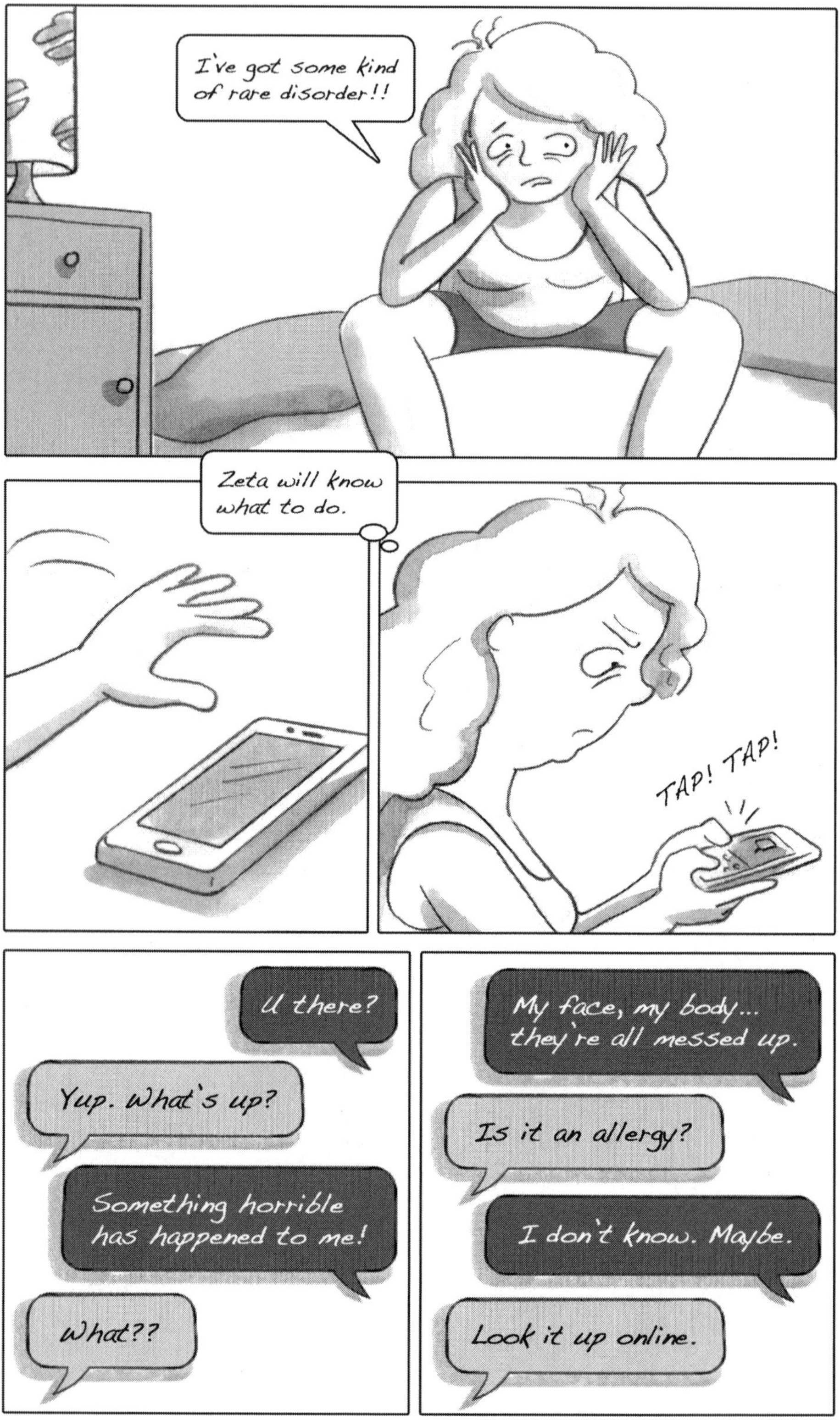
I've got some kind of rare disorder!!
Zeta will know what to do.
TAP! TAP!
U there?
Yup. What's up?
Something horrible has happened to me!
What??
My face, my body... they're all messed up.
Is it an allergy?
I don't know. Maybe.
Look it up online.

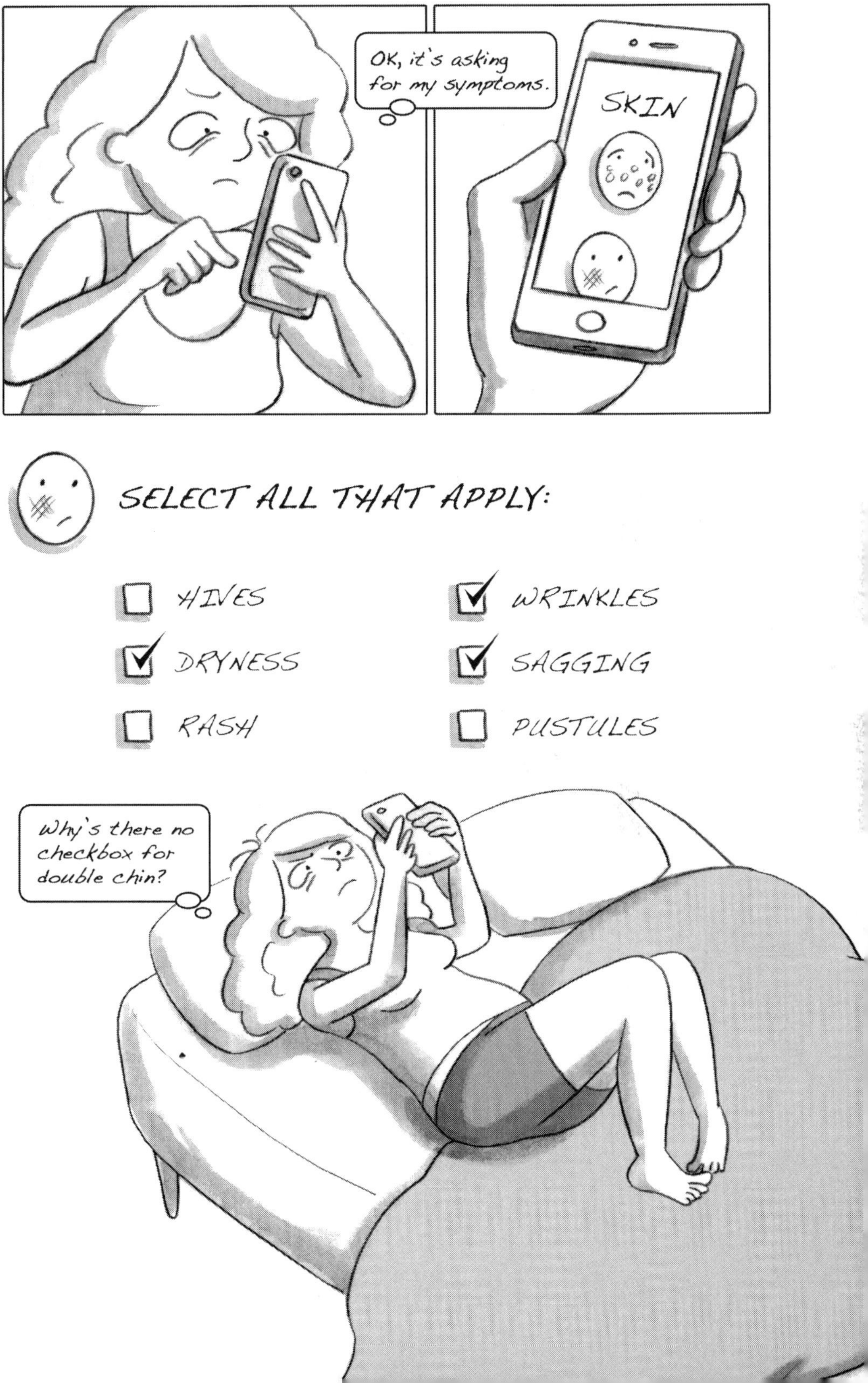
OK, it's asking for my symptoms.
SKIN
SELECT ALL THAT APPLY:
HIVES
DRYNESS
RASH
WRINKLES
SAGGING
PUSTULES
Why's there no checkbox for double chin?

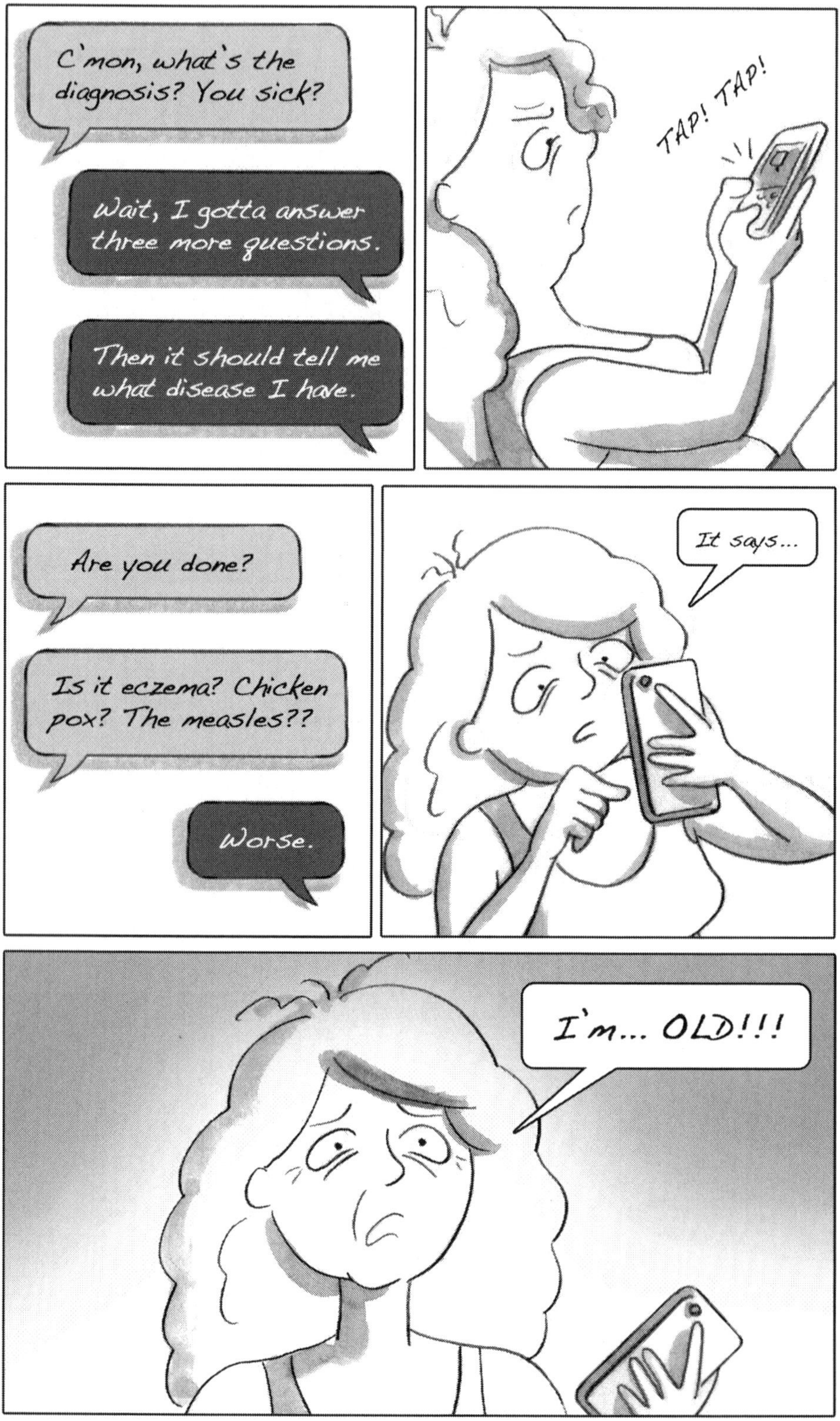
C'mon, what's the diagnosis? You sick?
Wait, I gotta answer three more questions.
Then it should tell me what disease I have.
TAP! TAP!
Are you done?
Is it eczema? Chicken pox? The measles??
Worse.
It says...
I'm... OLD!!!

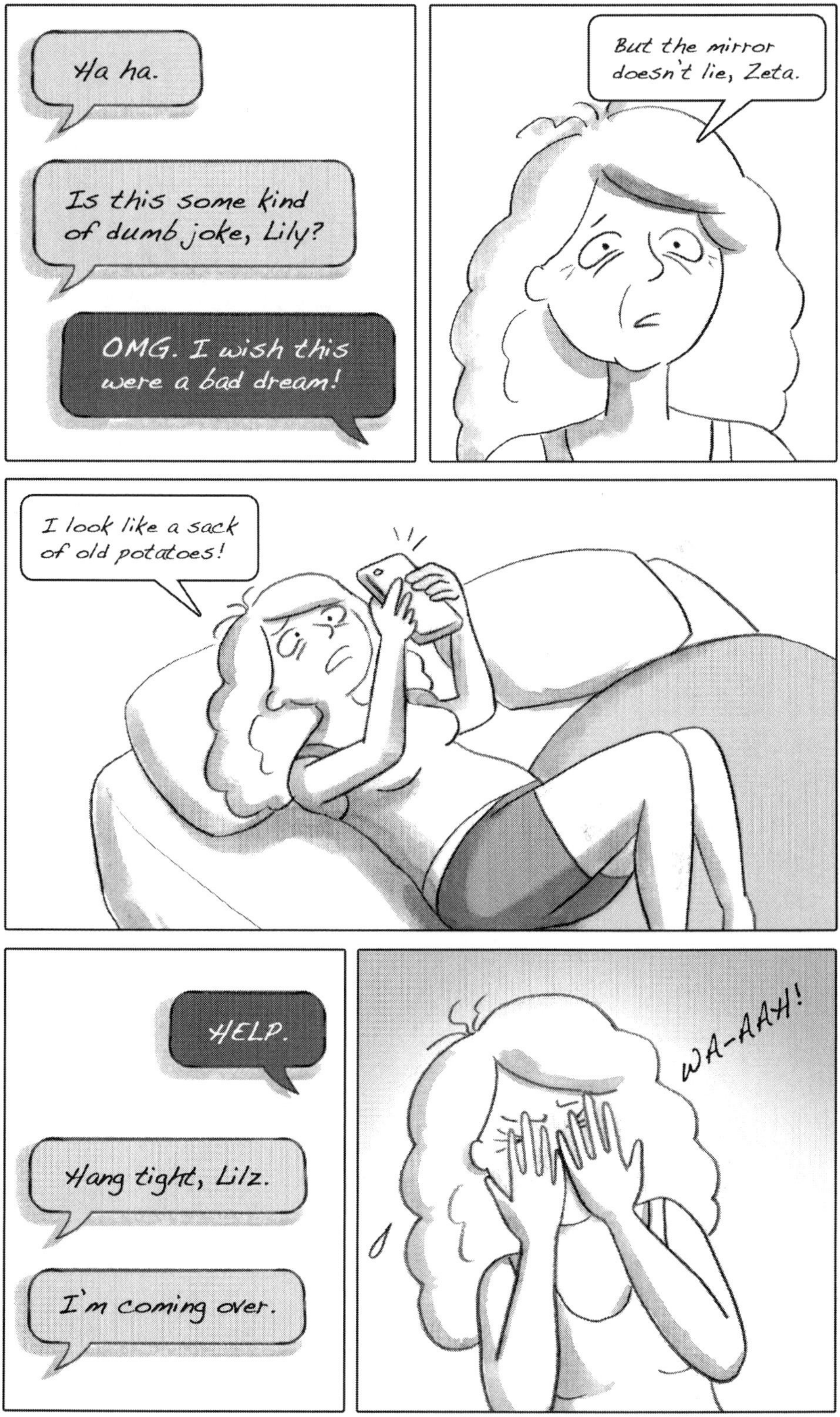
Ha ha.
Is this some kind of dumb joke, Lily?
OMG. I wish this were a bad dream!
But the mirror doesn't lie, Zeta.
I look like a sack of old potatoes!
HELP.
Hang tight, Lilz.
I'm coming over.
WA-AAH!

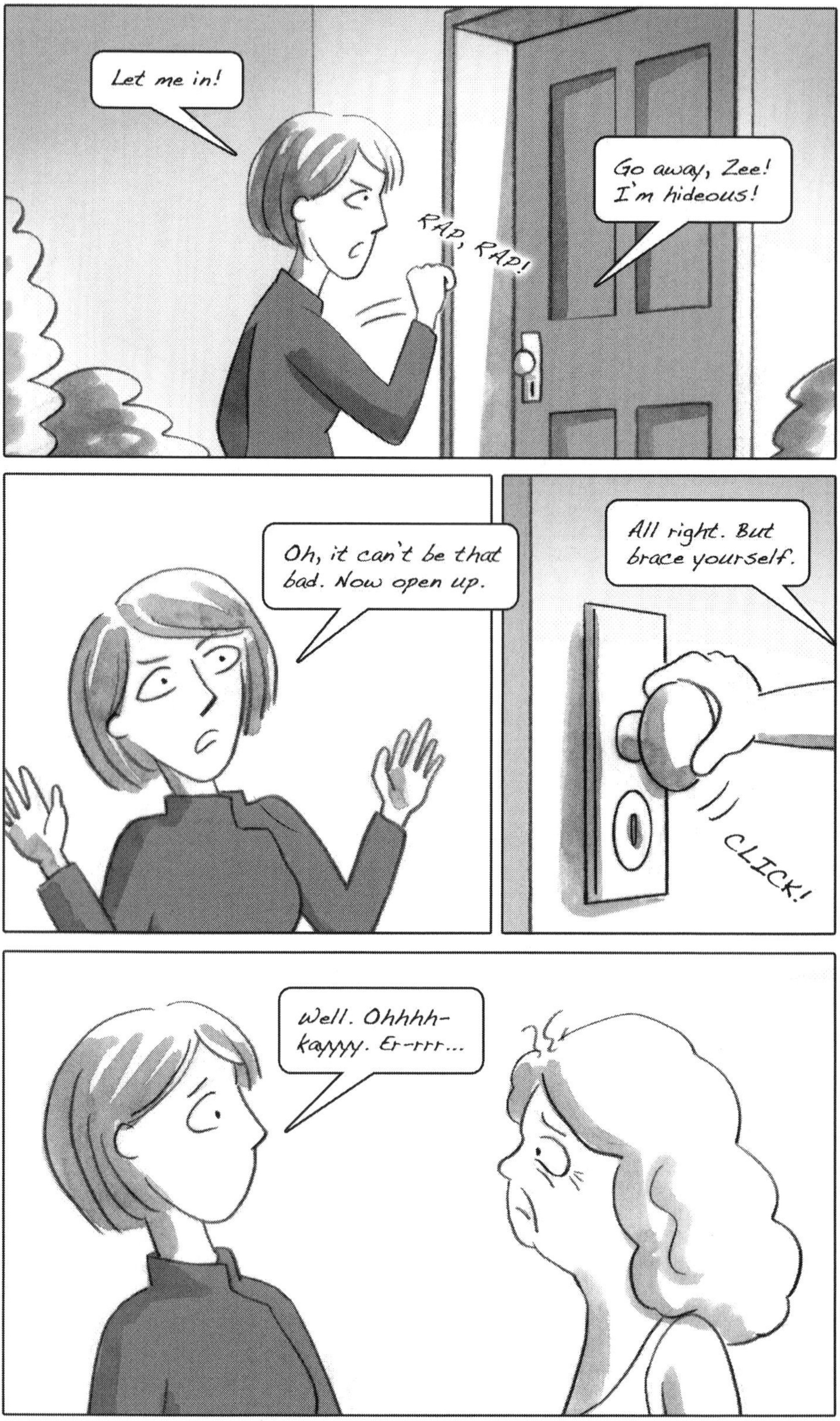
Let me in!
Go away, Zee! I'm hideous!
RAP, RAP!
Oh, it can't be that bad. Now open up.
All right. But brace yourself.
CLICK!
Well. Ohhhh-kayyyy. Er-rrr...

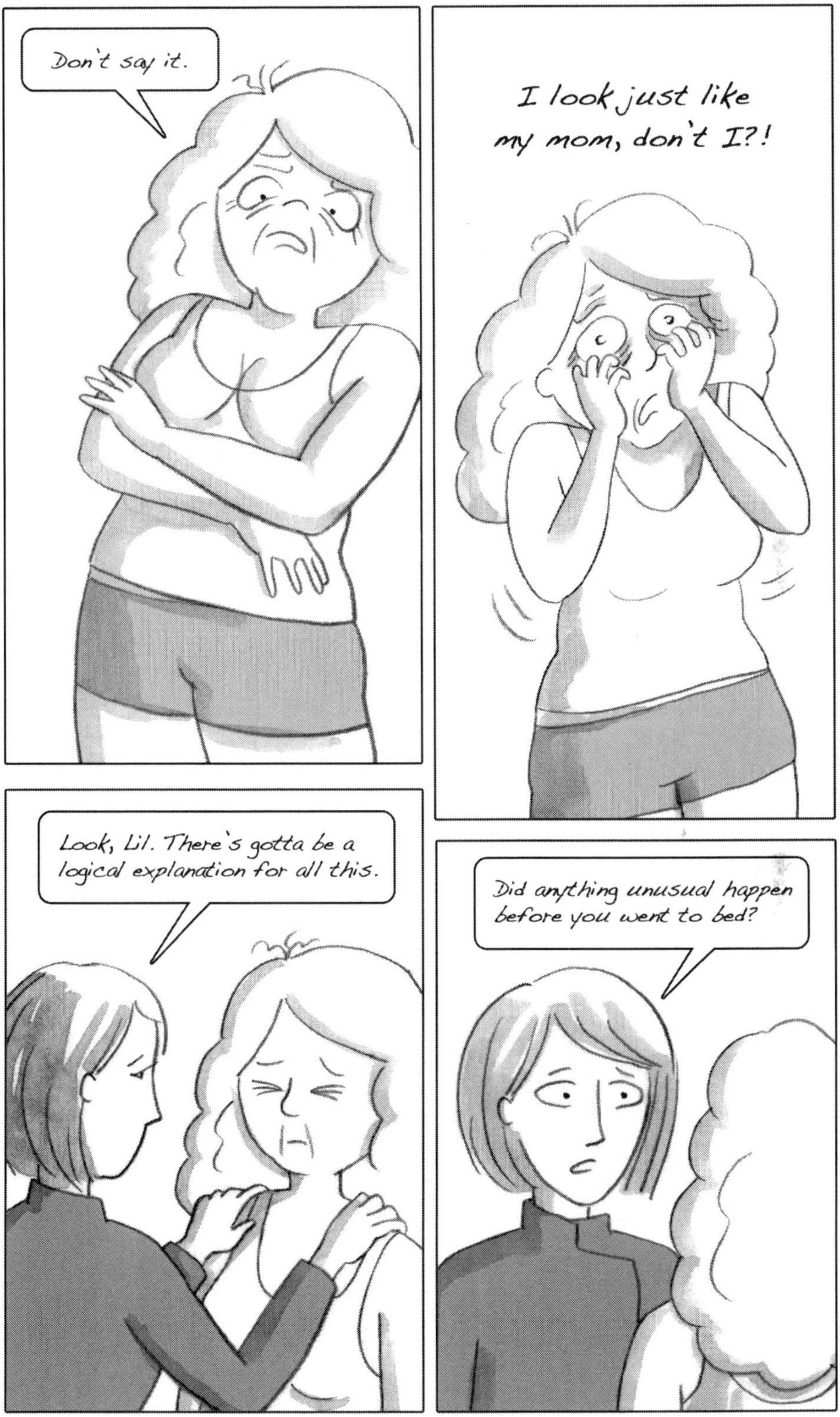
Don't say it.
I look just like my mom, don't I?!
Look, Lil. There's gotta be a logical explanation for all this.
Did anything unusual happen before you went to bed?

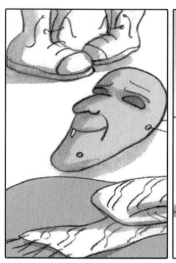

The only weird thing was at the party...

When that necklace you gave me started glowing.

Oh... no.

What?

It's the amulet! I told you it was magic.

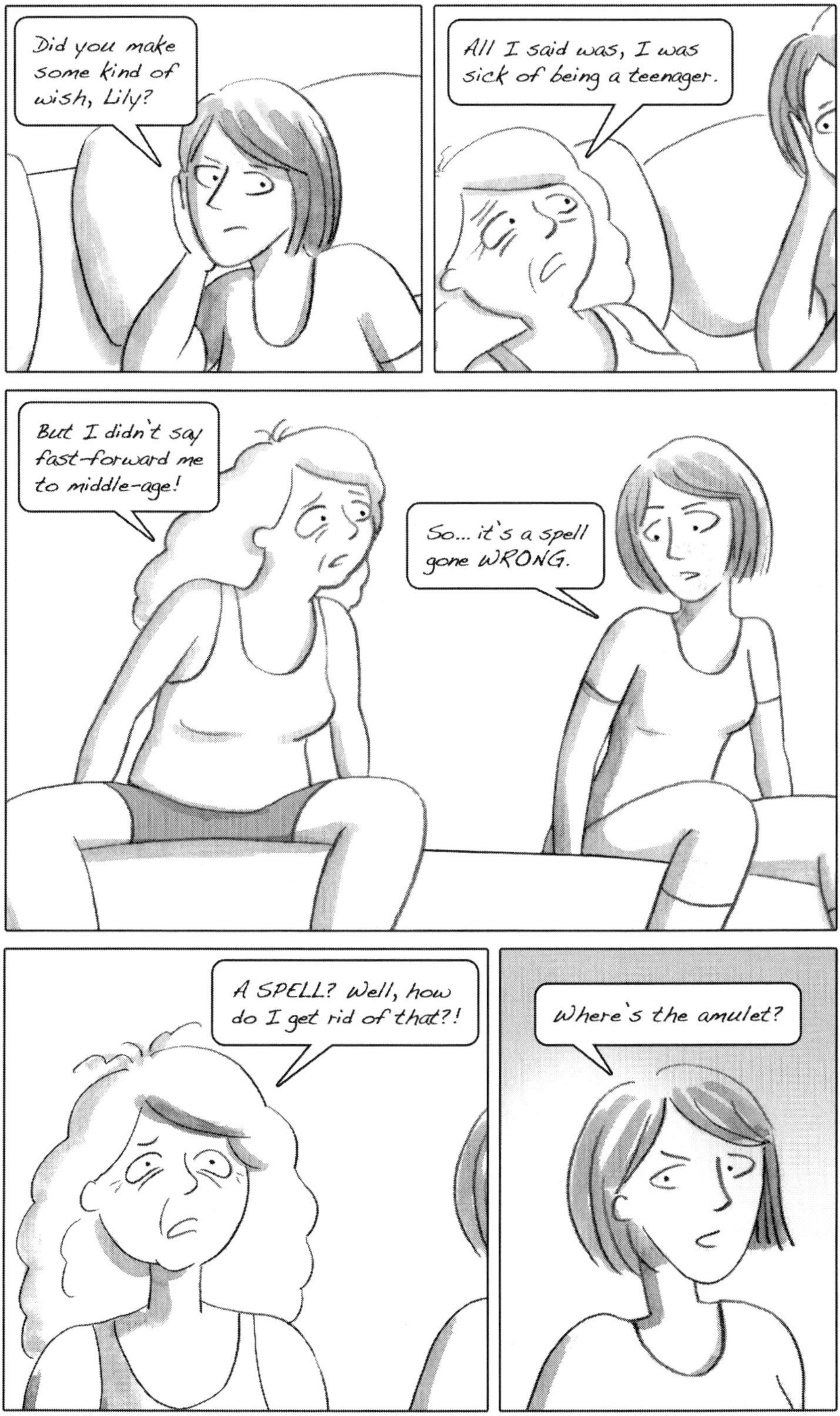
Did you make some kind of wish, Lily?
All I said was, I was sick of being a teenager.
But I didn't say fast-forward me to middle-age!
So... it's a spell gone WRONG.
A SPELL? Well, how do I get rid of that?!
Where's the amulet?

ONE HOUR LATER...

At least my feet still look young.

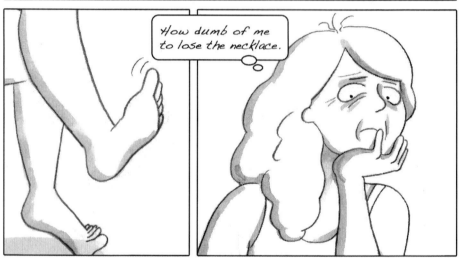

How dumb of me to lose the necklace.

But how would I know I'd need it to reverse a spell?

You still at Lynx's place?

Did you find it?

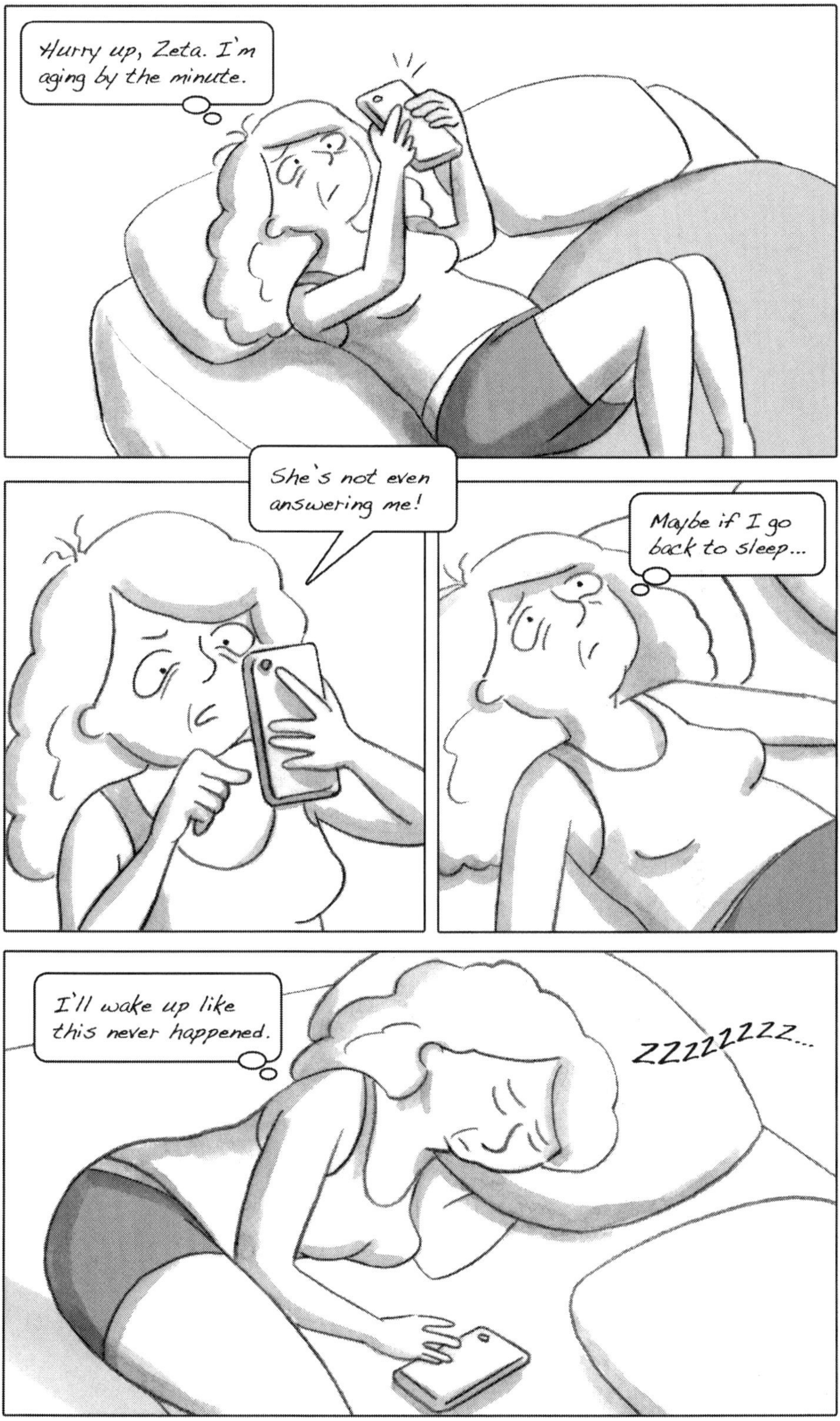
Hurry up, Zeta. I'm aging by the minute.
She's not even answering me!
Maybe if I go back to sleep...
I'll wake up like this never happened.
ZZZZZZZZ...

THE FIVE STAGES OF GRIEF

1) DENIAL

After a loss, the individual's first reaction is to deny reality, believe there's been a mistake and cling to false hope.

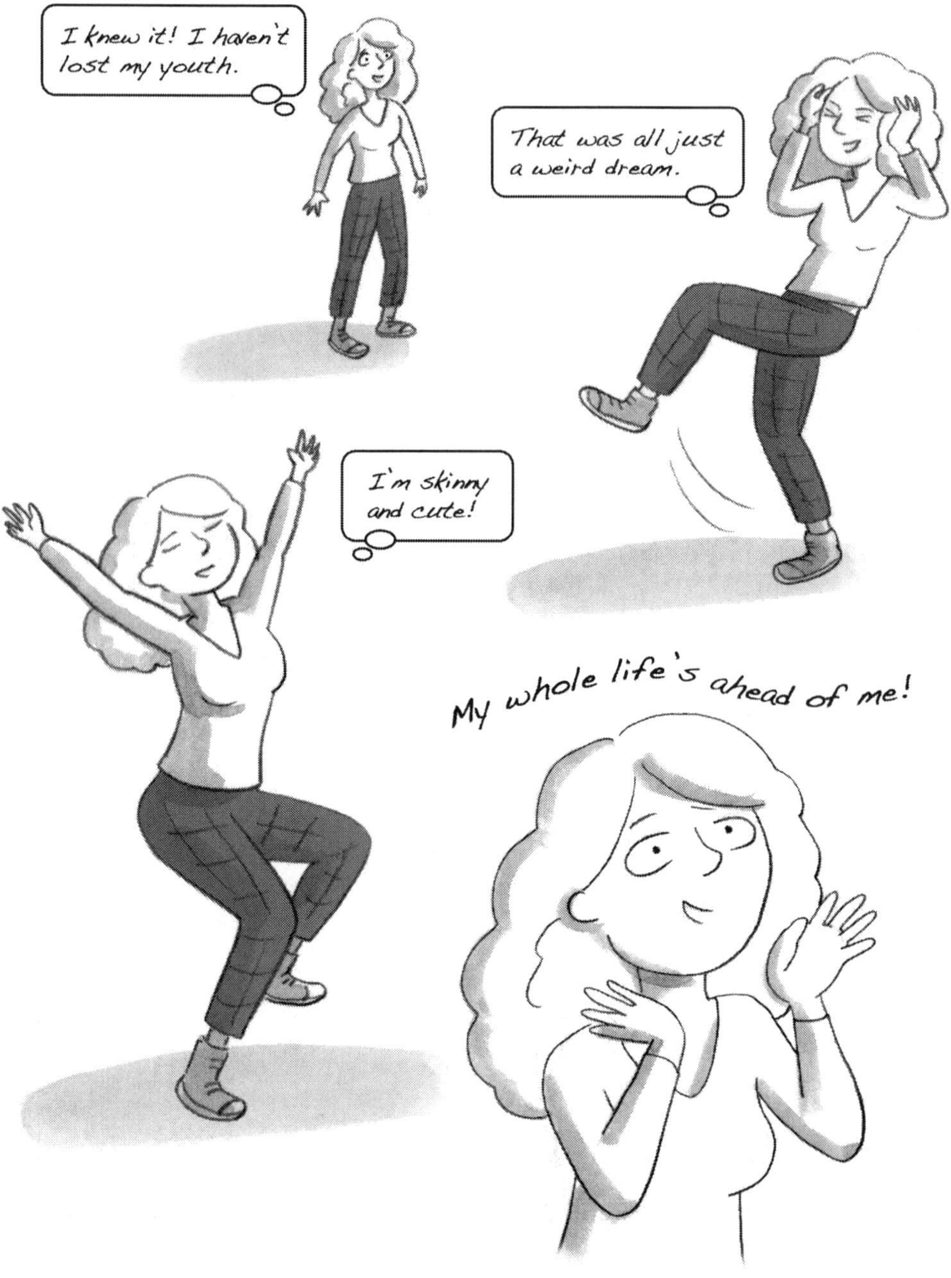
I knew it! I haven't lost my youth.
That was all just a weird dream.
I'm skinny and cute!
My whole life's ahead of me!

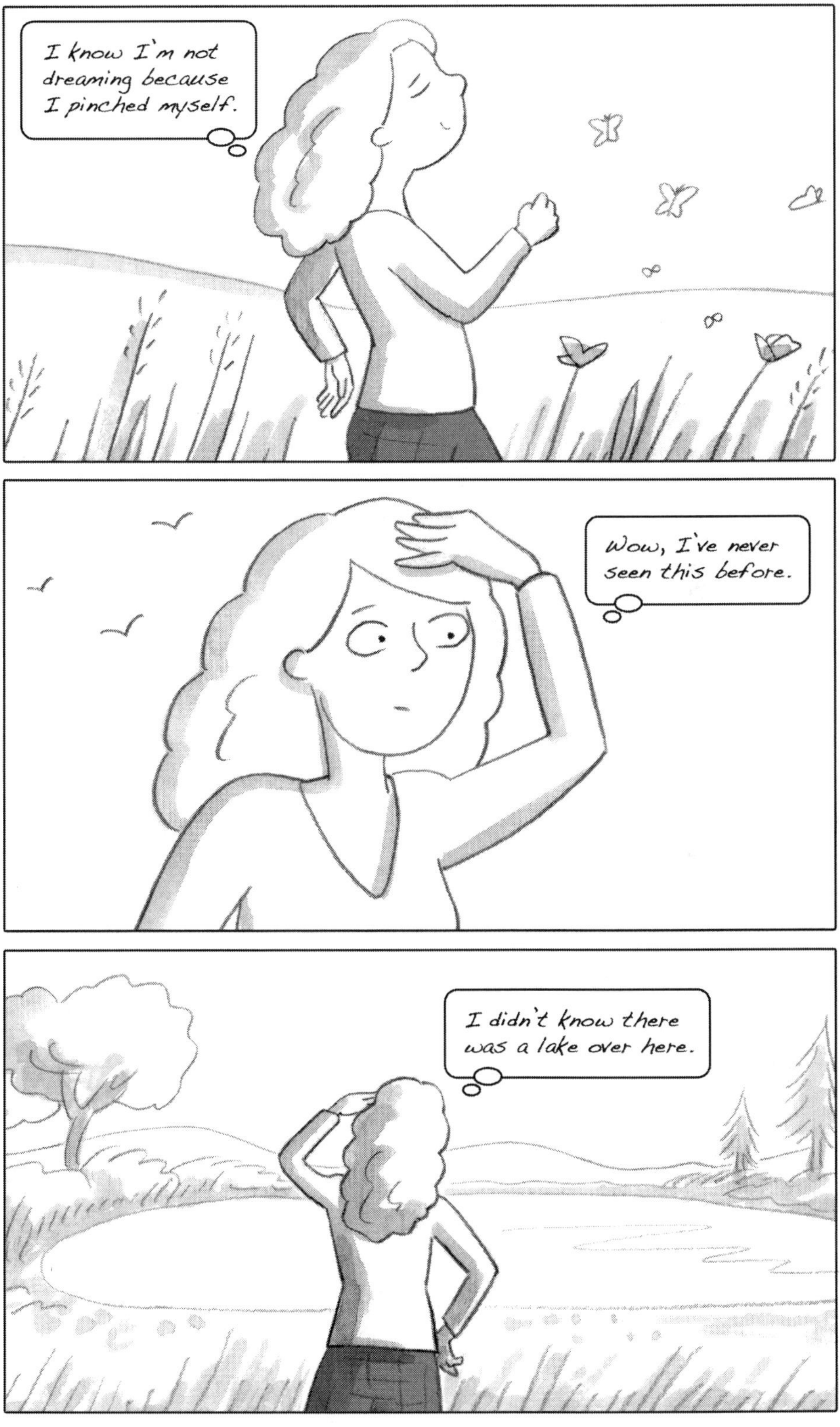
I know I'm not dreaming because I pinched myself.
Wow, I've never seen this before.
I didn't know there was a lake over here.

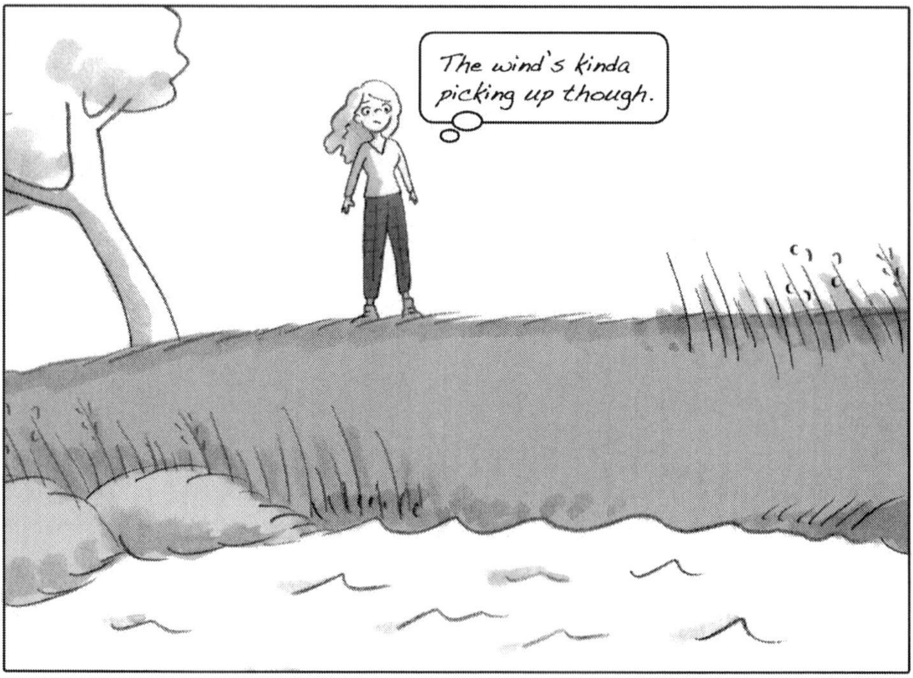
The wind's kinda picking up though.

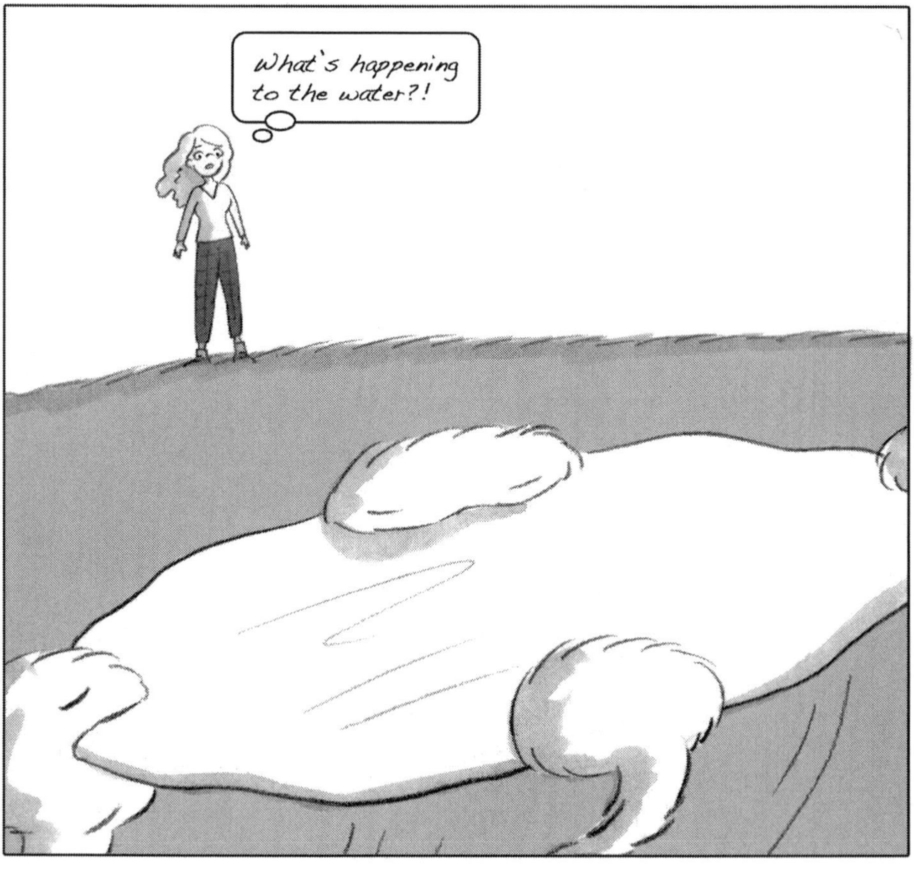
What's happening to the water?!

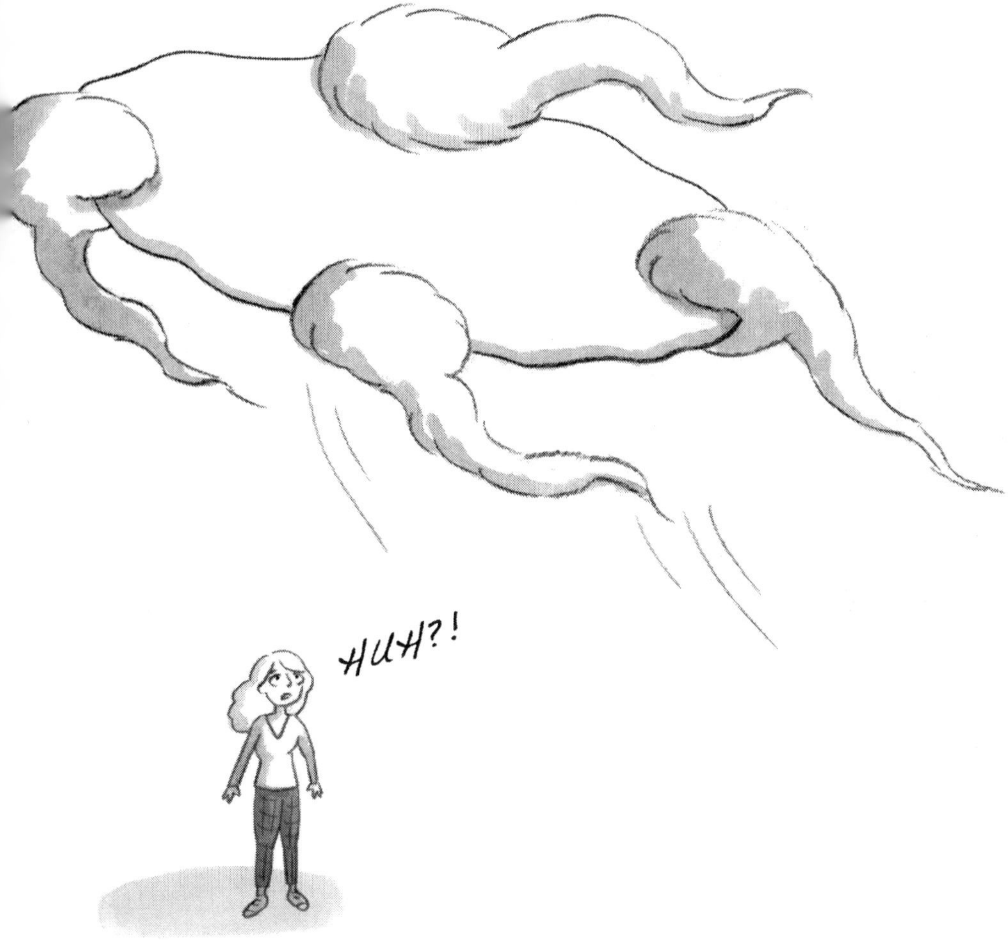
HUH?!

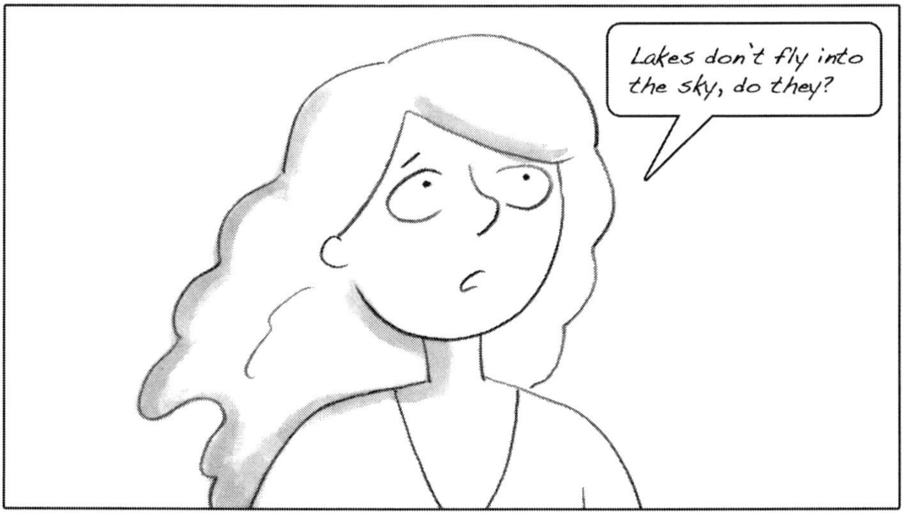
Lakes don't fly into the sky, do they?

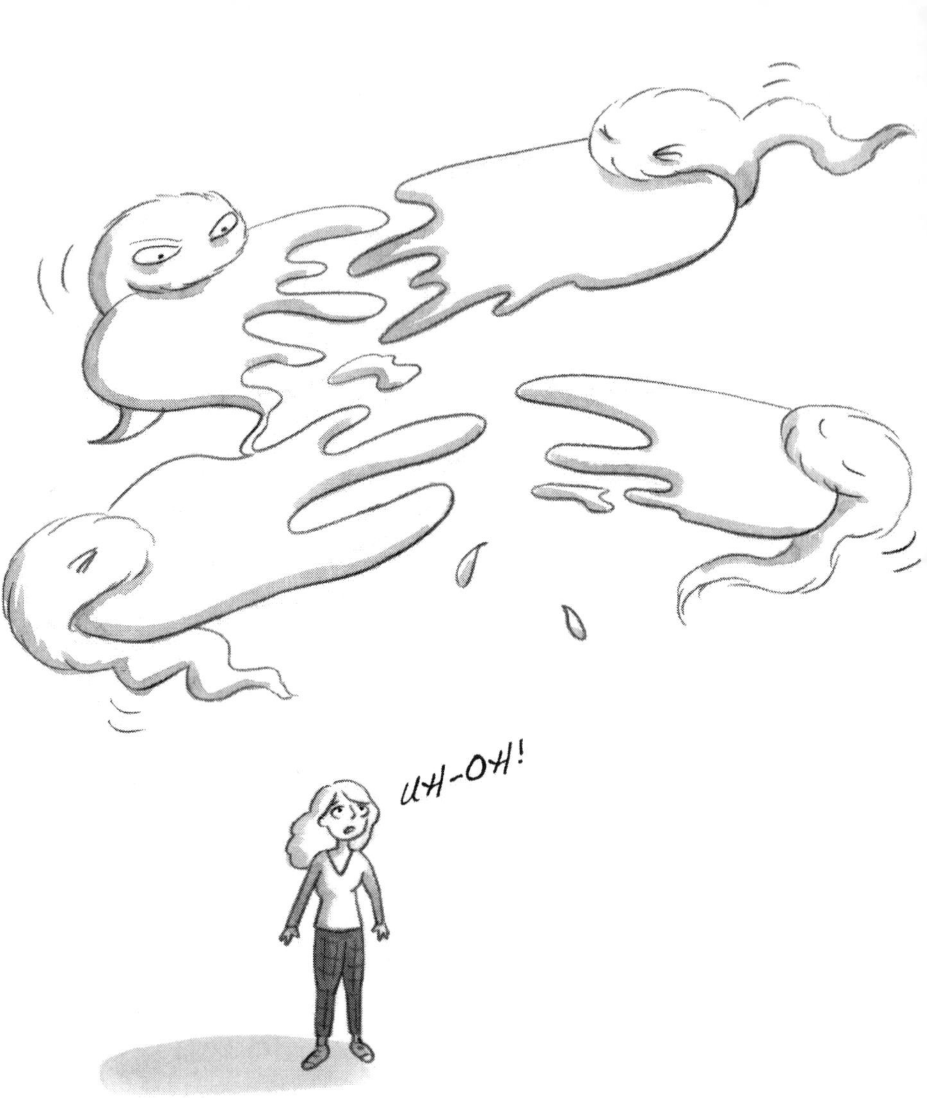
UH-OH!

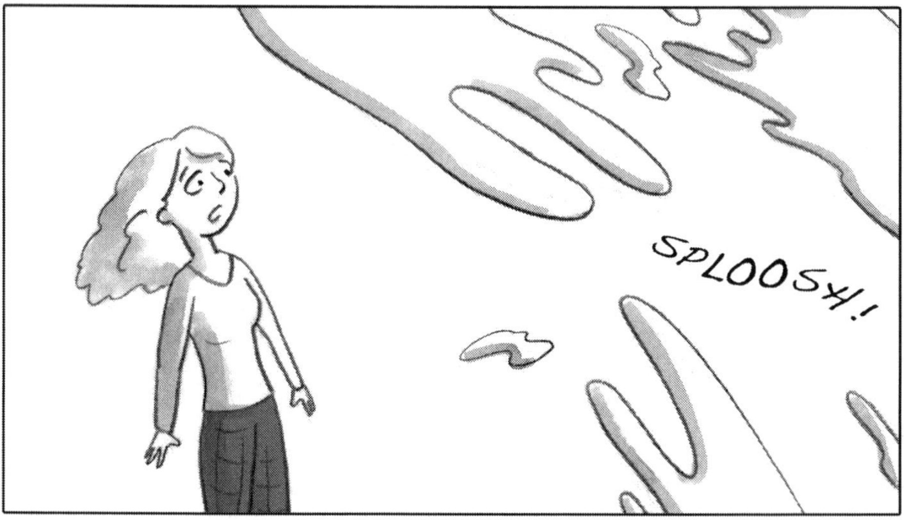
SPLOOSH!

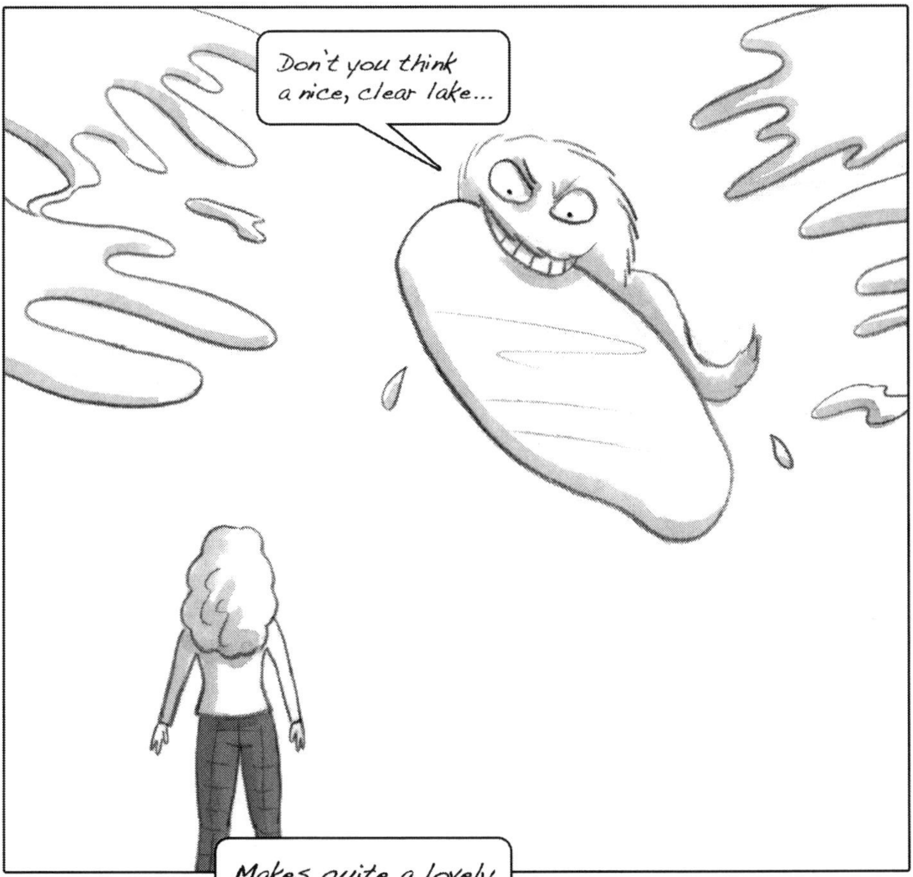
Don't you think a nice, clear lake...

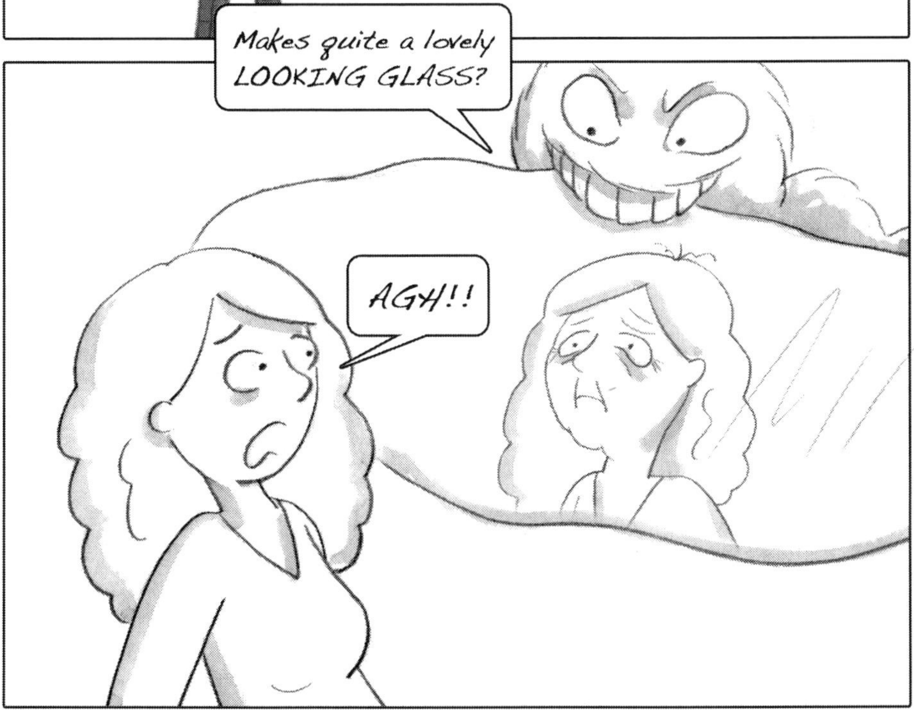
Makes quite a lovely LOOKING GLASS?
AGH!!

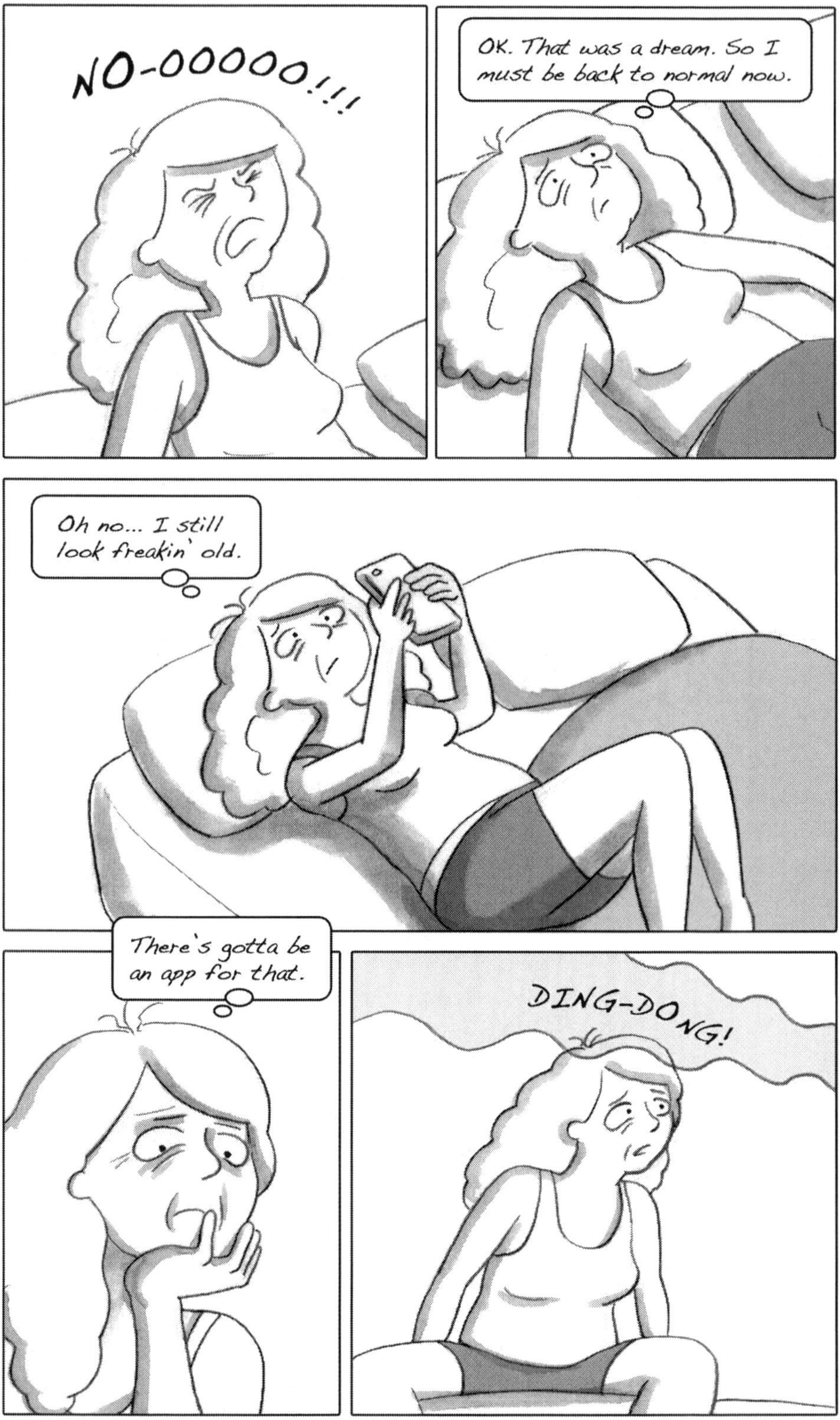
NO-OOOOO!!!!
OK. That was a dream. So I must be back to normal now.
Oh no... I still look freakin' old.
There's gotta be an app for that.
DING-DONG!

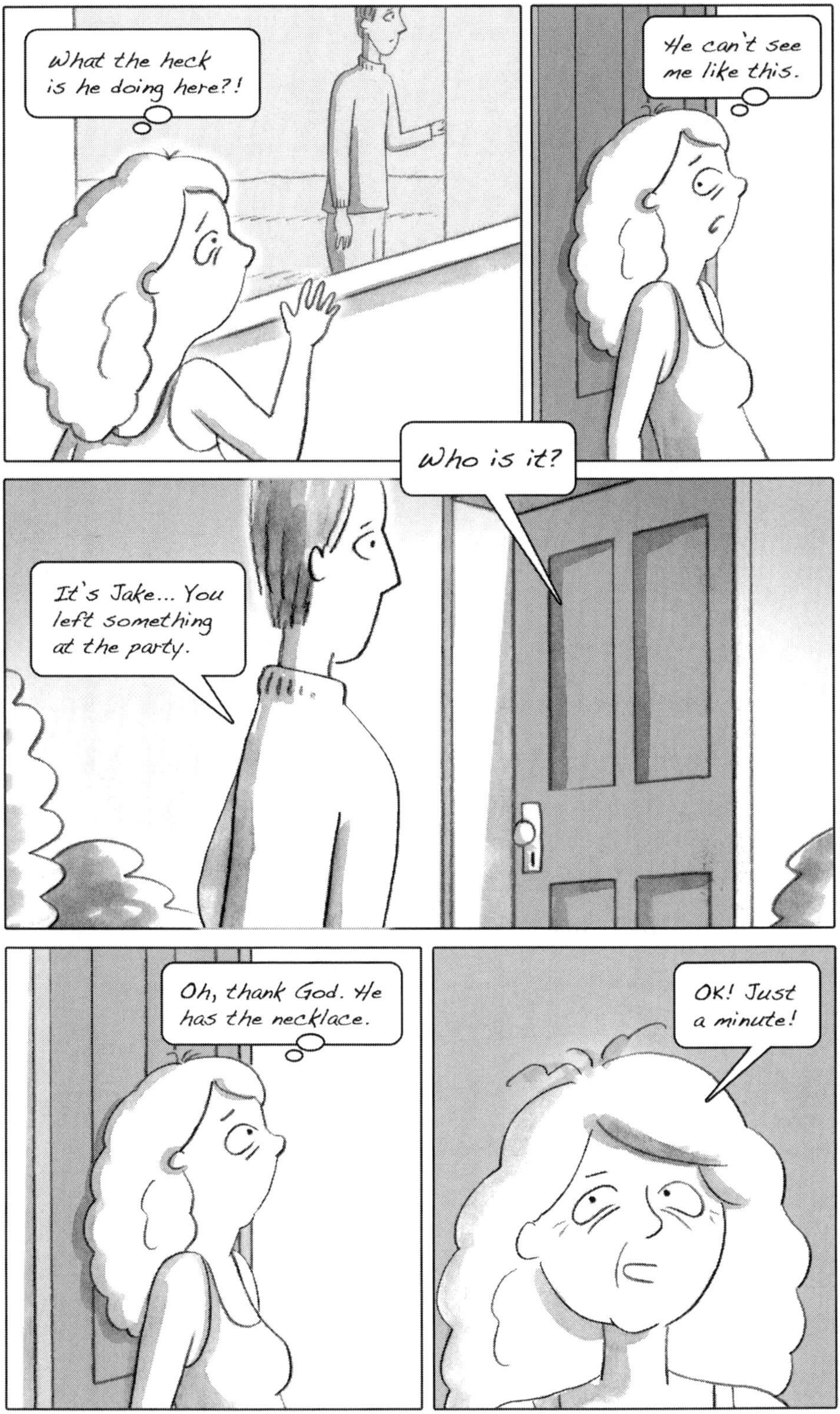
What the heck is he doing here?!
He can't see me like this.
Who is it?
It's Jake... You left something at the party.
Oh, thank God. He has the necklace.
OK! Just a minute!

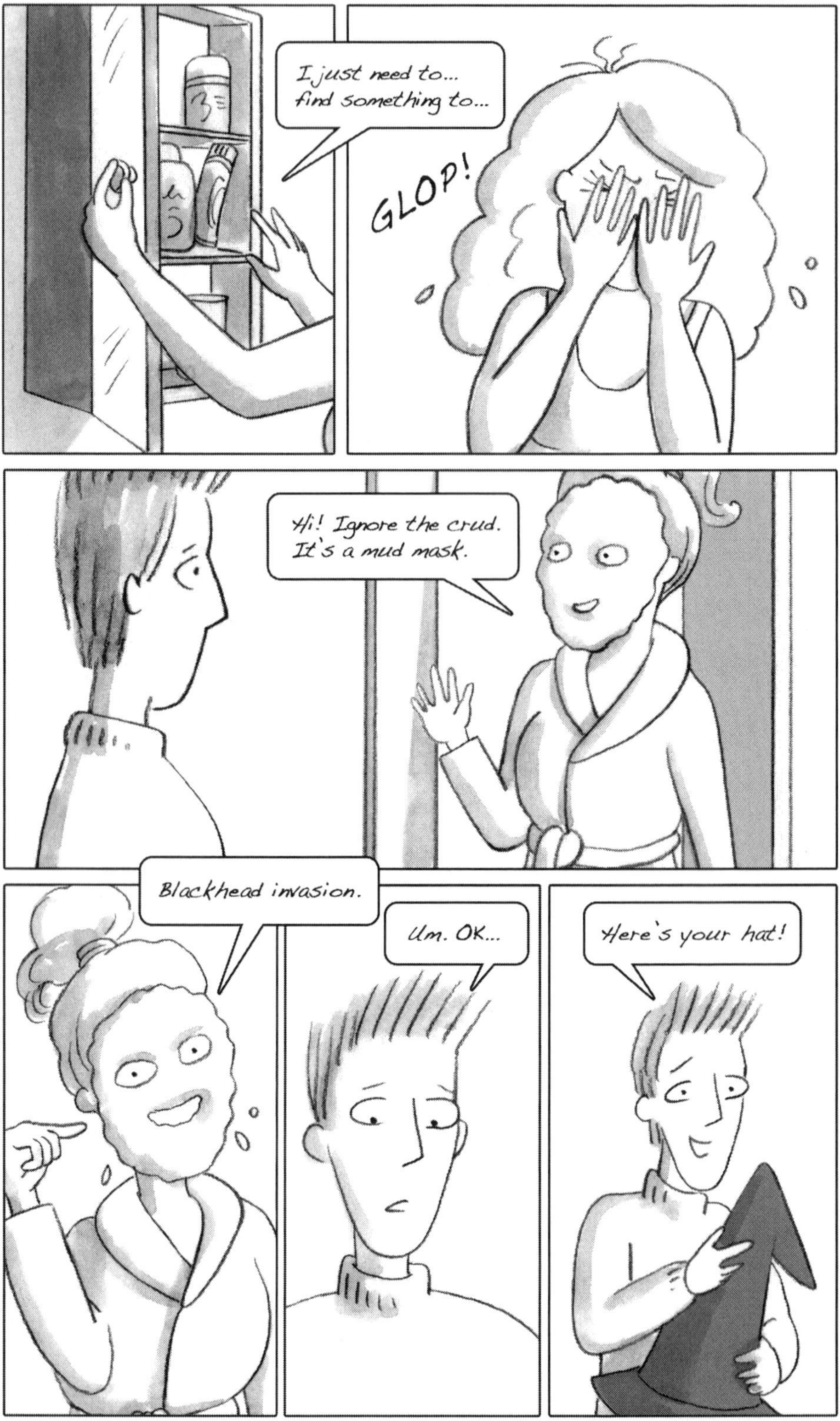
I just need to... find something to...
GLOP!
Hi! Ignore the crud. It's a mud mask.
Blackhead invasion.
Um. OK...
Here's your hat!

If you do not tell the truth
about yourself you cannot tell it
about other people.

VIRGINIA WOOLF

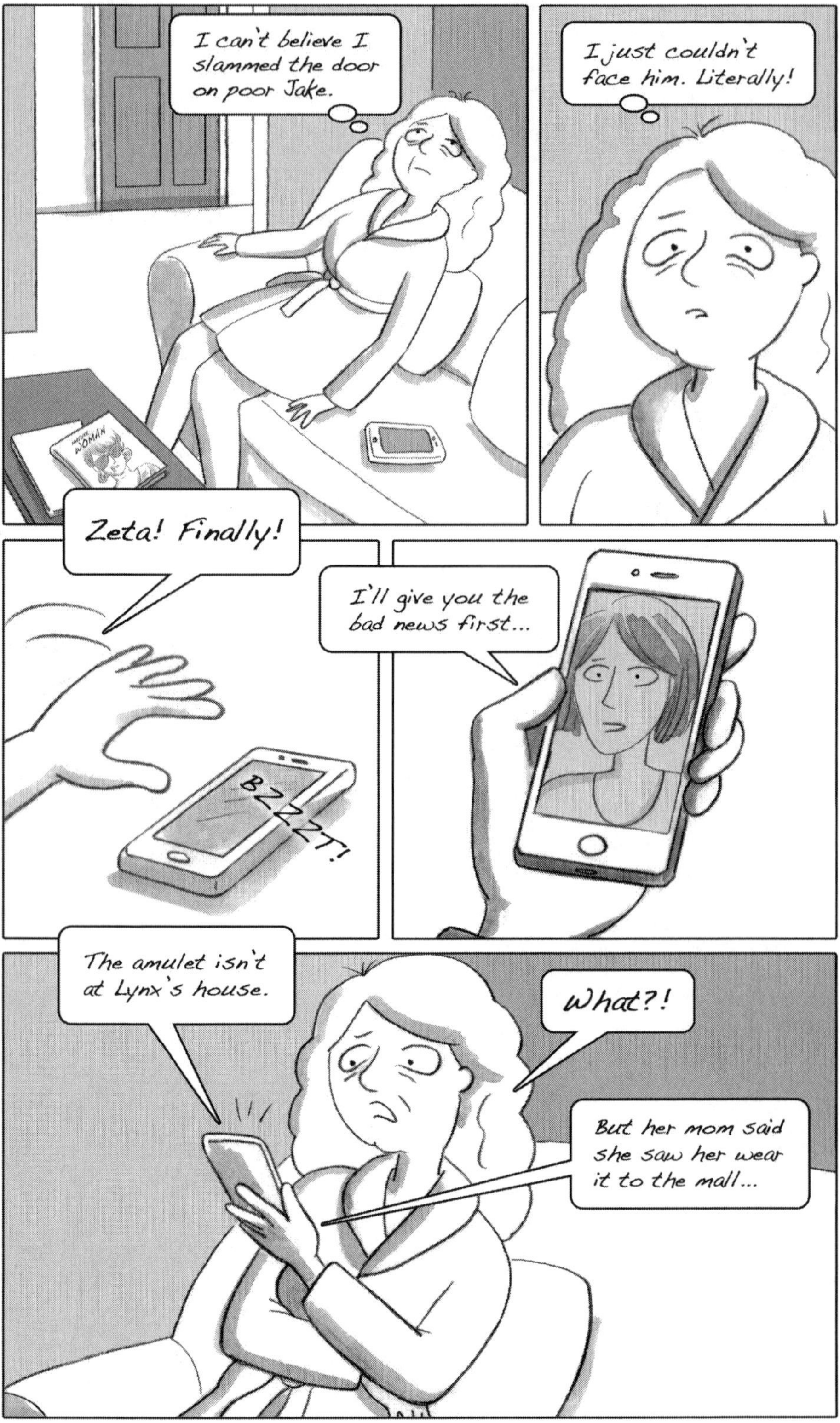
I can't believe I slammed the door on poor Jake.
I just couldn't face him. Literally!
Zeta! Finally!
BZZZT!
I'll give you the bad news first...
The amulet isn't at Lynx's house.
What?!
But her mom said she saw her wear it to the mall...

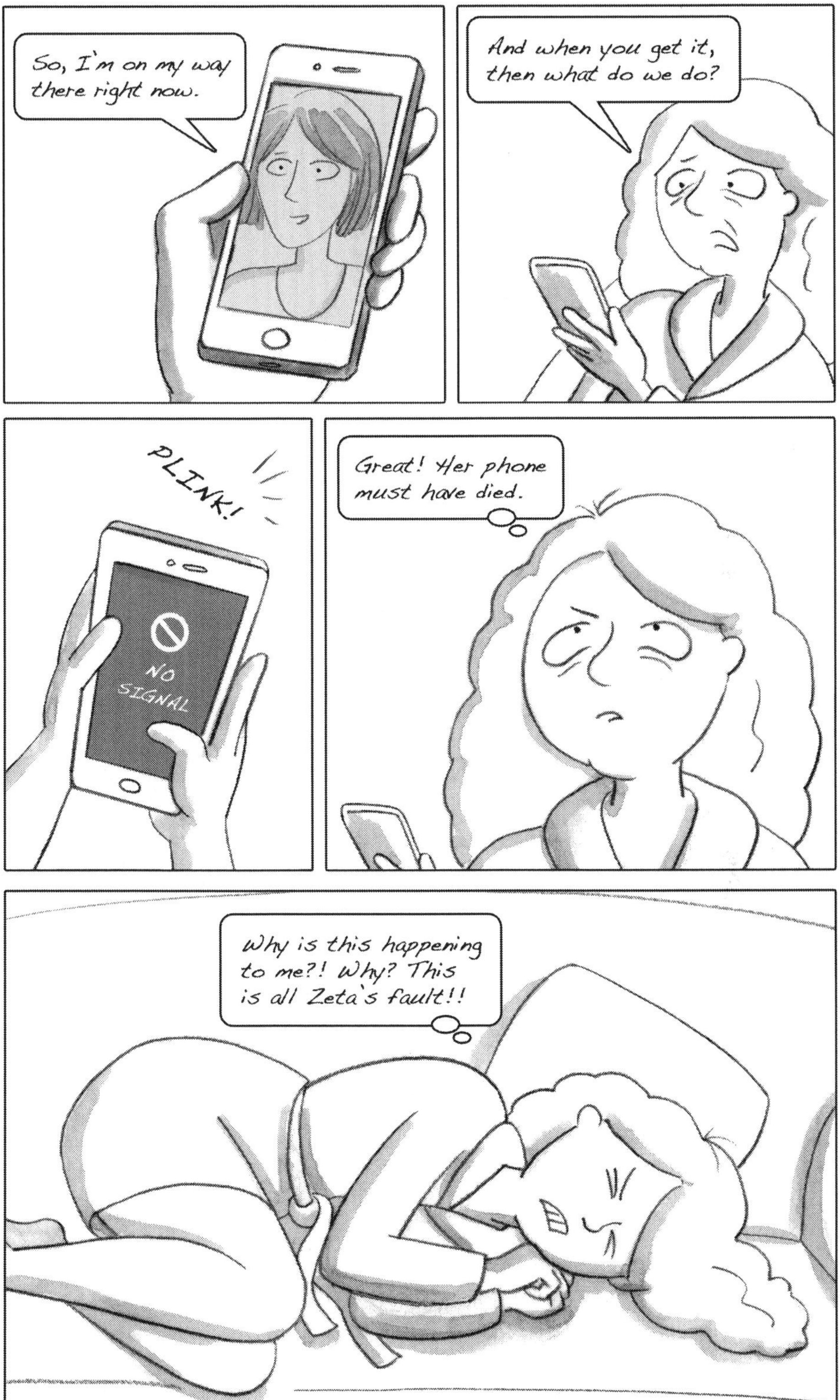
So, I'm on my way there right now.
And when you get it, then what do we do?
PLINK!
NO SIGNAL
Great! Her phone must have died.
Why is this happening to me?! Why? This is all Zeta's fault!!

THE FIVE STAGES OF GRIEF

2) ANGER

After coming out of denial, the individual seeks someone to blame for her condition.

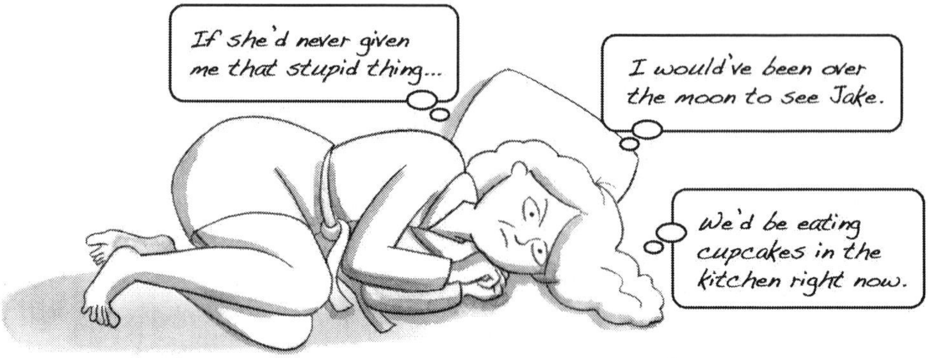
If she'd never given me that stupid thing...
I would've been over the moon to see Jake.
We'd be eating cupcakes in the kitchen right now.

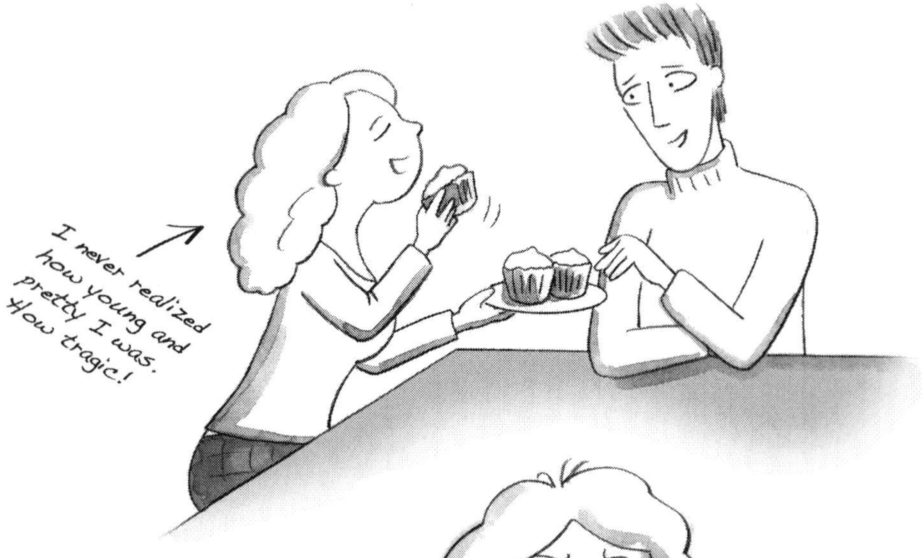
I never realized how young and pretty I was. How tragic!

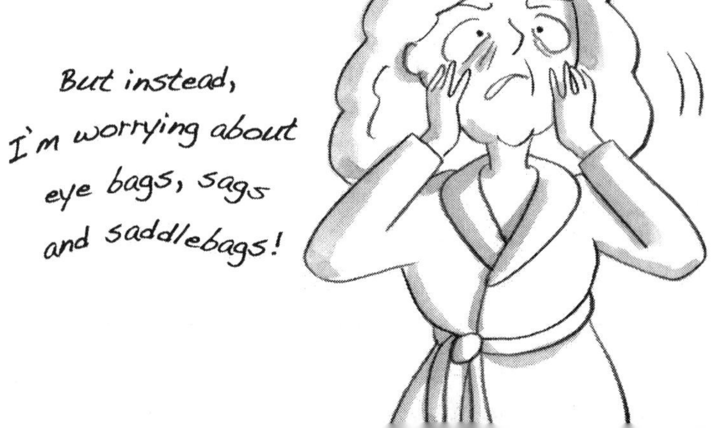
But instead, I'm worrying about eye bags, sags and saddlebags!

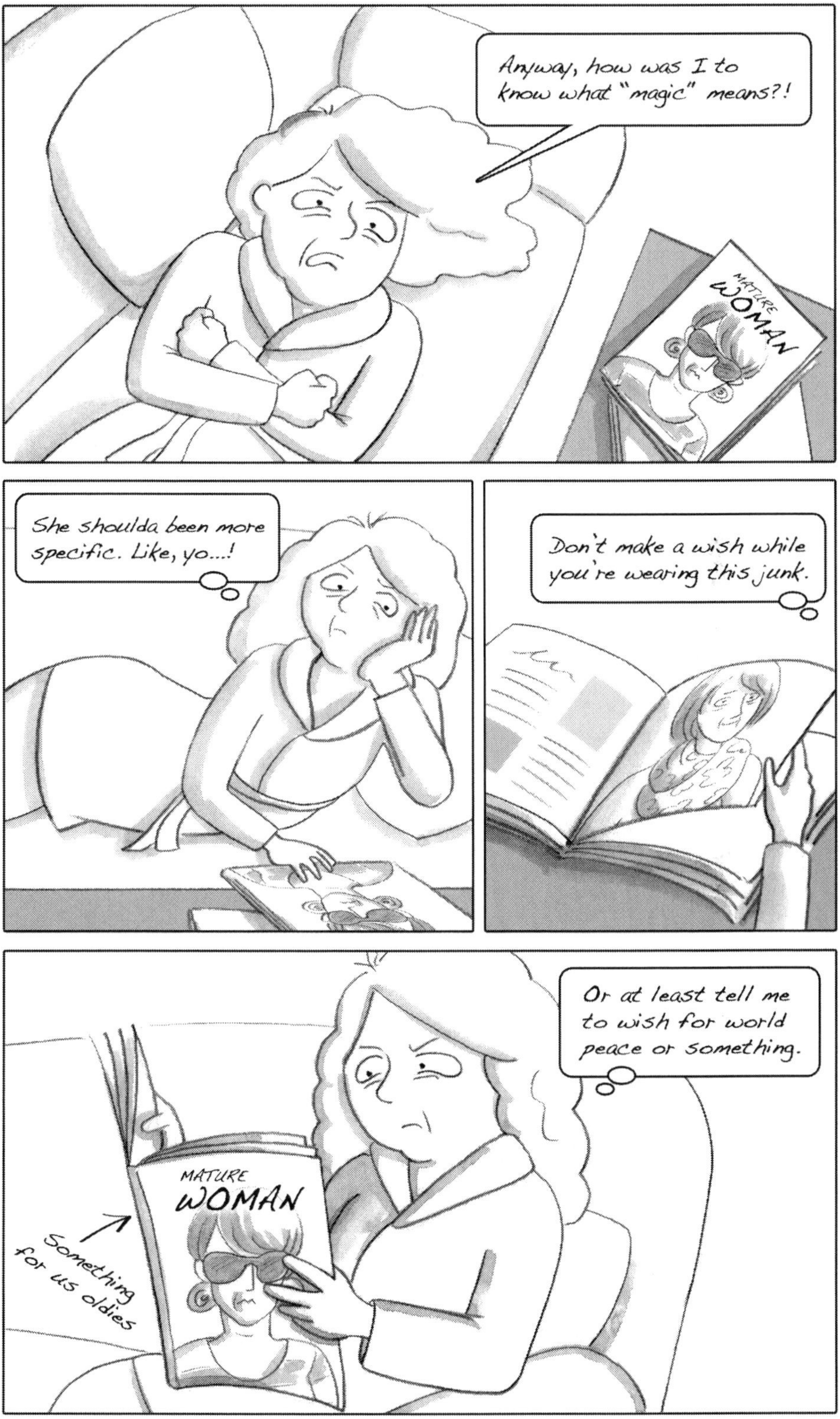
Anyway, how was I to know what "magic" means?!
MATURE WOMAN
She shoulda been more specific. Like, yo...!
Don't make a wish while you're wearing this junk.
Or at least tell me to wish for world peace or something.
MATURE WOMAN
Something for us oldies

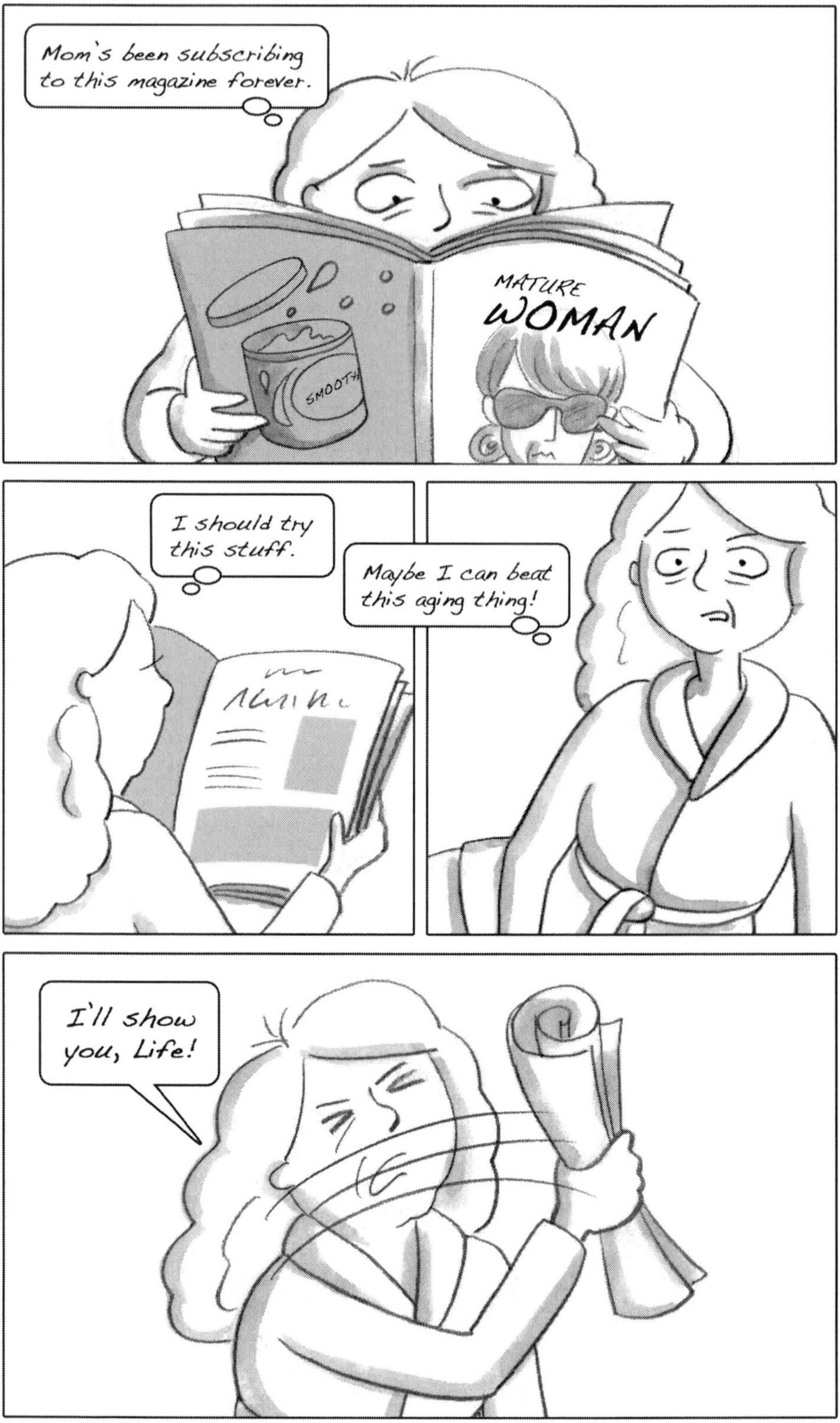
Mom's been subscribing to this magazine forever.
MATURE WOMAN
SMOOTH
I should try this stuff.
Maybe I can beat this aging thing!
I'll show you, Life!

AGELESS BEAUTY

LIVE YOUR BEST, WRINKLE-FREE LIFE!

Ever heard the expression, "You're as young as you FEEL?" Get real, ladies. We all know you're only as young as you LOOK.

That's why our in-house expert designed the AGELESS BEAUTY GUIDE to eliminate all your flaws.

Youthful, glowing skin, a toned tummy, perky appendages, and silky, soft hair... can all be yours with a little effort (and a wad of money).

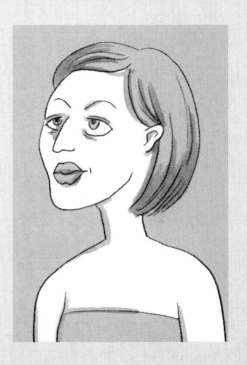

Ageless Expert
MS. MARGIE PLOOPS

Don't do as I do, do as I say! When I was young, I committed all manner of BEAUTY SINS! I laid out in the sun, I smiled too much, I drank coffee without using a straw, I ate trans fats... You name it, I did it.

But as a modern woman, you have a choice. You can enjoy your life... or commit to preserving your looks. Isn't it a no-brainer?

YOUR AGELESS BEAUTY GUIDE

BY MS. MARGIE PLOOPS

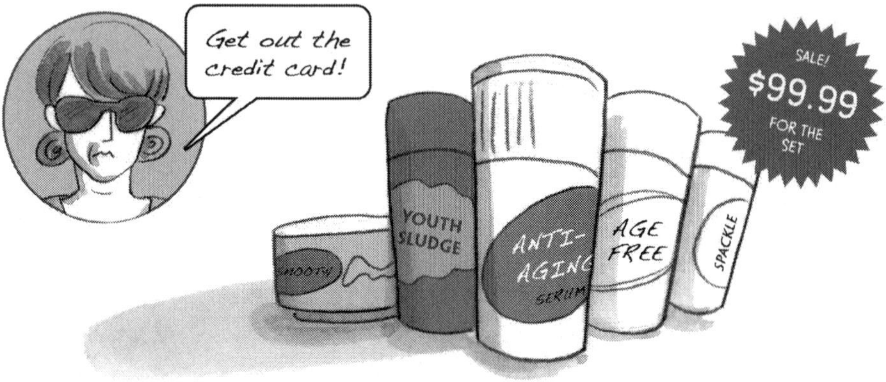

Get out the credit card!
SALE!
$99.99
FOR THE SET
SMOOTH
YOUTH SLUDGE
ANTI-AGING SERUM
AGE FREE
SPACKLE

Why settle for what life gave you?
With the right products, you can be in control of your aging journey... every step of the way!

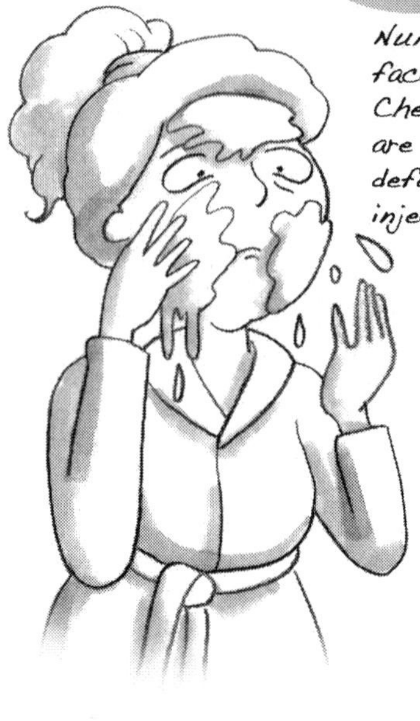

SKIN

Number one, get that face smoothed out. Chemical-laden potions are your first line of defense. (More on injecting them later.)

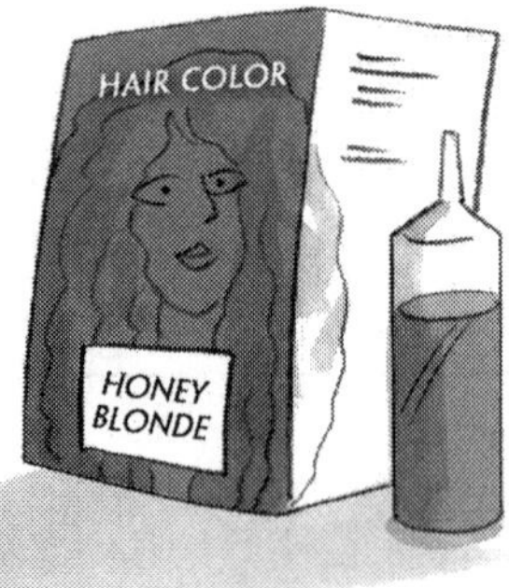

HAIR COLOR
HONEY BLONDE

HAIR

Your hair is no longer a D.I.Y. project. Gray coverage is now a job for a professional. You'll need a sizable hair budget, ladies.

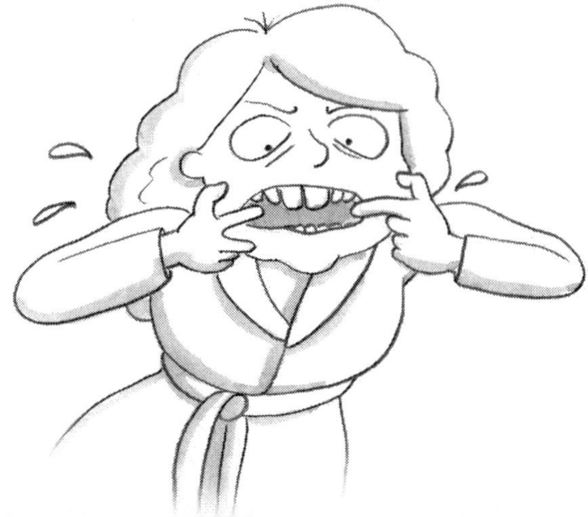

TEETH

There's one thing you don't want AU NATUREL, and that's your gnashers. Straighten them, whiten them or keep your mouth shut when you smile.

DO YOU MAKE THE CUT?

HOW TO GO FROM OLD COW TO NEW CALF

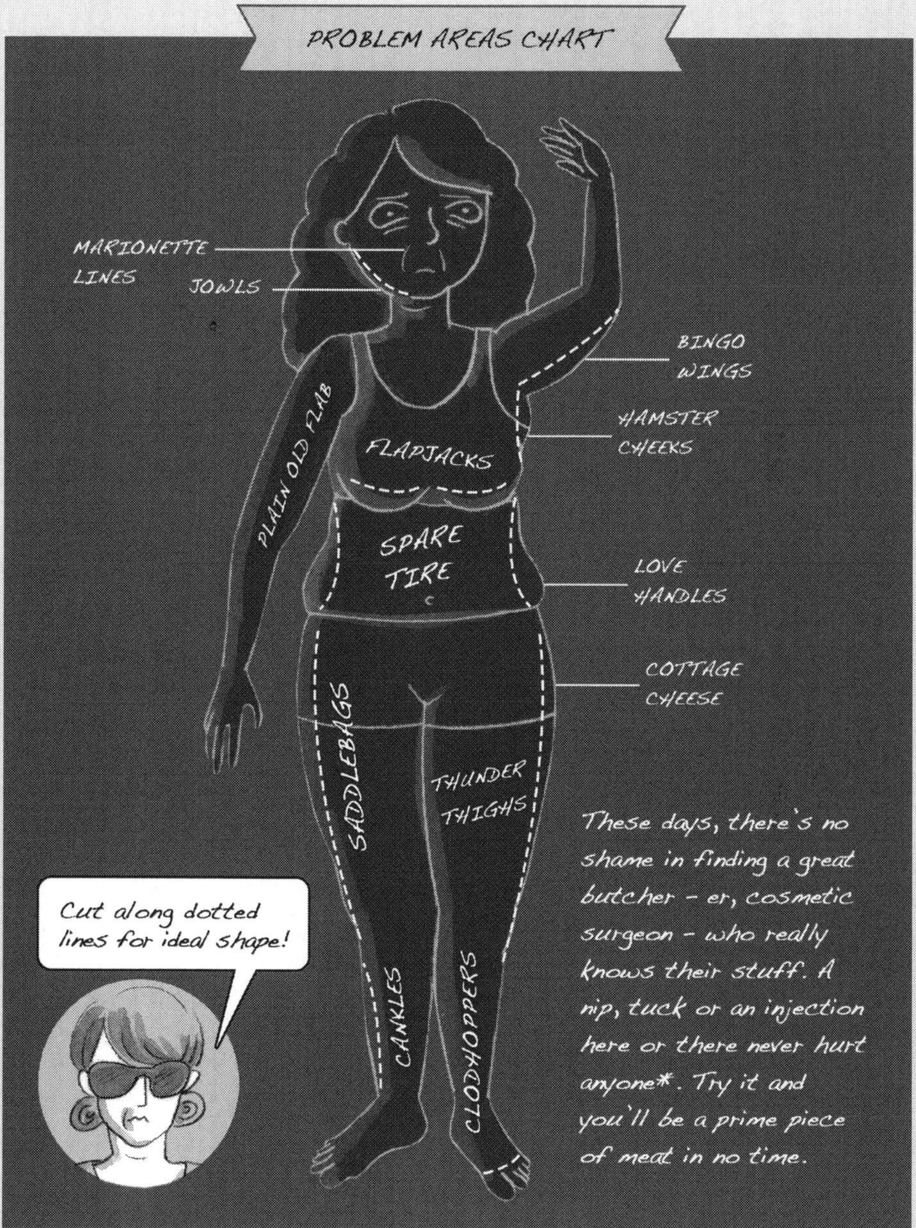
PROBLEM AREAS CHART
MARIONETTE LINES
JOWLS
BINGO WINGS
HAMSTER CHEEKS
PLAIN OLD FLAB
FLAPJACKS
SPARE TIRE
LOVE HANDLES
COTTAGE CHEESE
SADDLEBAGS
THUNDER THIGHS
CANKLES
CLODHOPPERS
Cut along dotted lines for ideal shape!
These days, there's no shame in finding a great butcher - er, cosmetic surgeon - who really knows their stuff. A nip, tuck or an injection here or there never hurt anyone*. Try it and you'll be a prime piece of meat in no time.

*We won't have accurate data on cosmetic injections for another twenty years, minimum. But, hey, you gotta die of something, right?

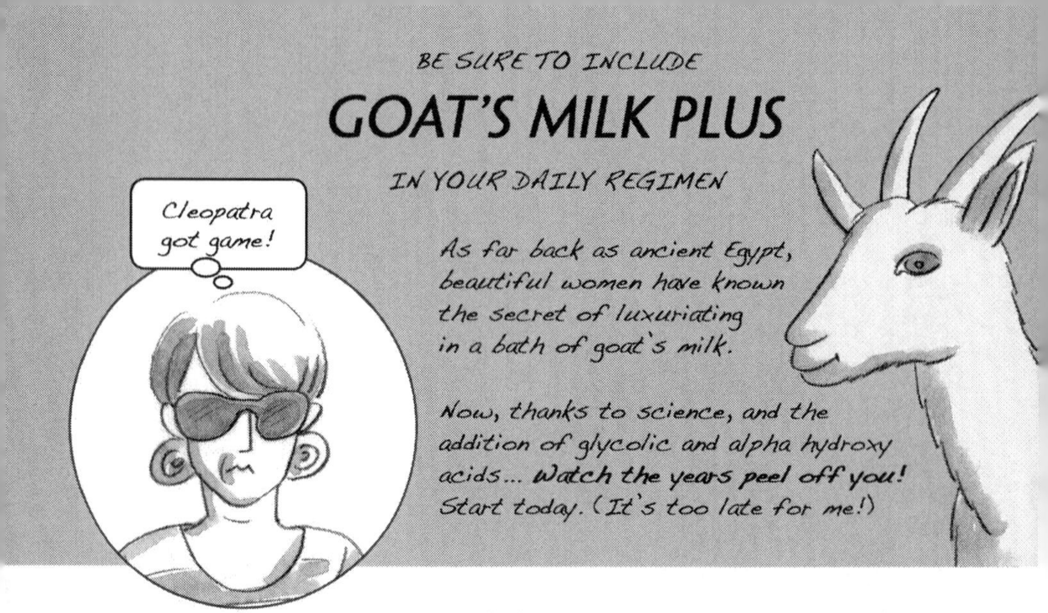
BE SURE TO INCLUDE
GOAT'S MILK PLUS
IN YOUR DAILY REGIMEN
Cleopatra got game!
As far back as ancient Egypt, beautiful women have known the secret of luxuriating in a bath of goat's milk.
Now, thanks to science, and the addition of glycolic and alpha hydroxy acids... Watch the years peel off you! Start today. (It's too late for me!)

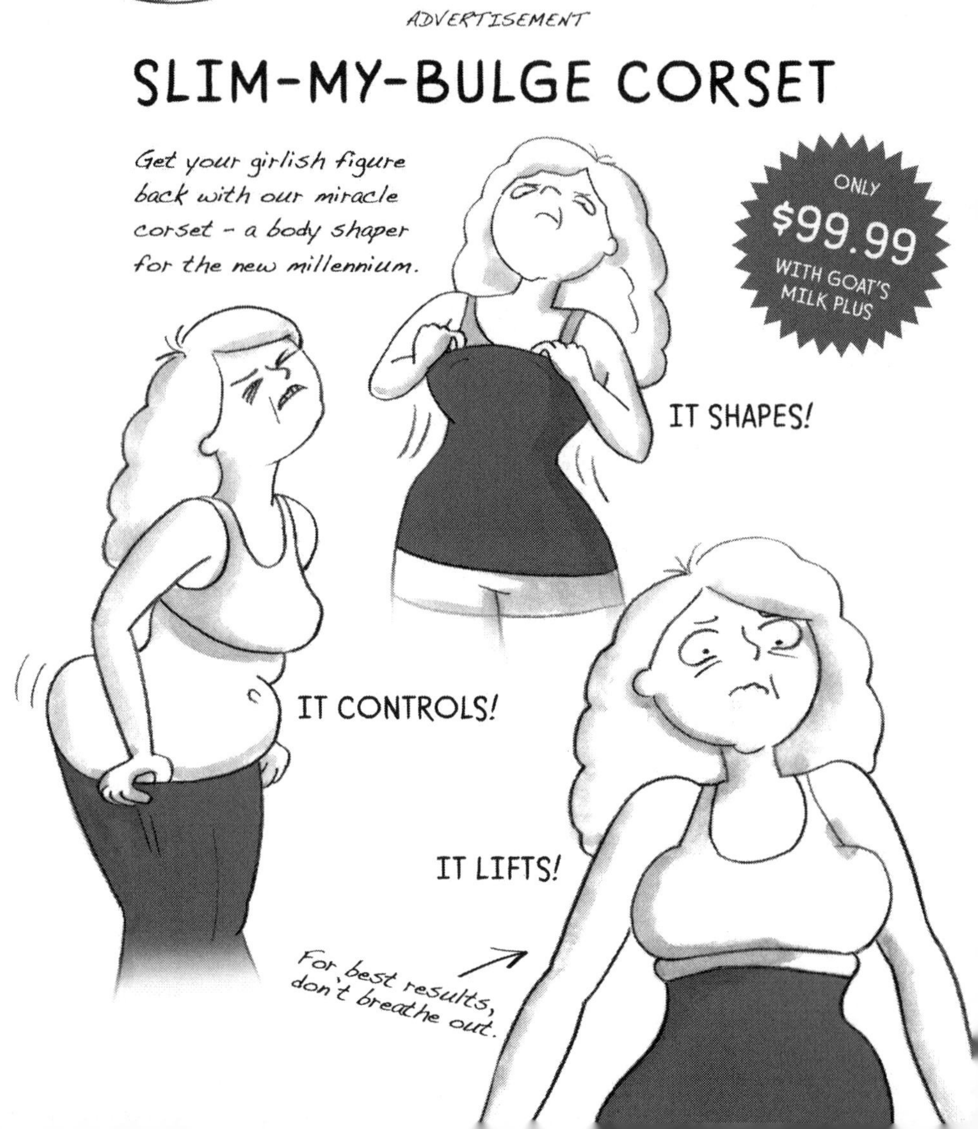
ADVERTISEMENT
SLIM-MY-BULGE CORSET
Get your girlish figure back with our miracle corset - a body shaper for the new millennium.
ONLY $99.99 WITH GOAT'S MILK PLUS
IT SHAPES!
IT CONTROLS!
IT LIFTS!
For best results, don't breathe out.

QUICK GUIDE

WHEN IN DOUBT, ALWAYS REMEMBER THE THREE ESSENTIALS:

ADVERTISEMENT

2 FOR 1!

BOTOXIC

PLUS LIPTOXIC FILLER

We'll turn your frown upside down with our state-of-the-art Botoxic wrinkle remover and Liptoxic facial filler.

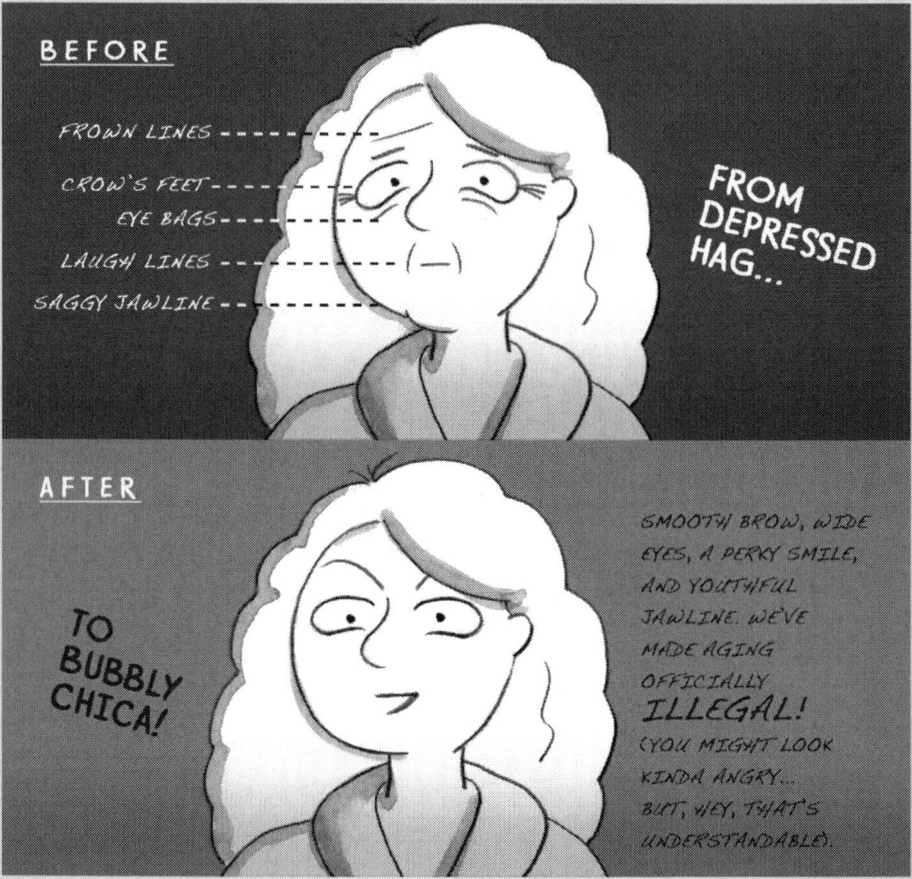
BEFORE
FROWN LINES
CROW'S FEET
EYE BAGS
LAUGH LINES
SAGGY JAWLINE
FROM DEPRESSED HAG...
AFTER
TO BUBBLY CHICA!
SMOOTH BROW, WIDE EYES, A PERKY SMILE, AND YOUTHFUL JAWLINE. WE'VE MADE AGING OFFICIALLY
ILLEGAL!
(YOU MIGHT LOOK KINDA ANGRY... BUT, HEY, THAT'S UNDERSTANDABLE).

COUPON

BOTOXIC + LIPTOXIC

ONLY $499.00*

2 FOR 1!

*All clients must sign Patient Consent Form advising of potential risks. (Horrific side effects or disfigurement are your own darn fault.)

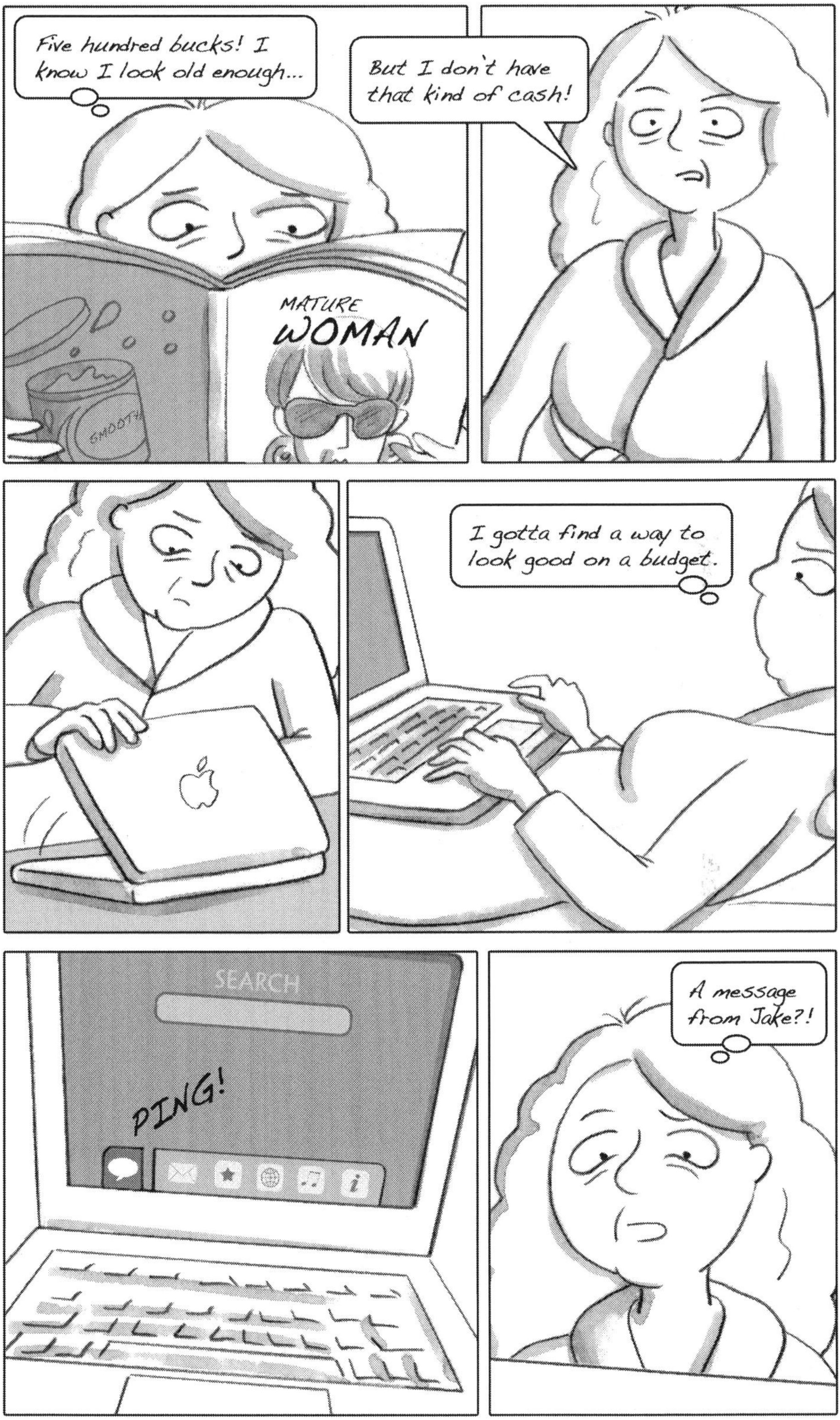
Five hundred bucks! I know I look old enough...
MATURE WOMAN
SMOOTH
But I don't have that kind of cash!
I gotta find a way to look good on a budget.
SEARCH
PING!
A message from Jake?!

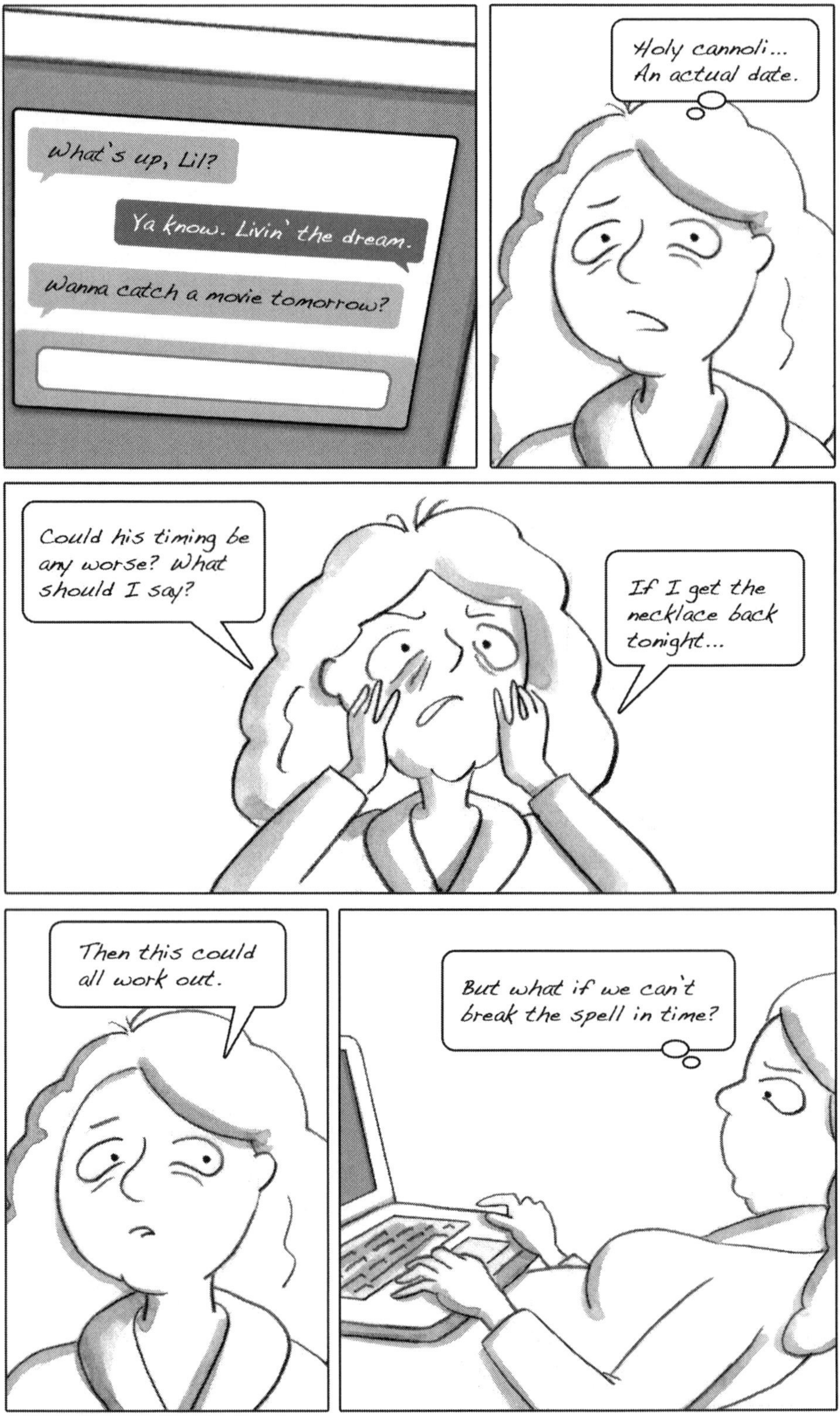
What's up, Lil?
Ya know. Livin' the dream.
Wanna catch a movie tomorrow?
Holy cannoli... An actual date.
Could his timing be any worse? What should I say?
If I get the necklace back tonight...
Then this could all work out.
But what if we can't break the spell in time?

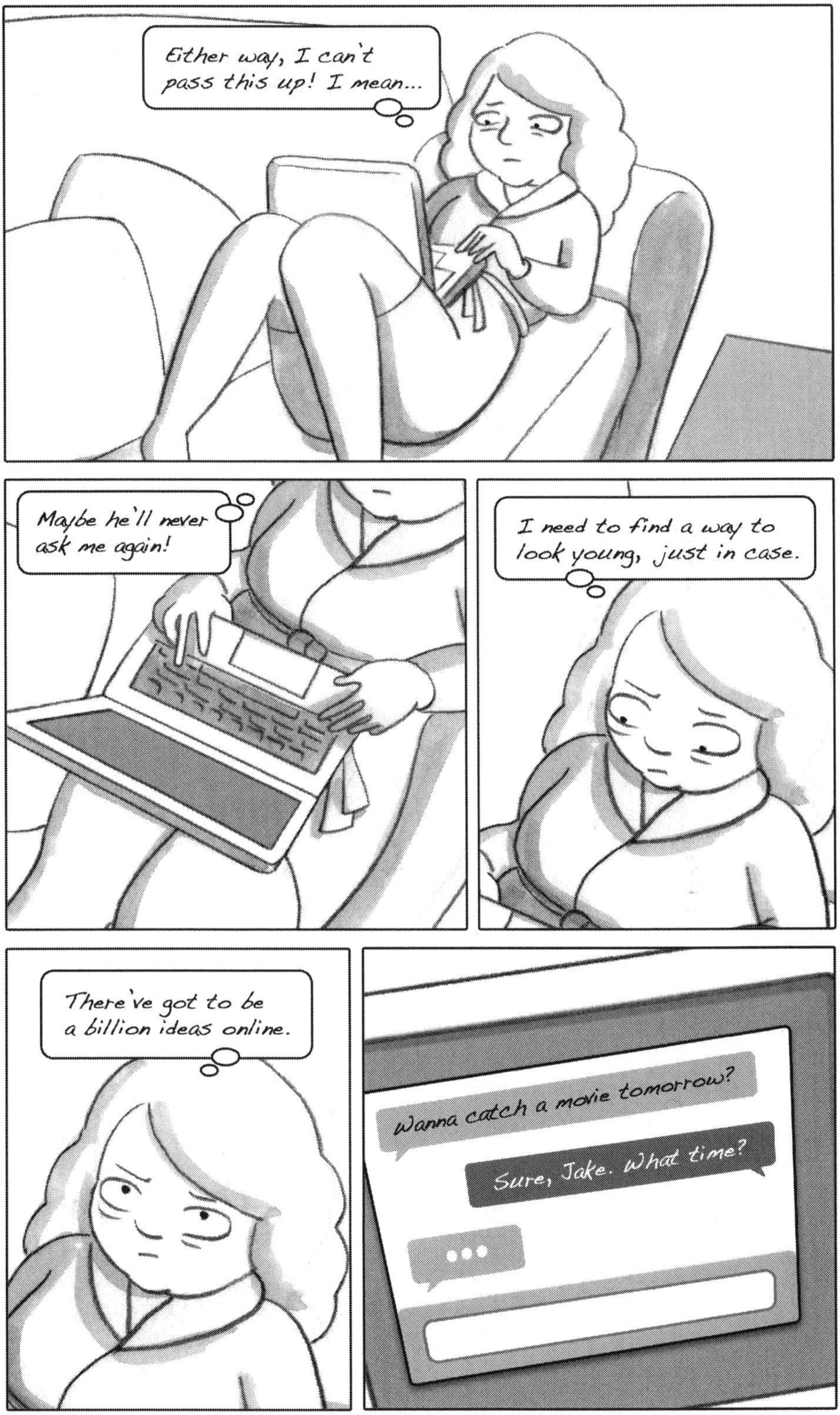
Either way, I can't pass this up! I mean...
Maybe he'll never ask me again!
I need to find a way to look young, just in case.
There've got to be a billion ideas online.
Wanna catch a movie tomorrow?
Sure, Jake. What time?

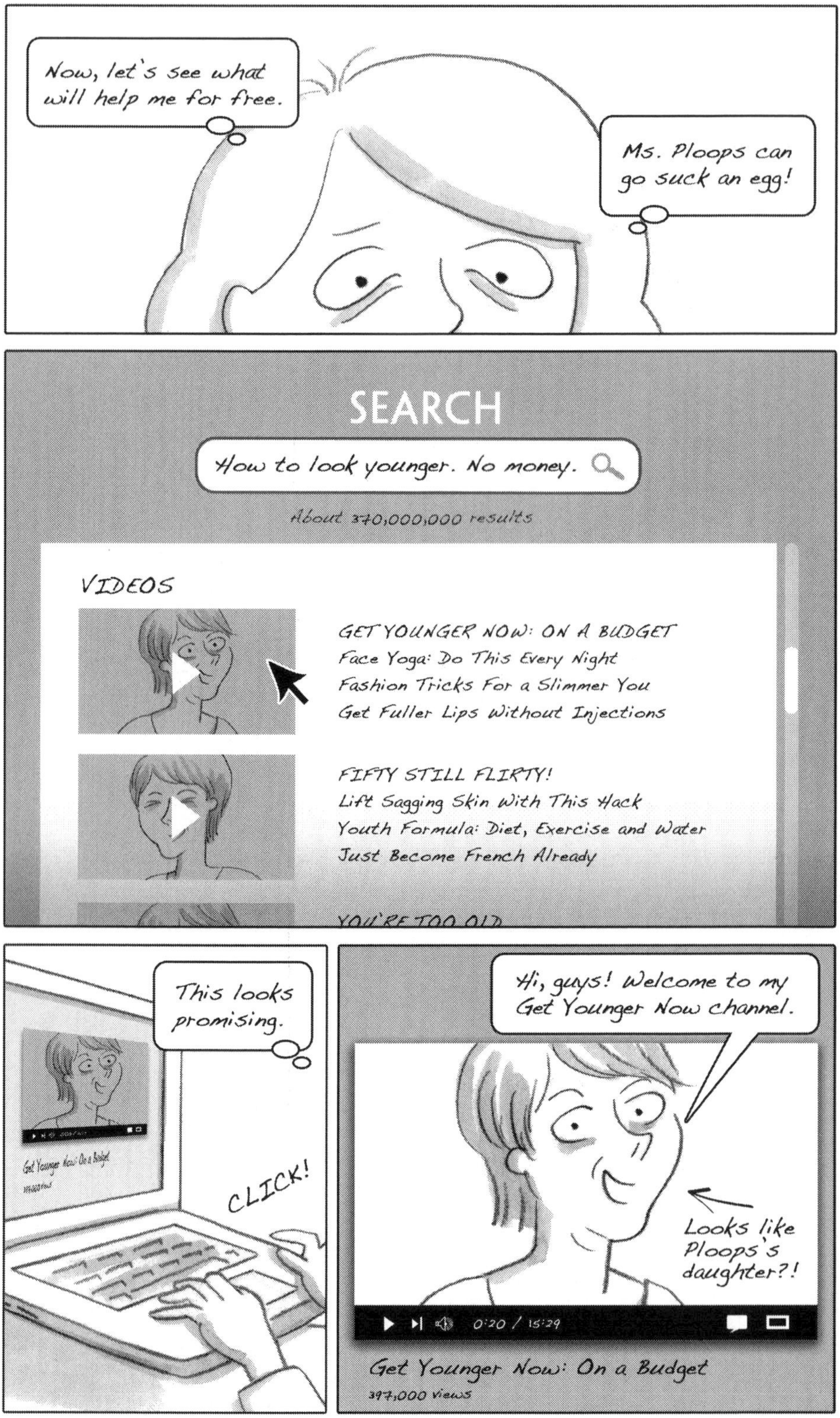
Now, let's see what will help me for free.
Ms. Ploops can go suck an egg!
SEARCH
How to look younger. No money.
About 370,000,000 results
VIDEOS
GET YOUNGER NOW: ON A BUDGET
Face Yoga: Do This Every Night
Fashion Tricks For a Slimmer You
Get Fuller Lips Without Injections
FIFTY STILL FLIRTY!
Lift Sagging Skin With This Hack
Youth Formula: Diet, Exercise and Water
Just Become French Already
This looks promising.
CLICK!
Hi, guys! Welcome to my Get Younger Now channel.
Looks like Ploops's daughter?!
0:20 / 15:29
Get Younger Now: On a Budget
397,000 views

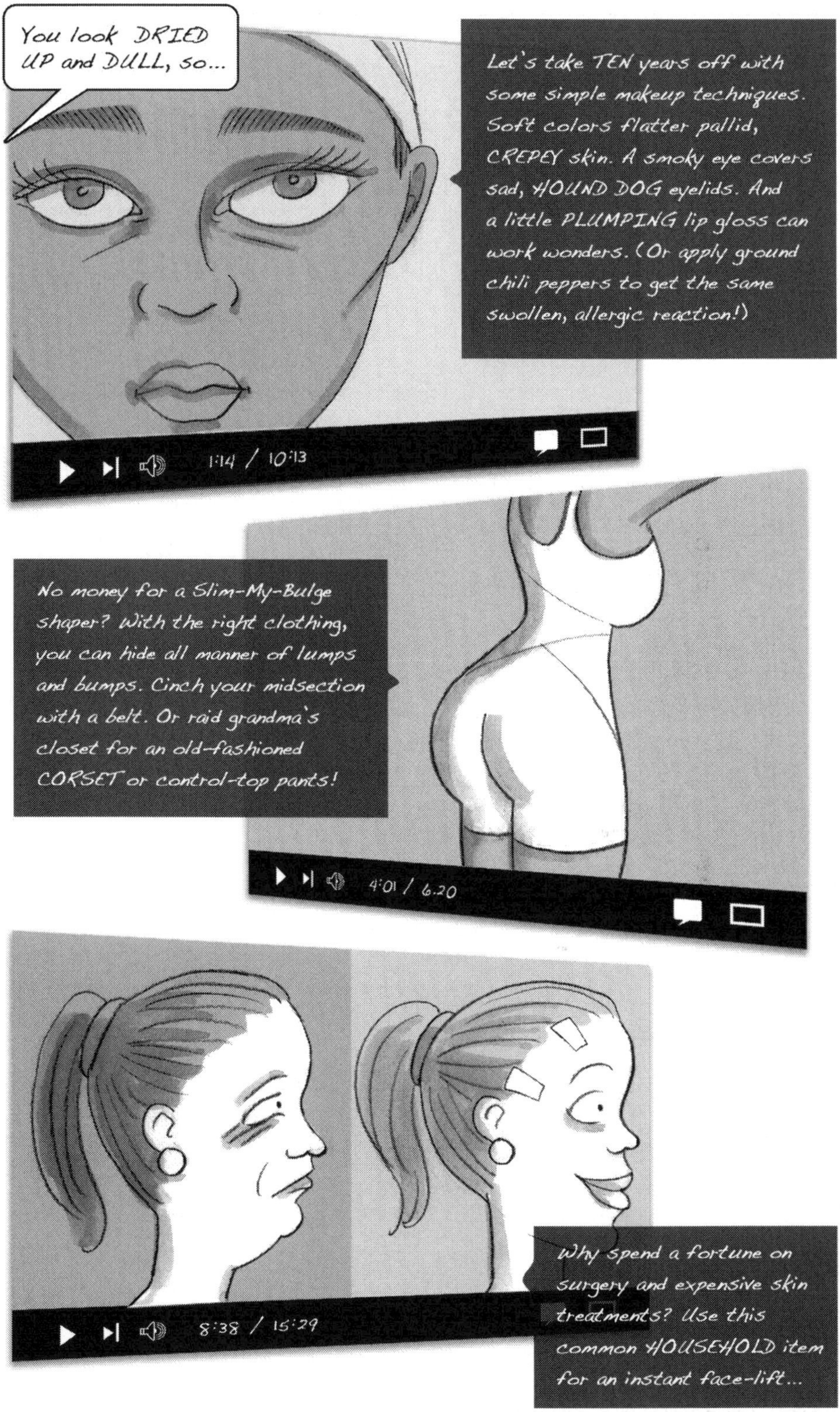
You look DRIED UP and DULL, so...
Let's take TEN years off with some simple makeup techniques. Soft colors flatter pallid, CREPEY skin. A smoky eye covers sad, HOUND DOG eyelids. And a little PLUMPING lip gloss can work wonders. (Or apply ground chili peppers to get the same swollen, allergic reaction!)
1:14 / 10:13
No money for a Slim-My-Bulge shaper? With the right clothing, you can hide all manner of lumps and bumps. Cinch your midsection with a belt. Or raid grandma's closet for an old-fashioned CORSET or control-top pants!
4:01 / 6:20
8:38 / 15:29
Why spend a fortune on surgery and expensive skin treatments? Use this common HOUSEHOLD item for an instant face-lift...

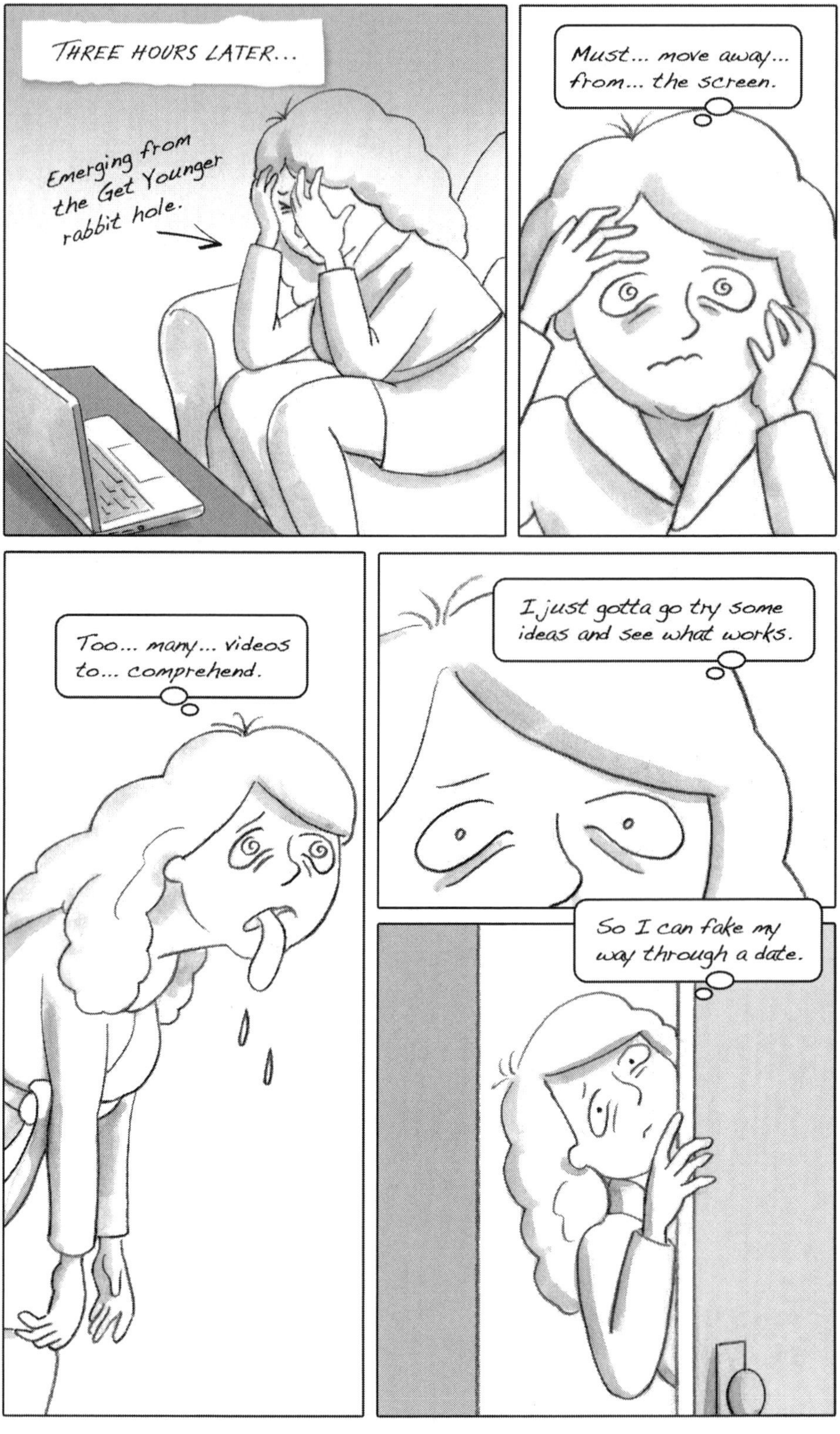
THREE HOURS LATER...
Emerging from the Get Younger rabbit hole.
Must... move away... from... the screen.
Too... many... videos to... comprehend.
I just gotta go try some ideas and see what works.
So I can fake my way through a date.

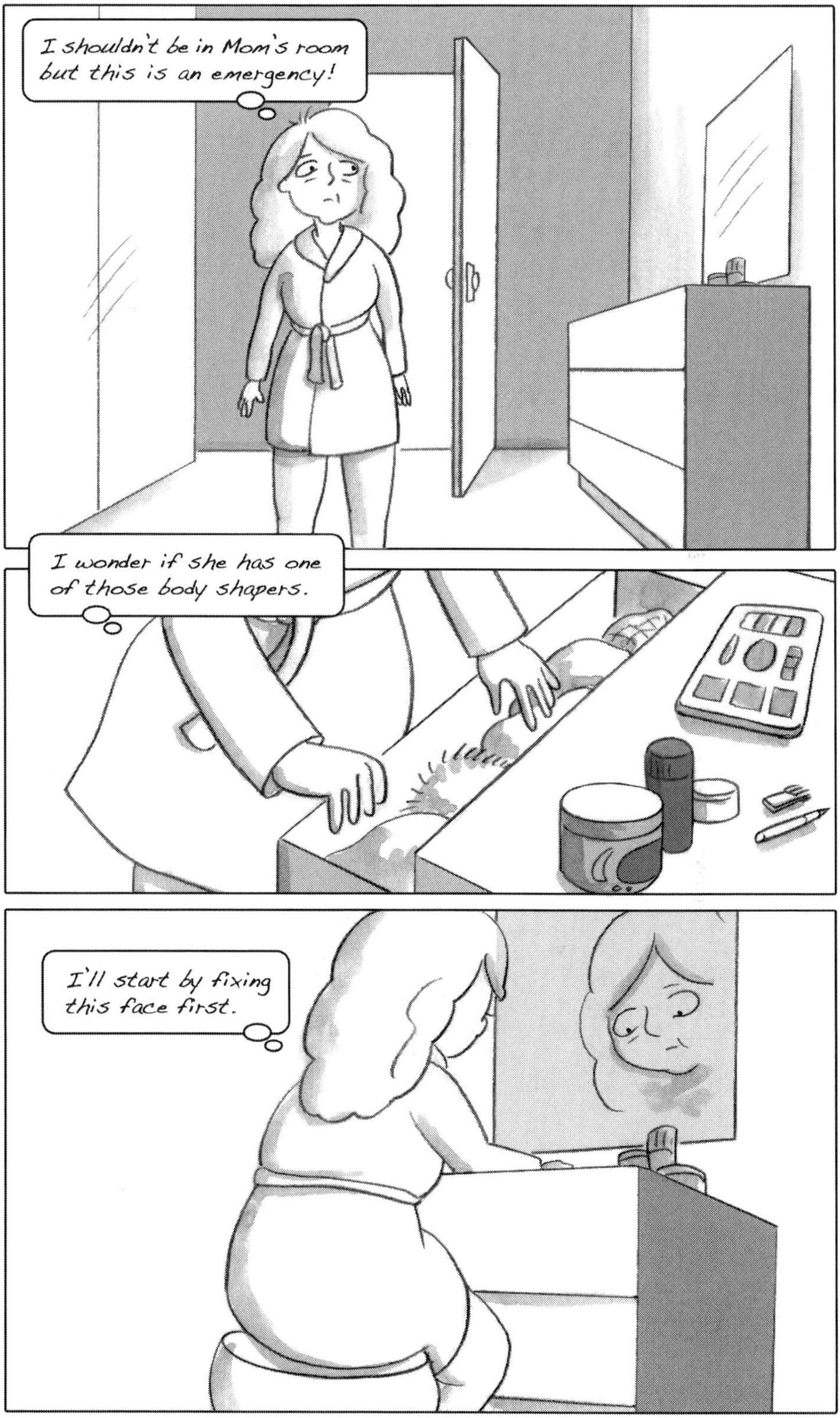
I shouldn't be in Mom's room but this is an emergency!
I wonder if she has one of those body shapers.
I'll start by fixing this face first.

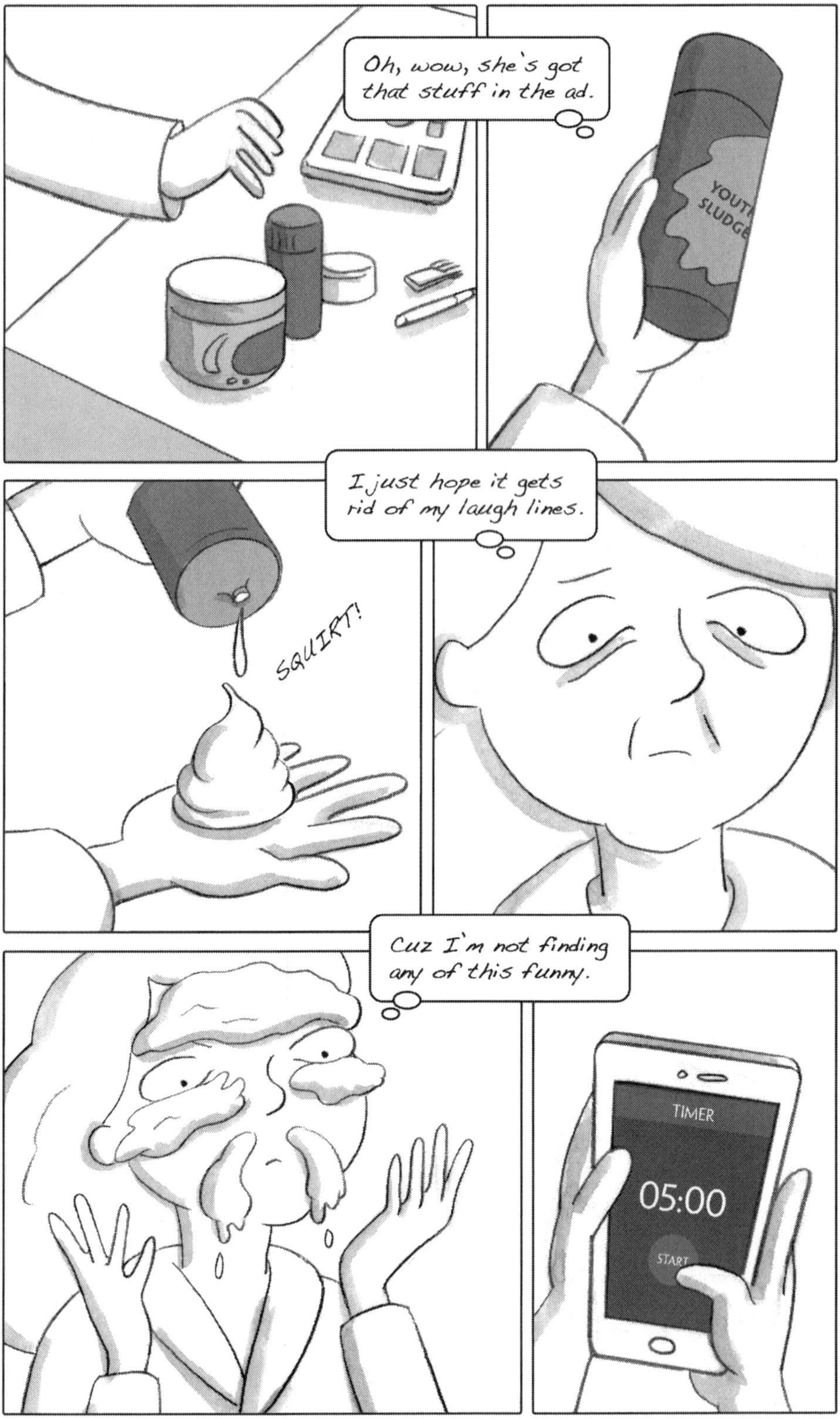
Oh, wow, she's got that stuff in the ad.
YOUTH SLUDGE
I just hope it gets rid of my laugh lines.
SQUIRT!
Cuz I'm not finding any of this funny.
TIMER
05:00
START

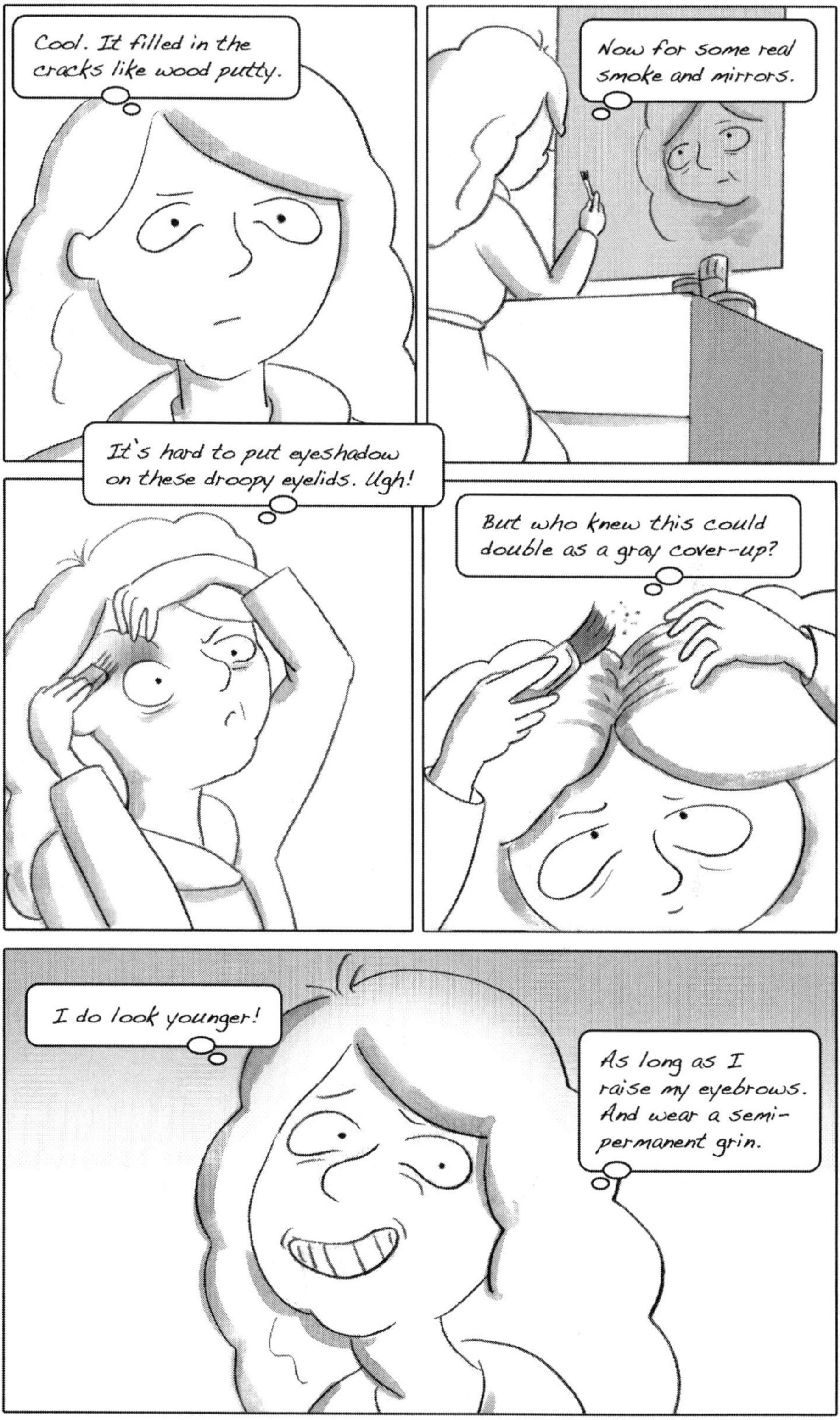
Cool. It filled in the cracks like wood putty.
Now for some real smoke and mirrors.
It's hard to put eyeshadow on these droopy eyelids. Ugh!
But who knew this could double as a gray cover-up?
I do look younger!
As long as I raise my eyebrows. And wear a semi-permanent grin.

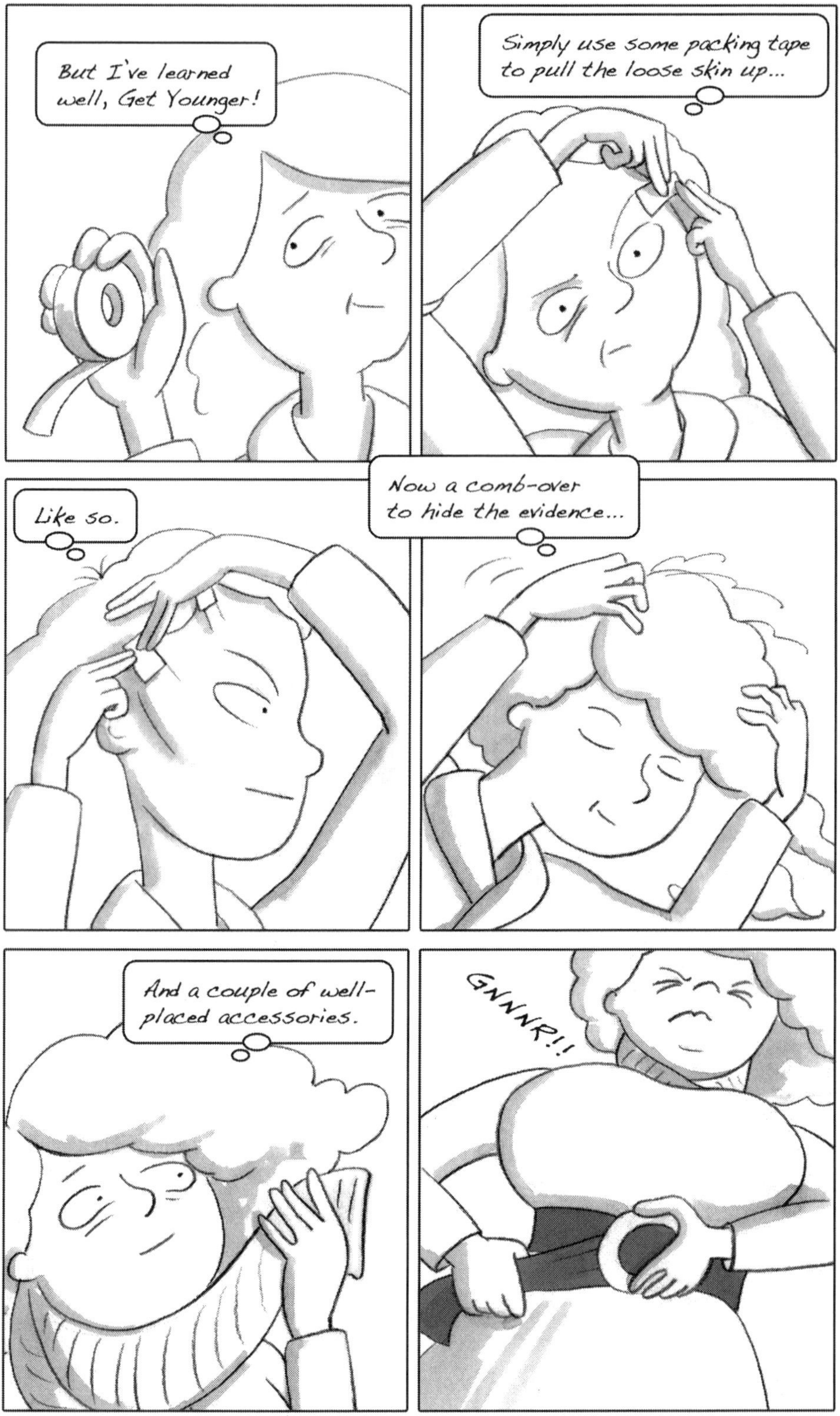
But I've learned well, Get Younger!
Simply use some packing tape to pull the loose skin up...
Like so.
Now a comb-over to hide the evidence...
And a couple of well-placed accessories.
GNNNR!!

Some heels to slim the legs...
And my age-defying makeover is complete.
Hey, not bad! I could maybe pass for a teenager.
Has successfully simulated the angry Botoxic eyebrow.
Just keep the lights down low.

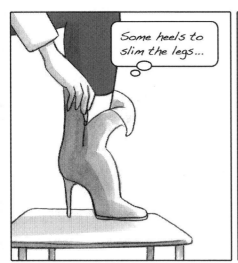

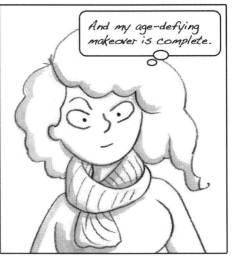

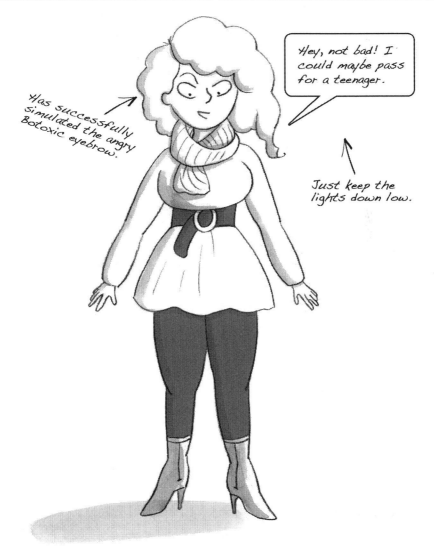

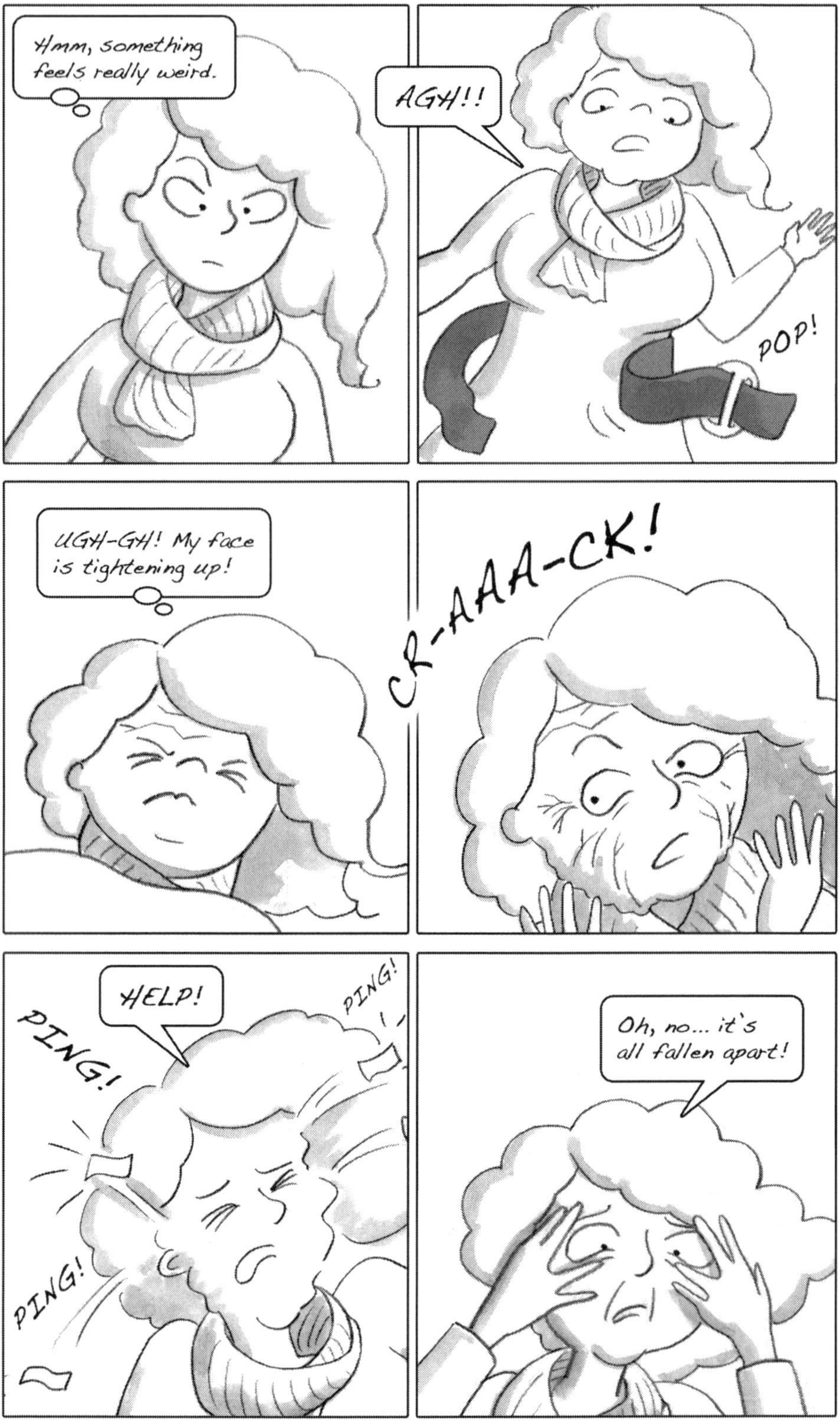
Hmm, something feels really weird.
AGH!!
POP!
UGH-GH! My face is tightening up!
CR-AAA-CK!
HELP!
PING!
PING!
PING!
Oh, no... it's all fallen apart!

THE FIVE STAGES OF GRIEF

3) BARGAINING

The individual tries to negotiate a deal in exchange for getting her former life back.

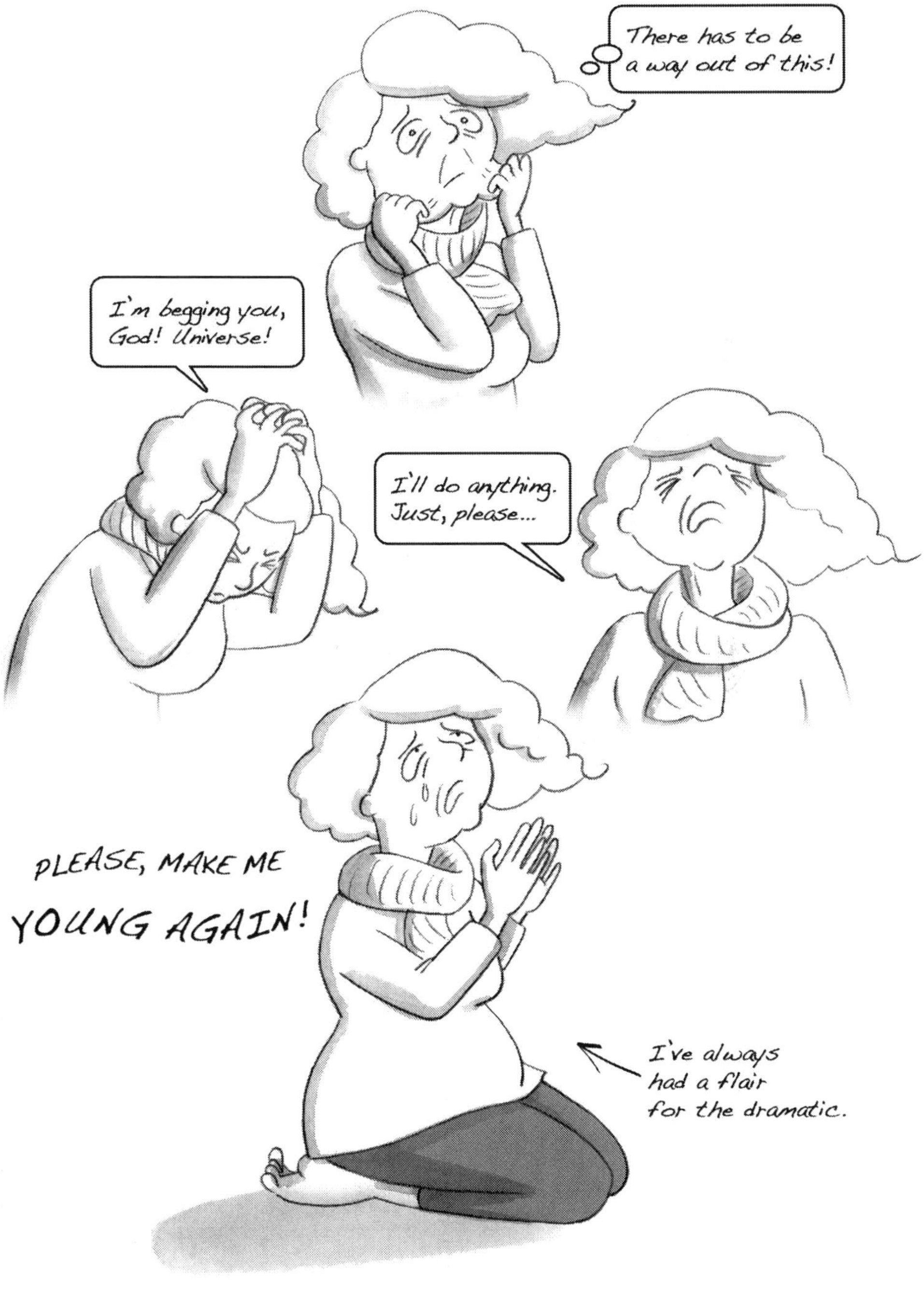
There has to be a way out of this!
I'm begging you, God! Universe!
I'll do anything. Just, please...
PLEASE, MAKE ME YOUNG AGAIN!
I've always had a flair for the dramatic.

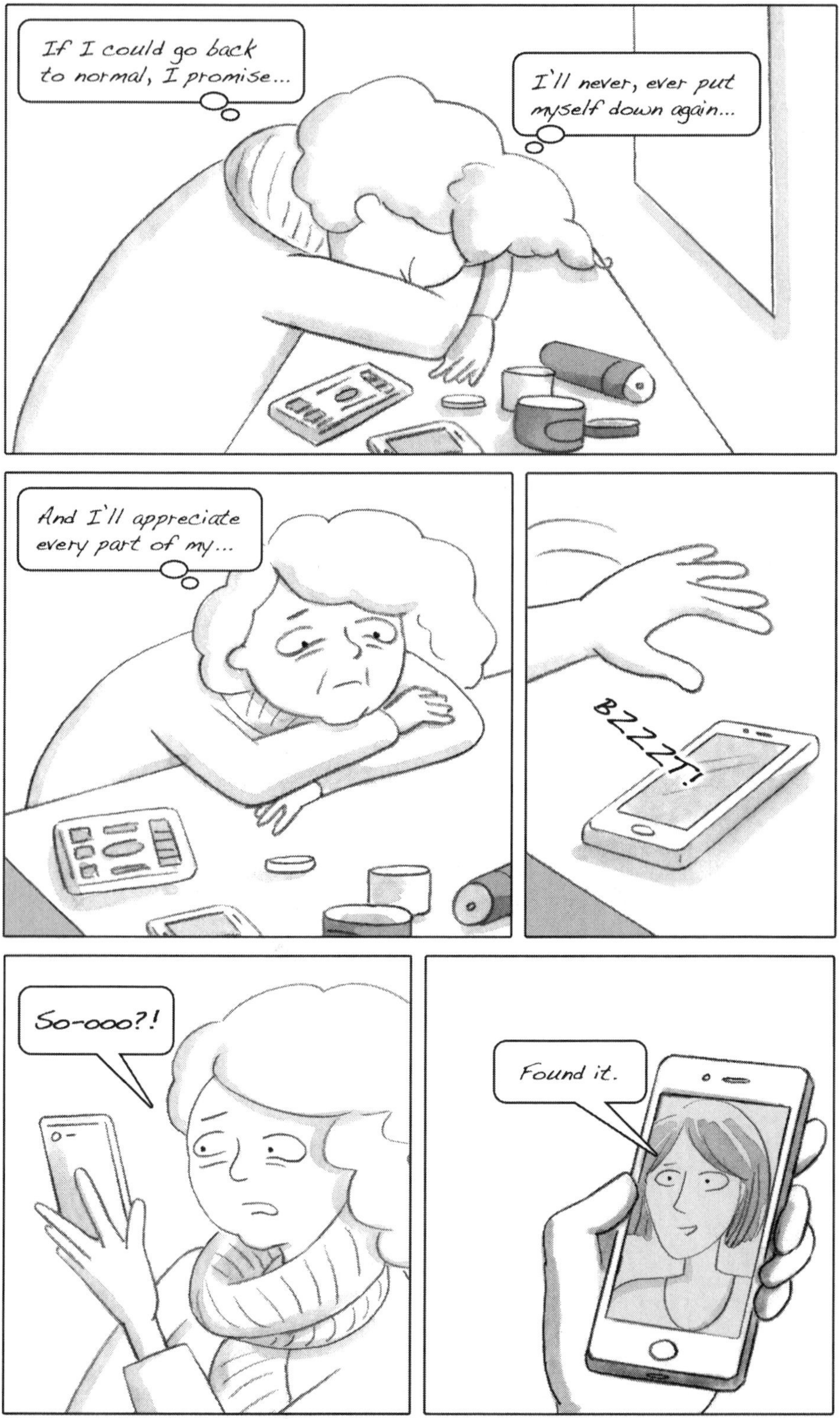
If I could go back to normal, I promise...
I'll never, ever put myself down again...
And I'll appreciate every part of my...
BZZZT!
So-ooo?!
Found it.

We are the mirror,

as well as the face in it.

RUMI

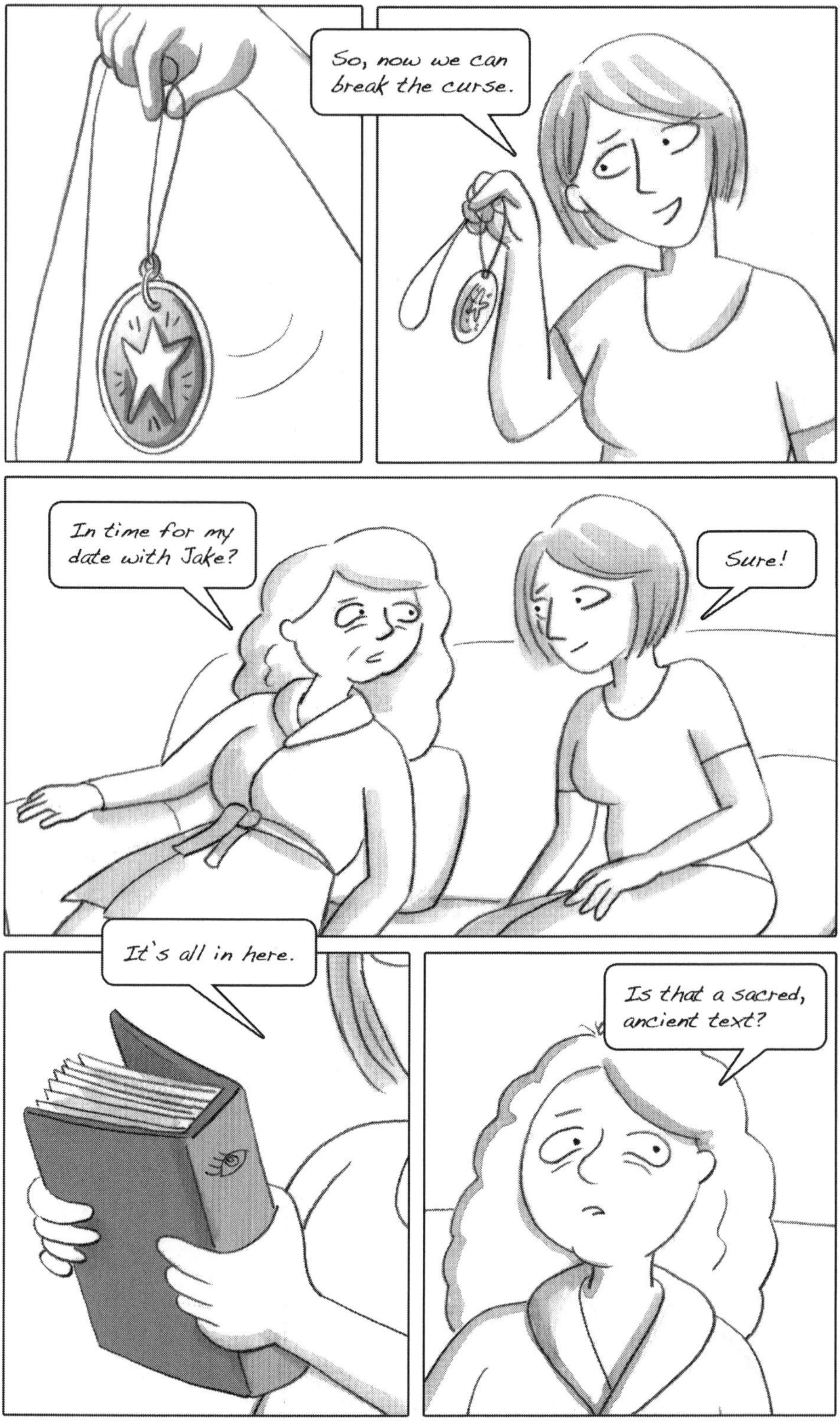
So, now we can break the curse.
In time for my date with Jake?
Sure!
It's all in here.
Is that a sacred, ancient text?

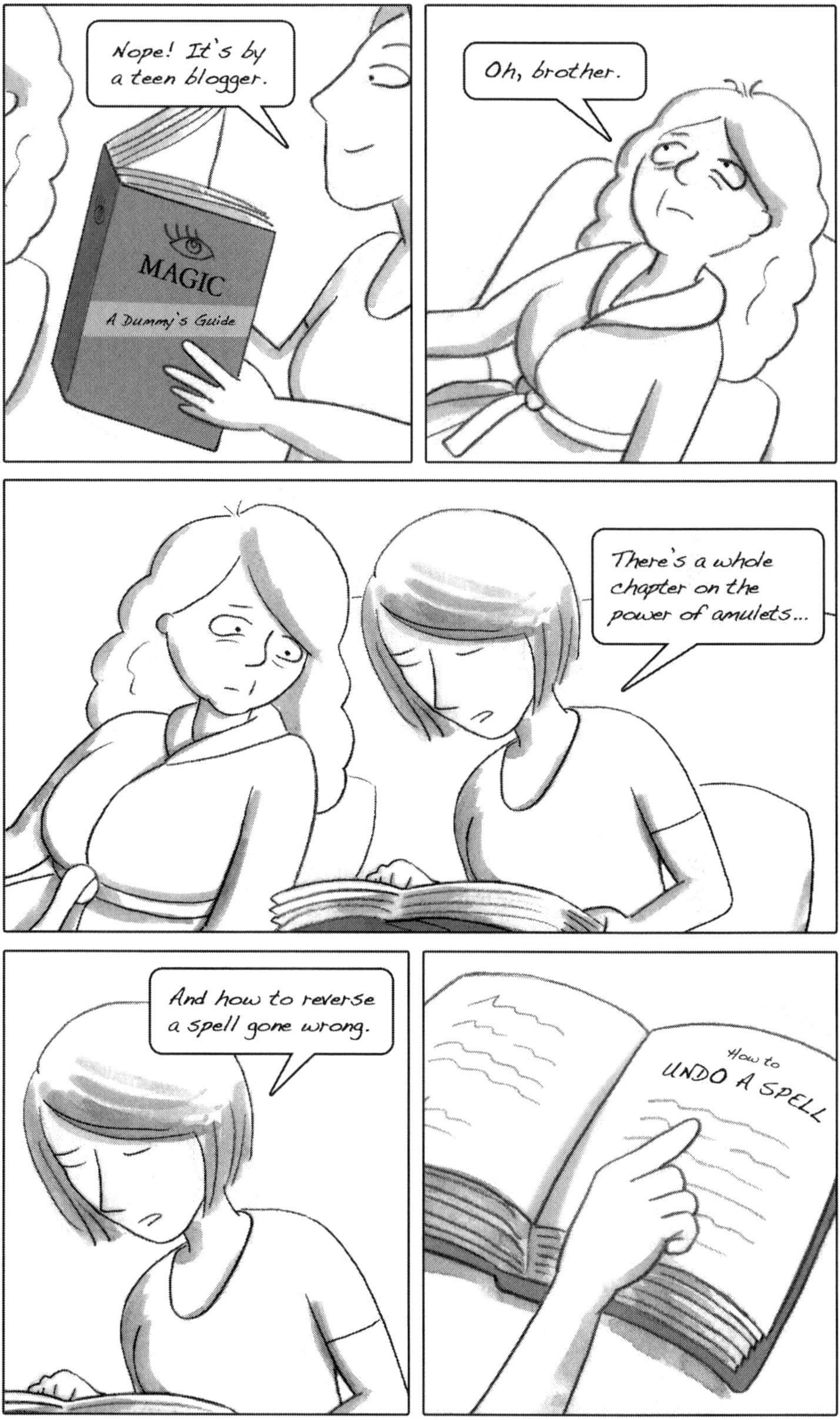
Nope! It's by a teen blogger.
MAGIC
A Dummy's Guide
Oh, brother.
There's a whole chapter on the power of amulets...
And how to reverse a spell gone wrong.
How to UNDO A SPELL

THE MAGIC CANDLE

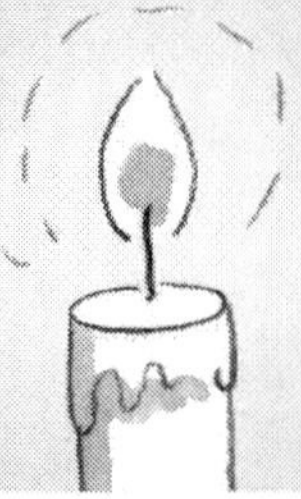

WHAT YOU WILL NEED:

Ceramic bowl
Small candle
Patience

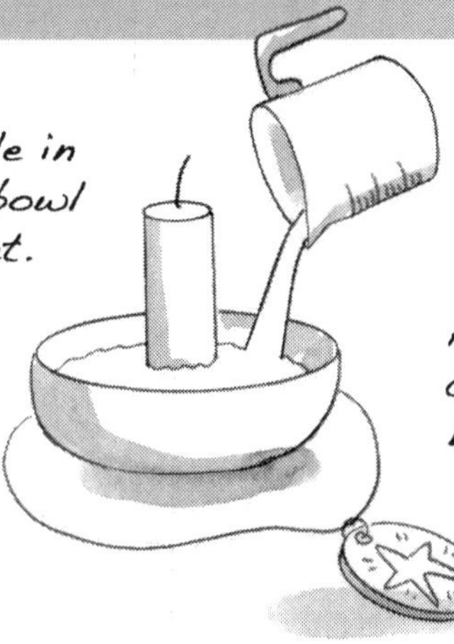

Place candle in center of bowl with amulet.

Pour water into bowl, covering half the candle. Light candle and say:

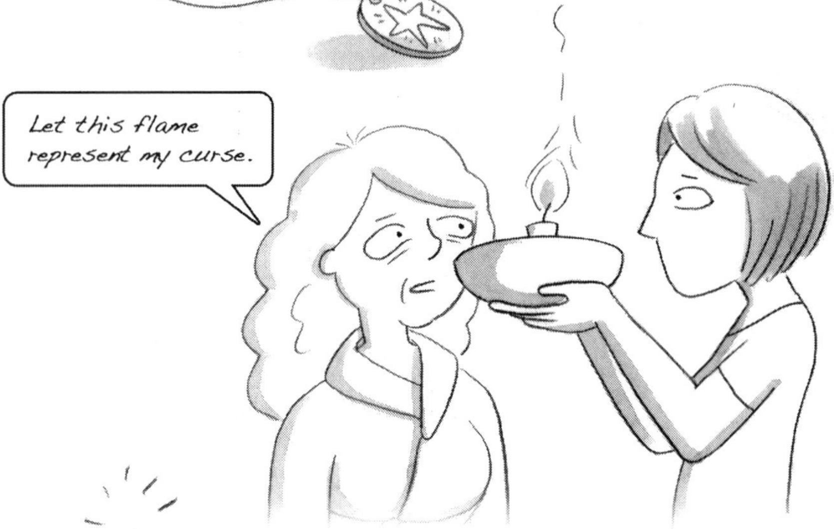
Let this flame represent my curse.

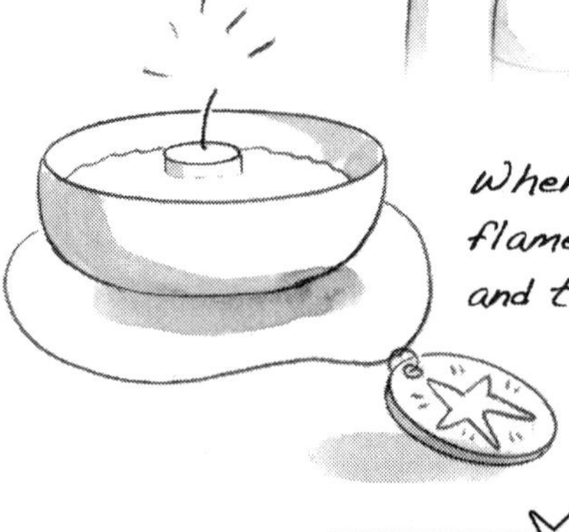

When candle burns down, flame will extinguish, and then, POOF...

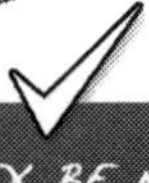

YO' HEX BE NIXED!

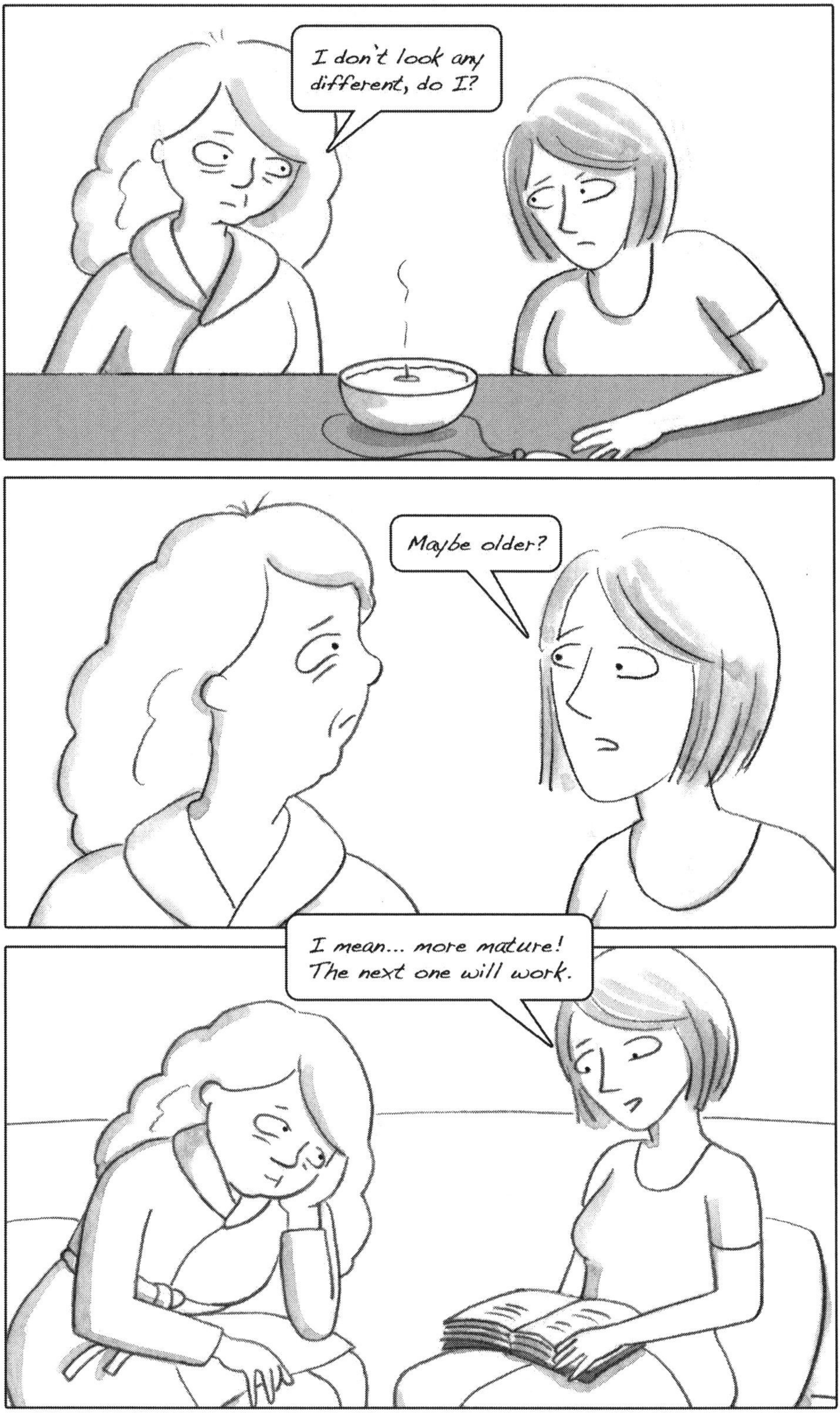
I don't look any different, do I?
Maybe older?
I mean... more mature! The next one will work.

SAGE AND SALT

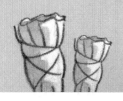

WHAT YOU WILL NEED:
Sage smudge stick
Celtic sea salt
No shame

Place amulet on bed of
sea salt inside small box.

Light sage stick
and waft over
box, chanting:

I purify this amulet
of all negative energy!

It helps if you
prance around.

Place amulet around neck,
then make a new wish. And now...

YO' SPELL BE GONE!

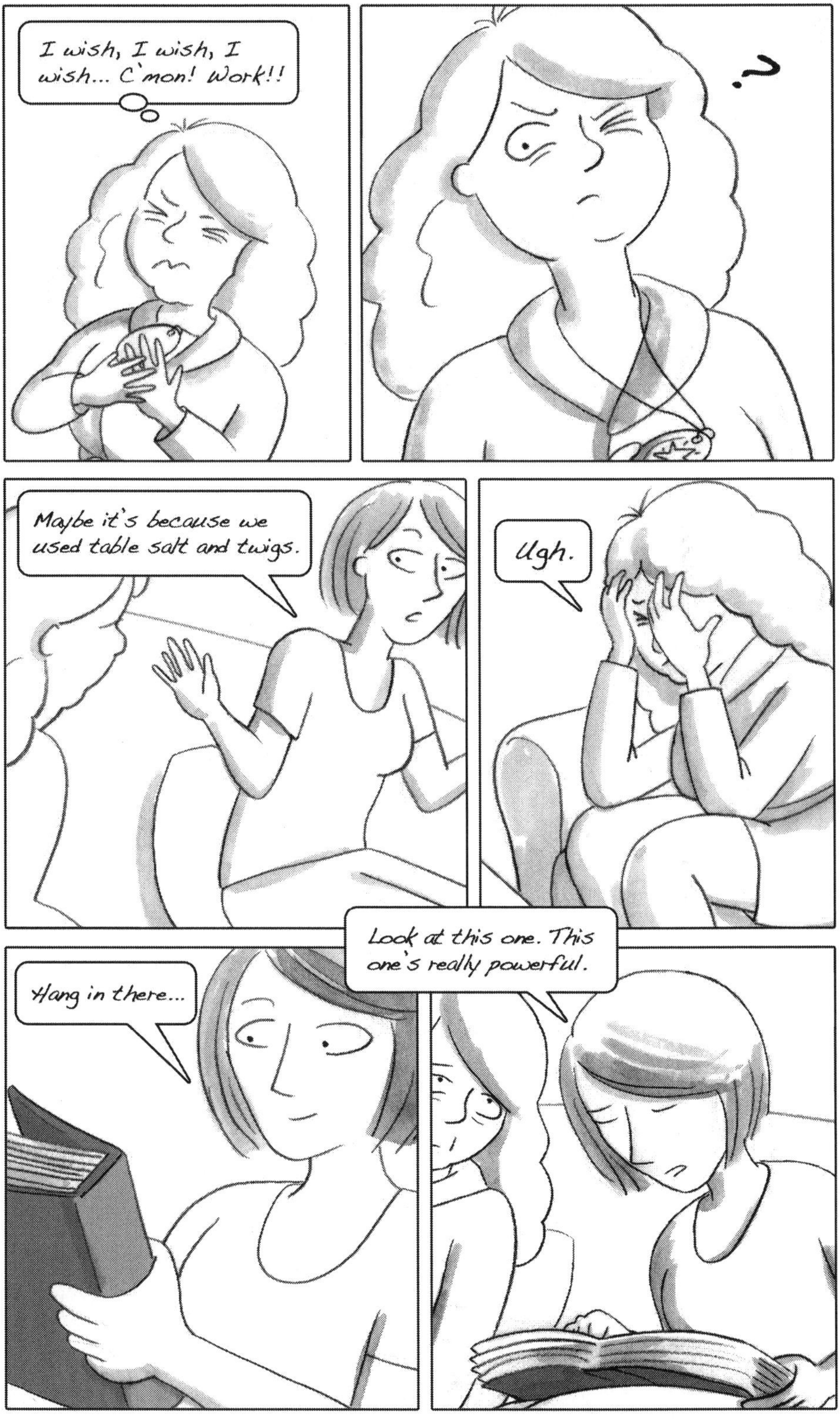
I wish, I wish, I wish... C'mon! Work!!
?
Maybe it's because we used table salt and twigs.
Ugh.
Hang in there...
Look at this one. This one's really powerful.

MINI-ME / DECOY DOLL

 WHAT YOU WILL NEED:
Doll or poppet
Mirror, notepaper, quill
Blind faith

Create doll in your own likeness,
so spell will be cast on doll
instead of you.

Place doll in front of
mirror and write these
words on notepaper:

> May you receive this
> affliction in my place.

Wrap doll and amulet
in notepaper. Bury in earth.
And so be it...

✓

YO' CURSE BE CANCELED!

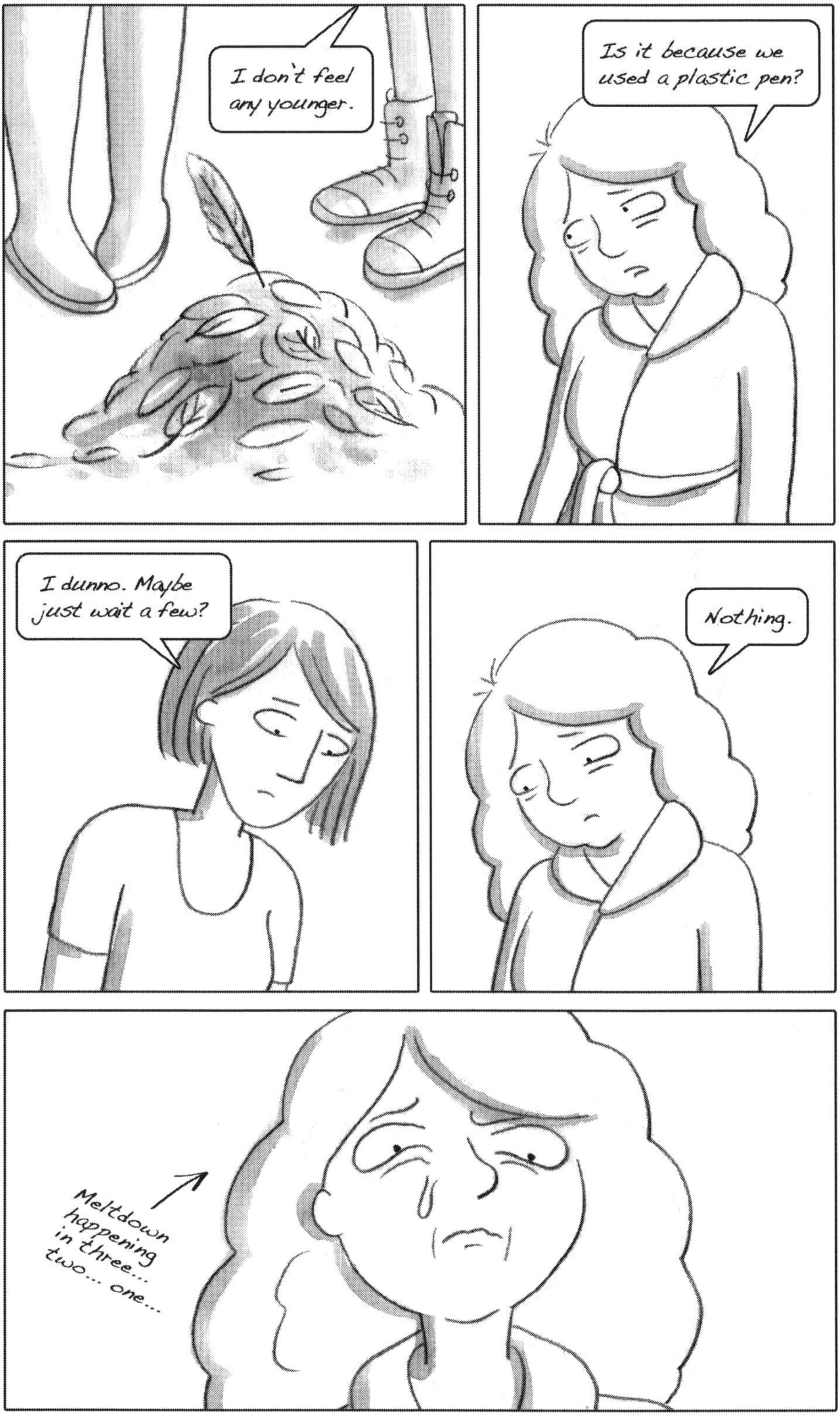
I don't feel any younger.
Is it because we used a plastic pen?
I dunno. Maybe just wait a few?
Nothing.
Meltdown happening in three... two... one...

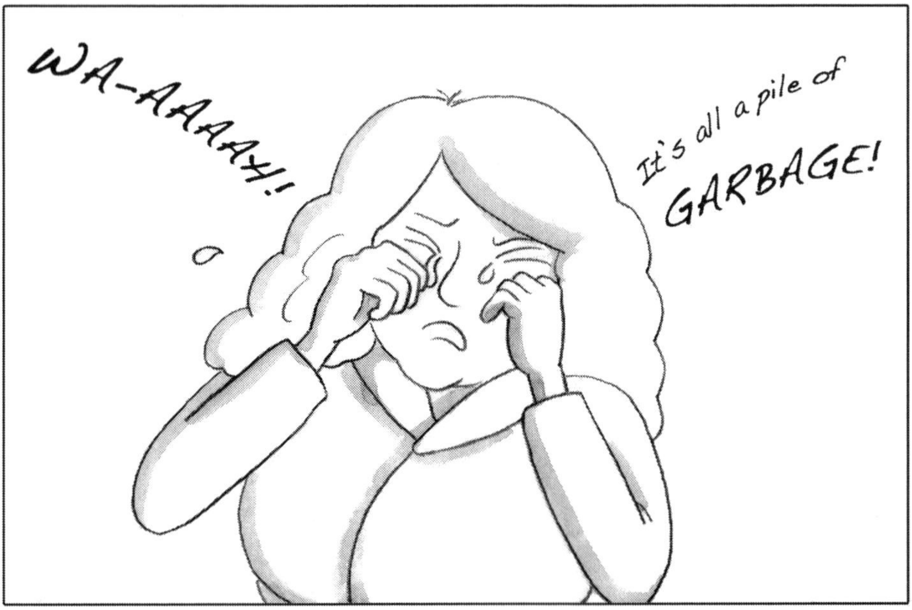
WA-AAAAAH!
It's all a pile of GARBAGE!

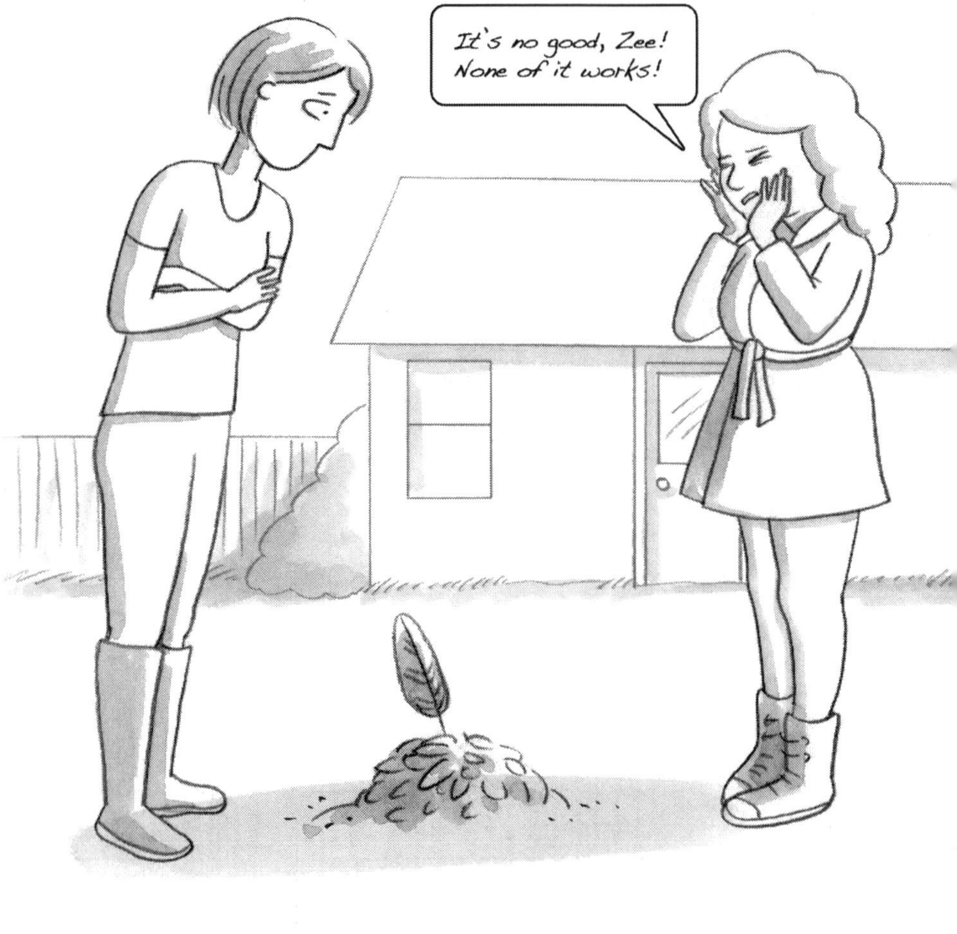
It's no good, Zee! None of it works!

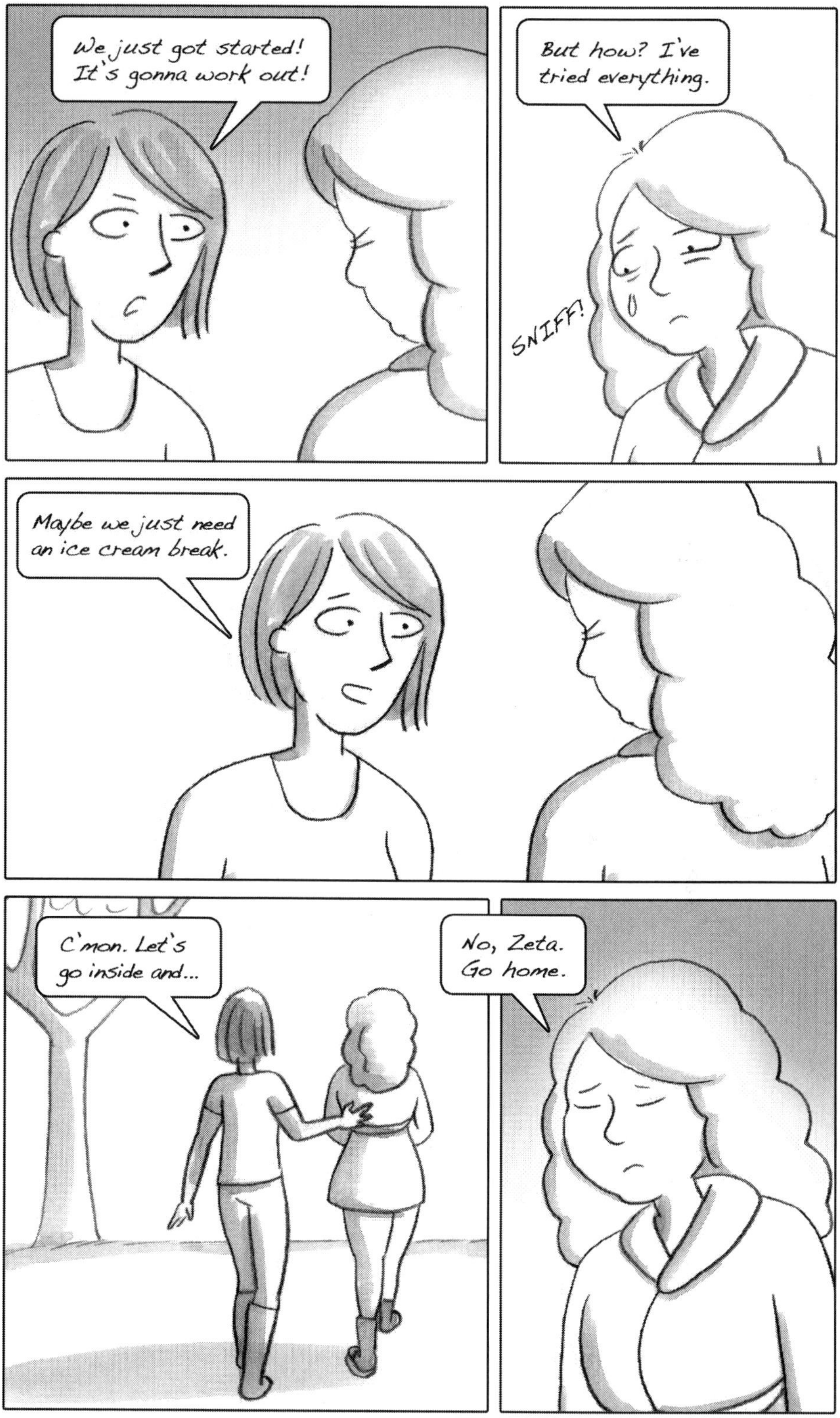
We just got started! It's gonna work out!
But how? I've tried everything.
SNIFF!
Maybe we just need an ice cream break.
C'mon. Let's go inside and...
No, Zeta. Go home.

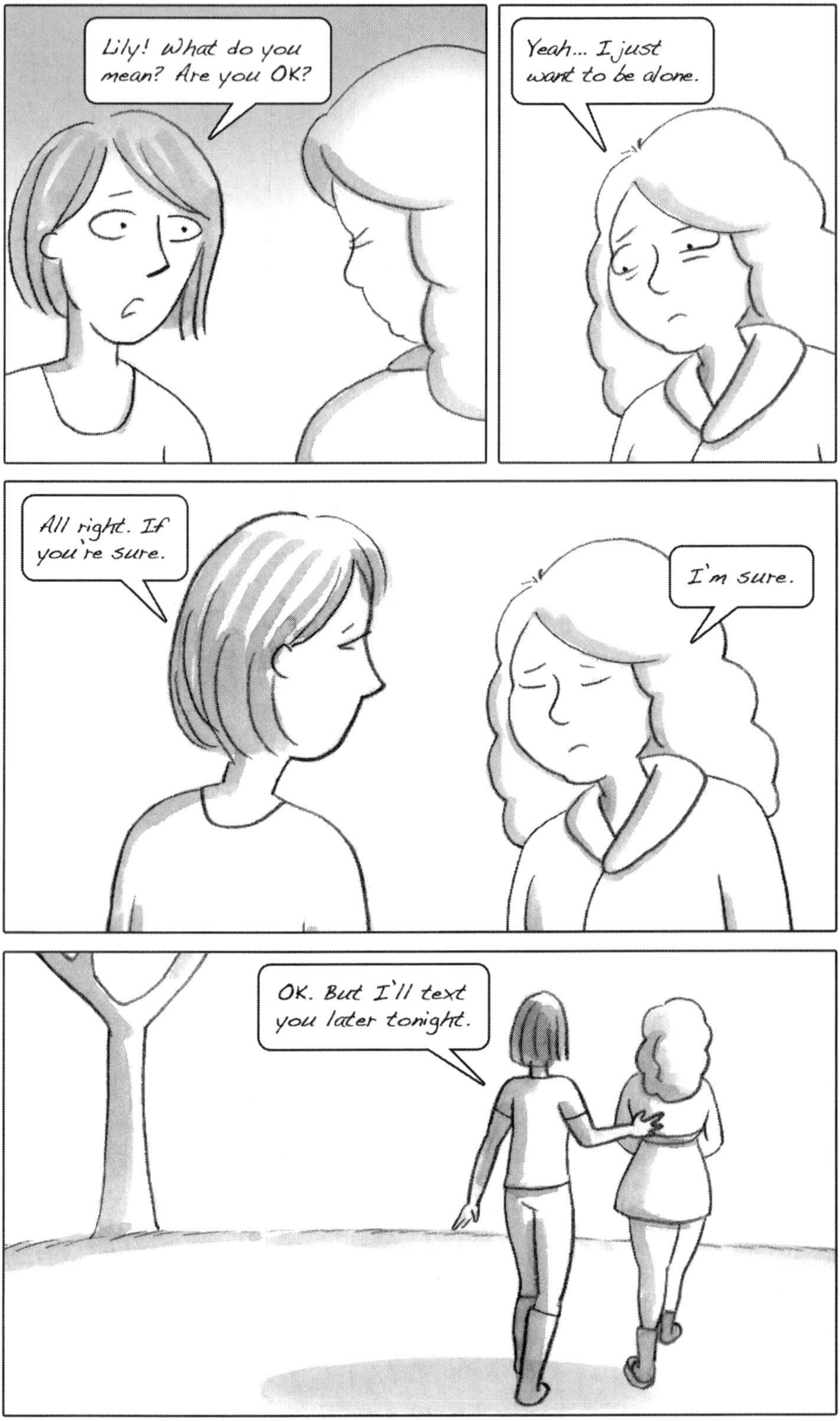
Lily! What do you mean? Are you OK?
Yeah... I just want to be alone.
All right. If you're sure.
I'm sure.
OK. But I'll text you later tonight.

THE FIVE STAGES OF GRIEF

4) DEPRESSION

In the fourth stage, despair hits. The individual decides her situation is futile, becomes sullen and withdraws.

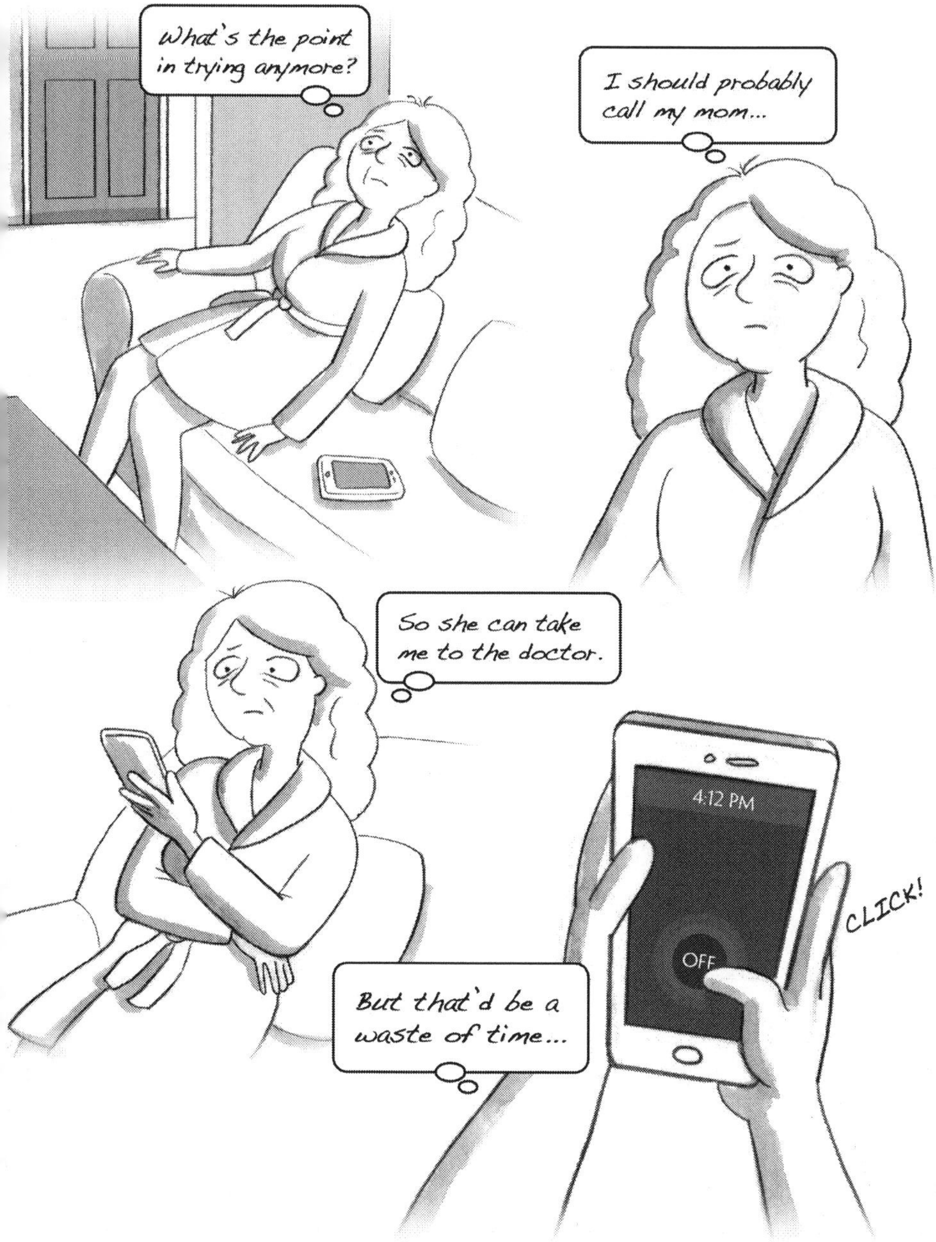

What's the point in trying anymore?
I should probably call my mom...
So she can take me to the doctor.
4:12 PM
OFF
But that'd be a waste of time...
CLICK!

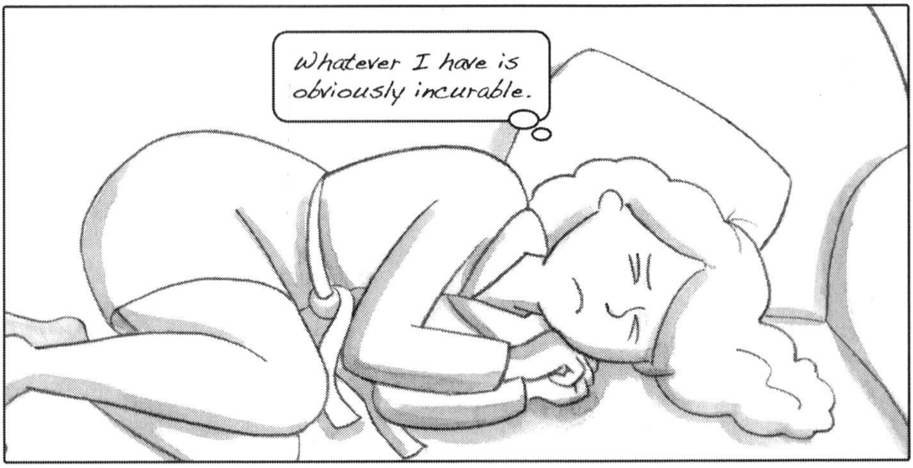
Whatever I have is obviously incurable.

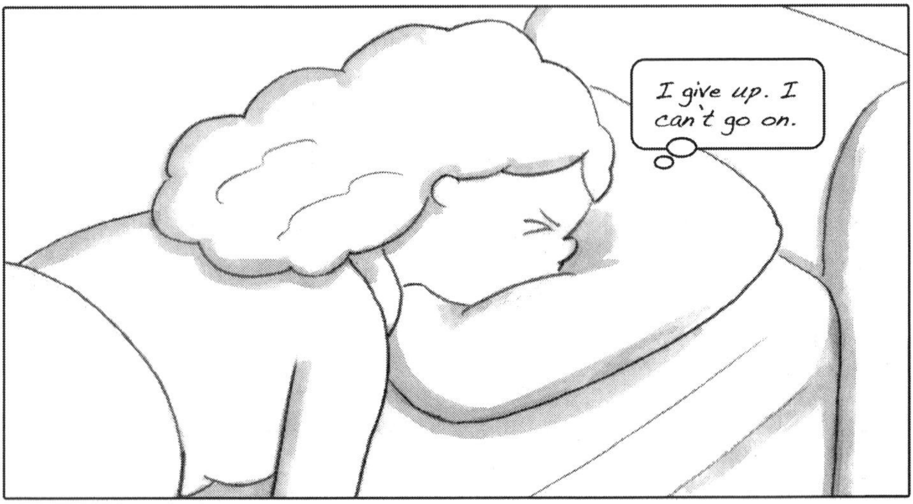
I give up. I can't go on.

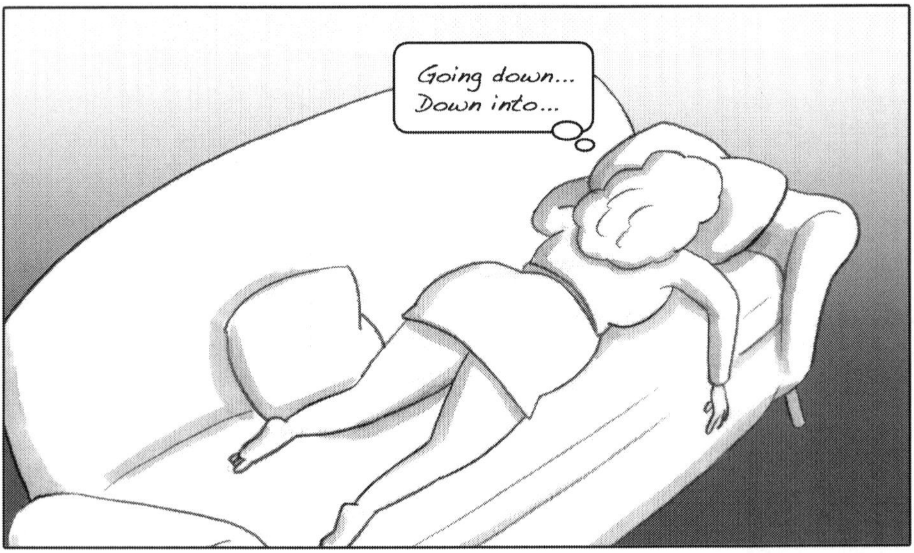
Going down...
Down into...

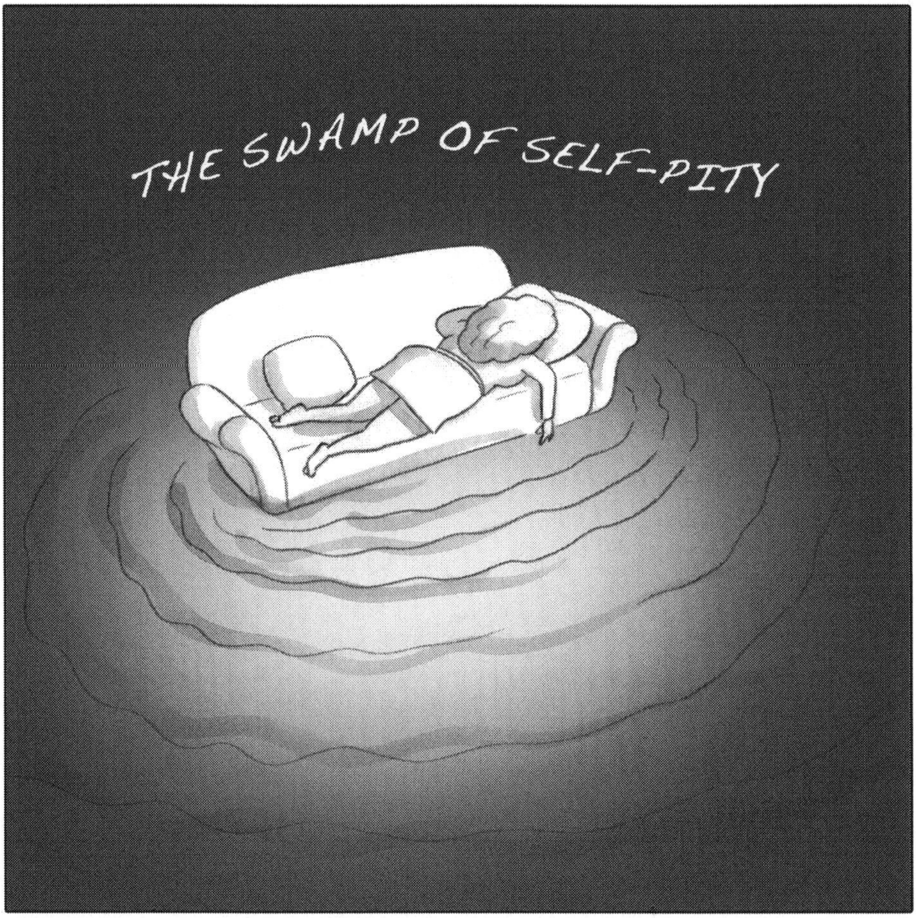
THE SWAMP OF SELF-PITY

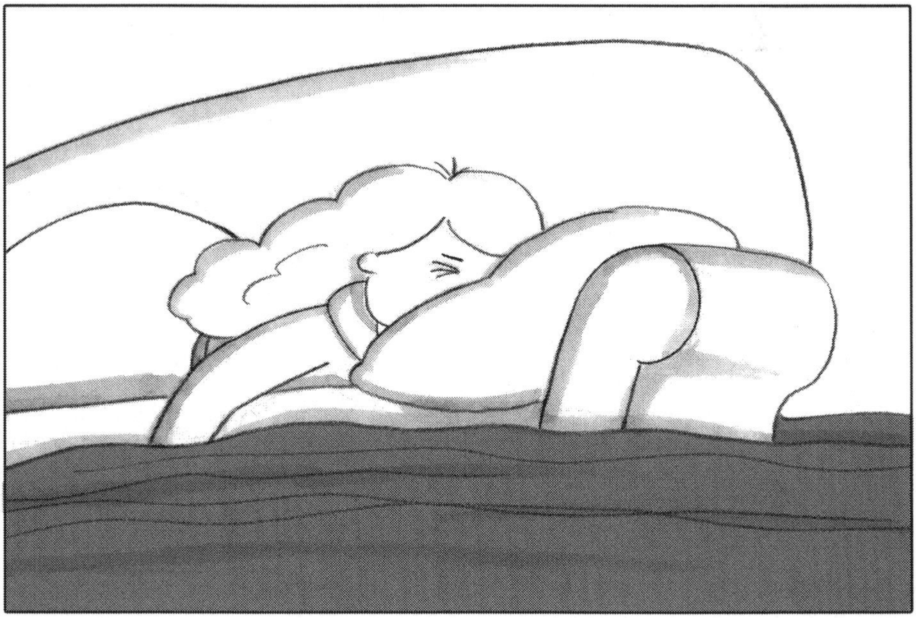

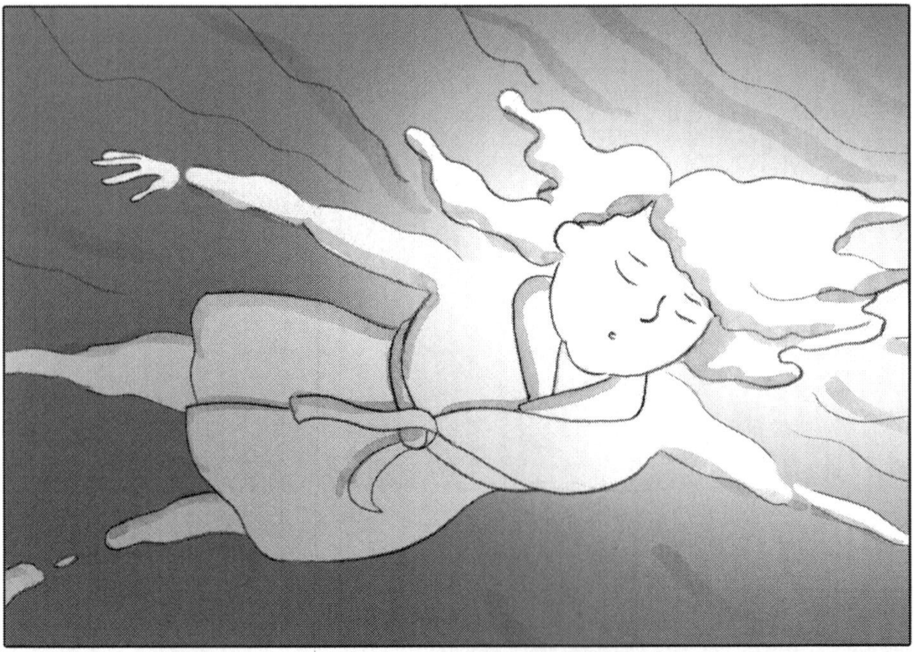

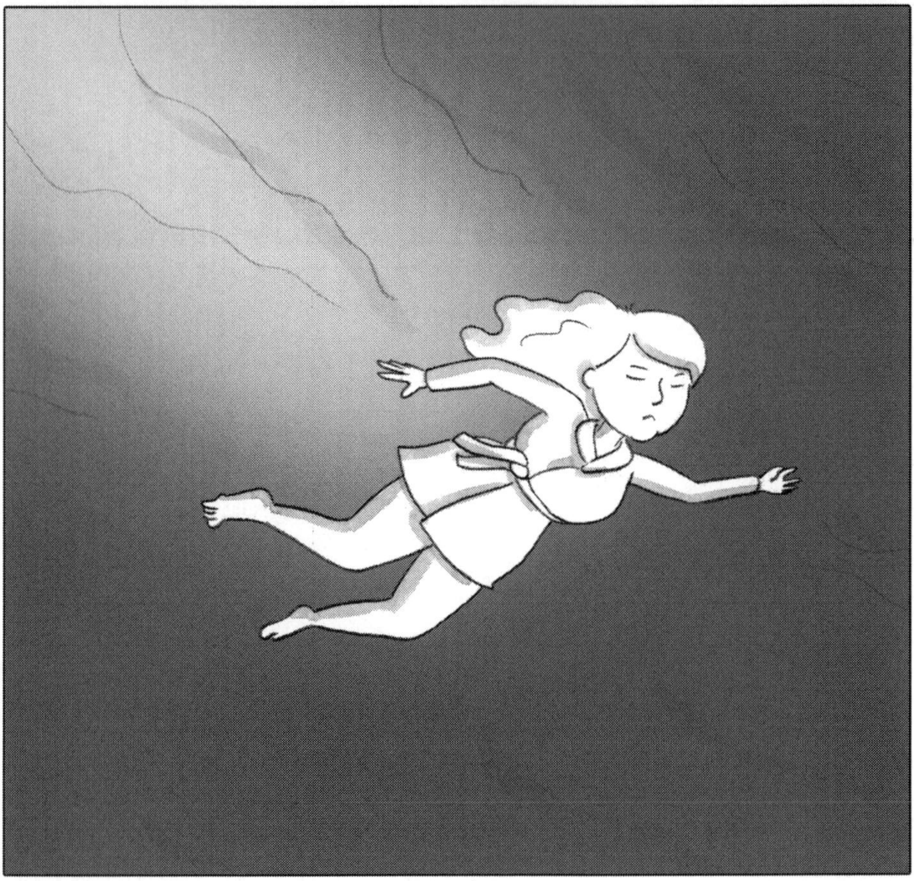

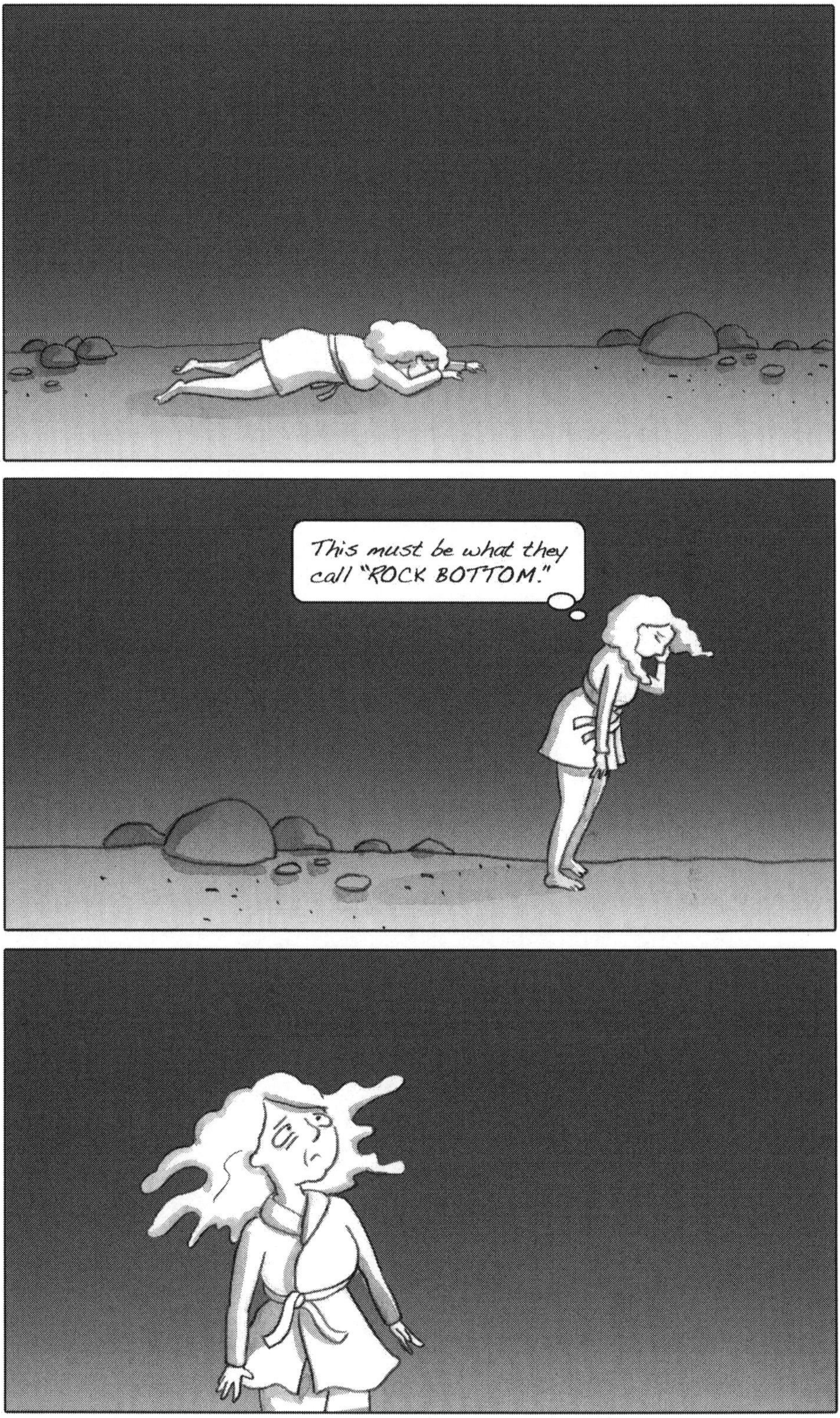
This must be what they call "ROCK BOTTOM."

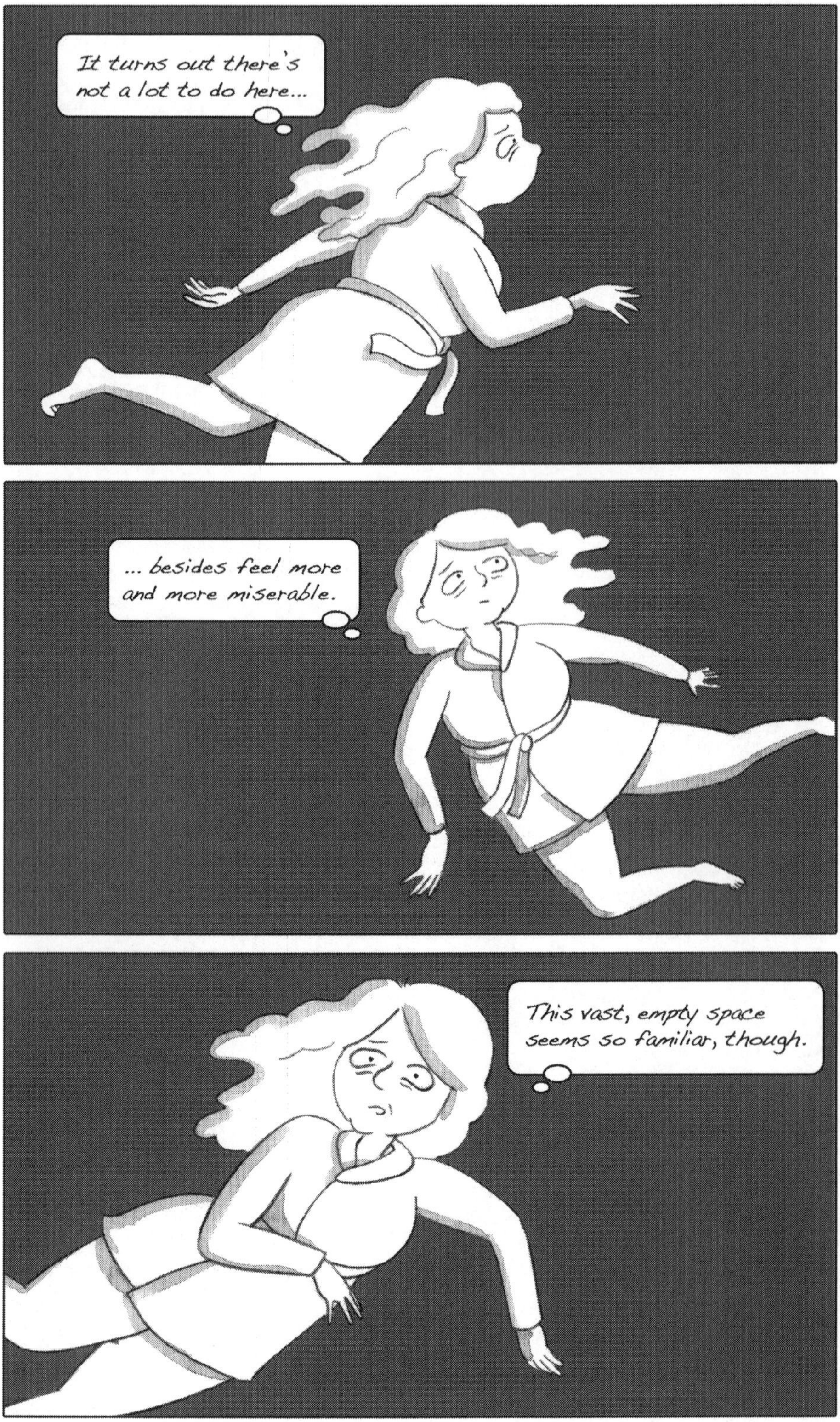
It turns out there's not a lot to do here...
... besides feel more and more miserable.
This vast, empty space seems so familiar, though.

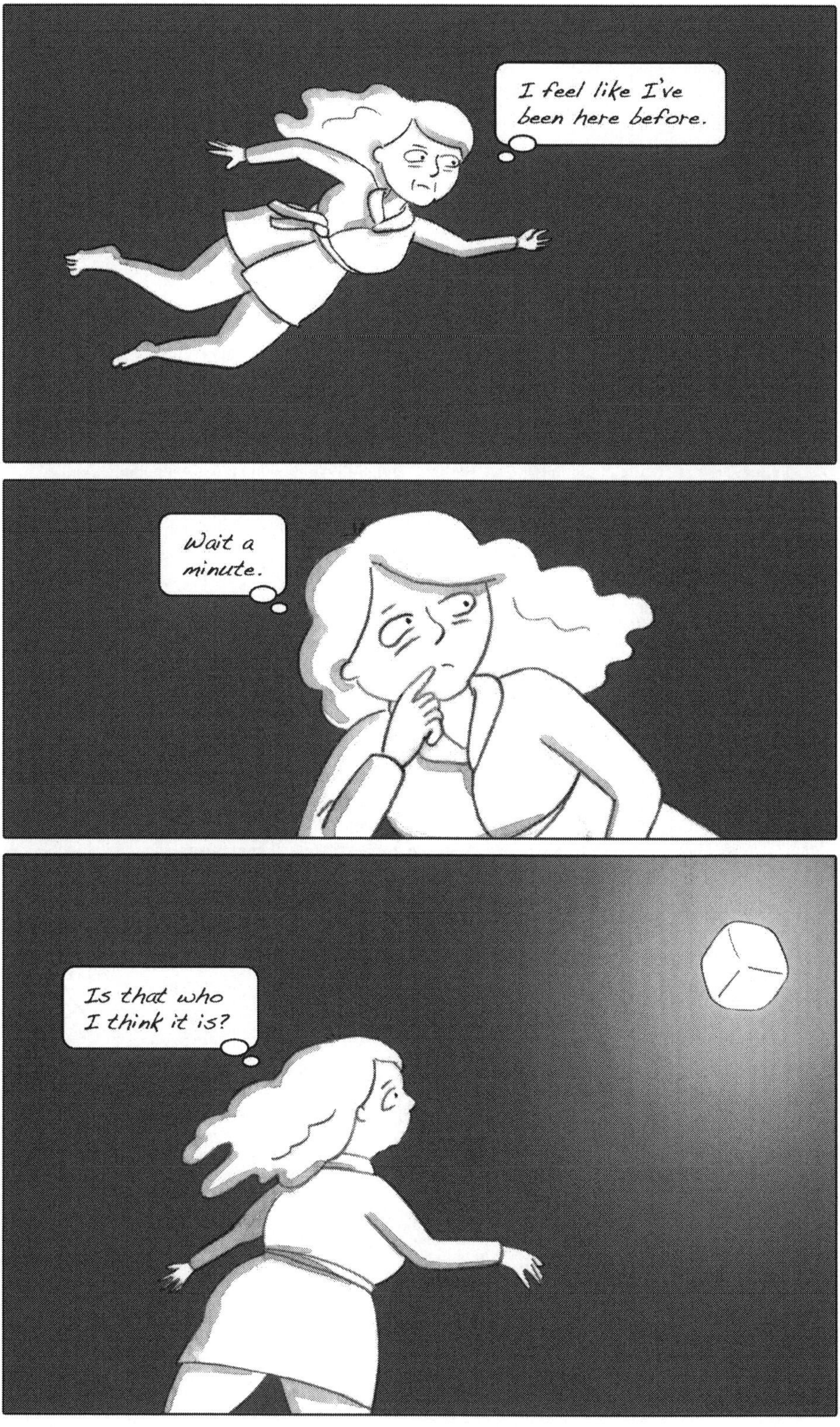
I feel like I've been here before.
Wait a minute.
Is that who I think it is?

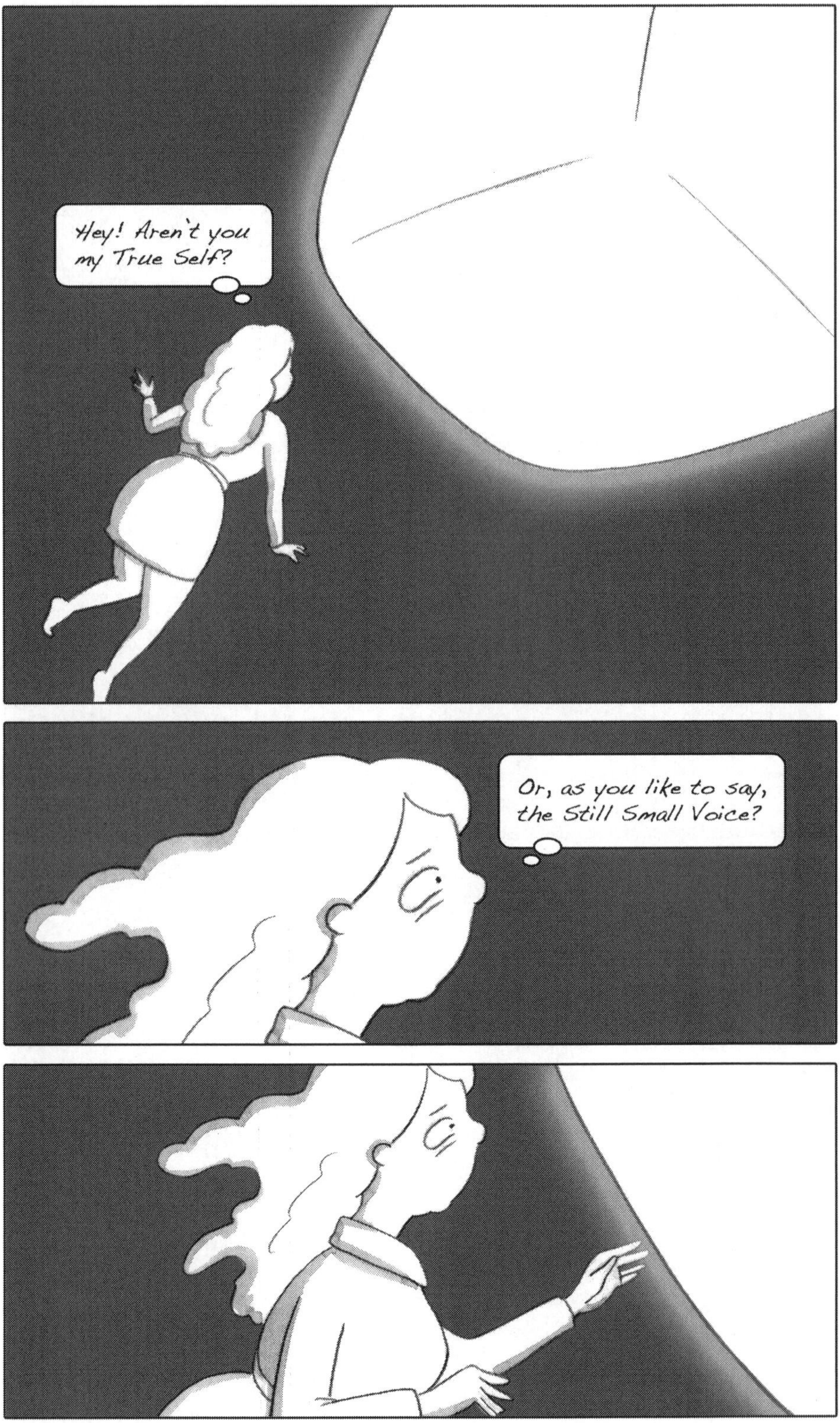
Hey! Aren't you my True Self?
Or, as you like to say, the Still Small Voice?

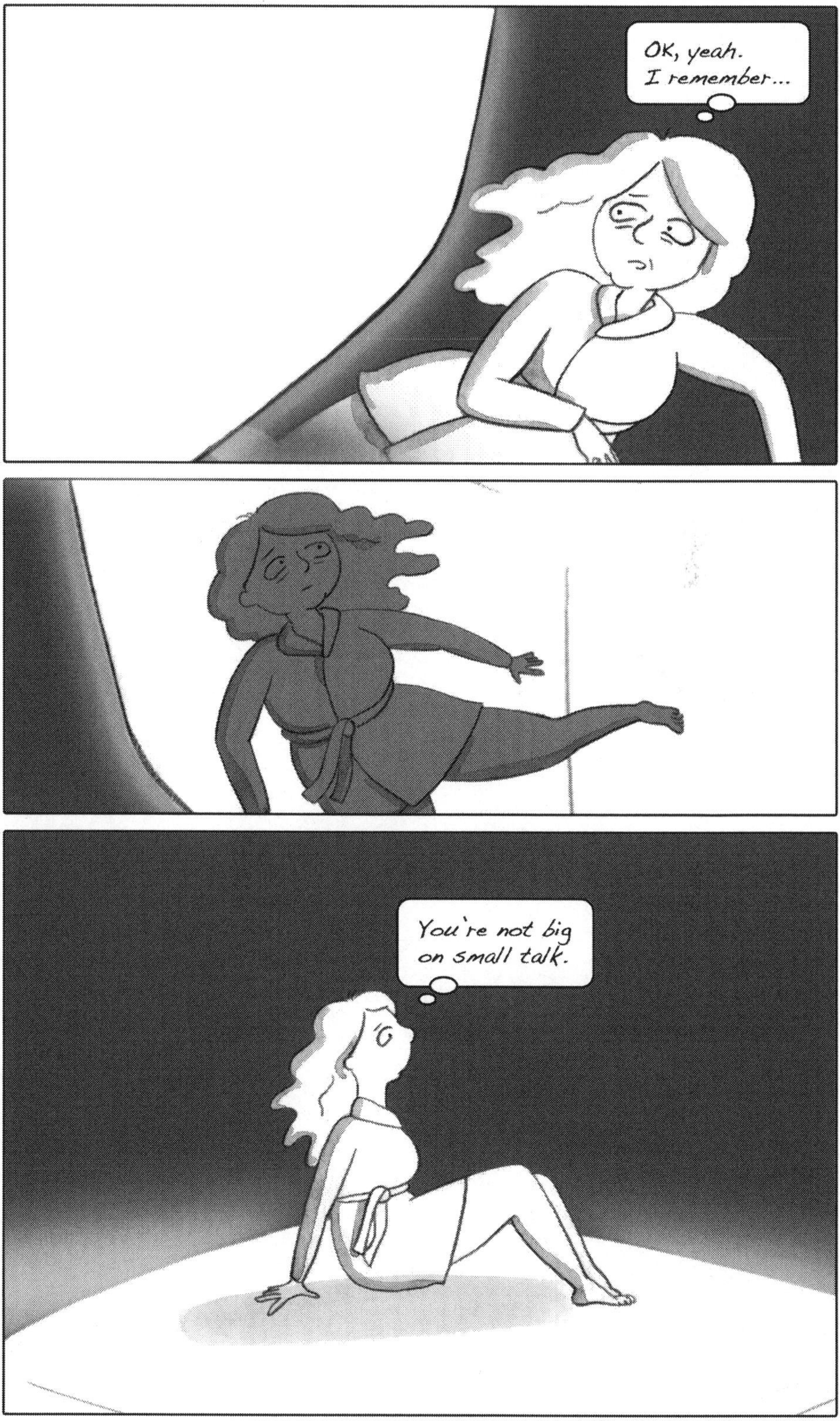
OK, yeah.
I remember...
You're not big
on small talk.

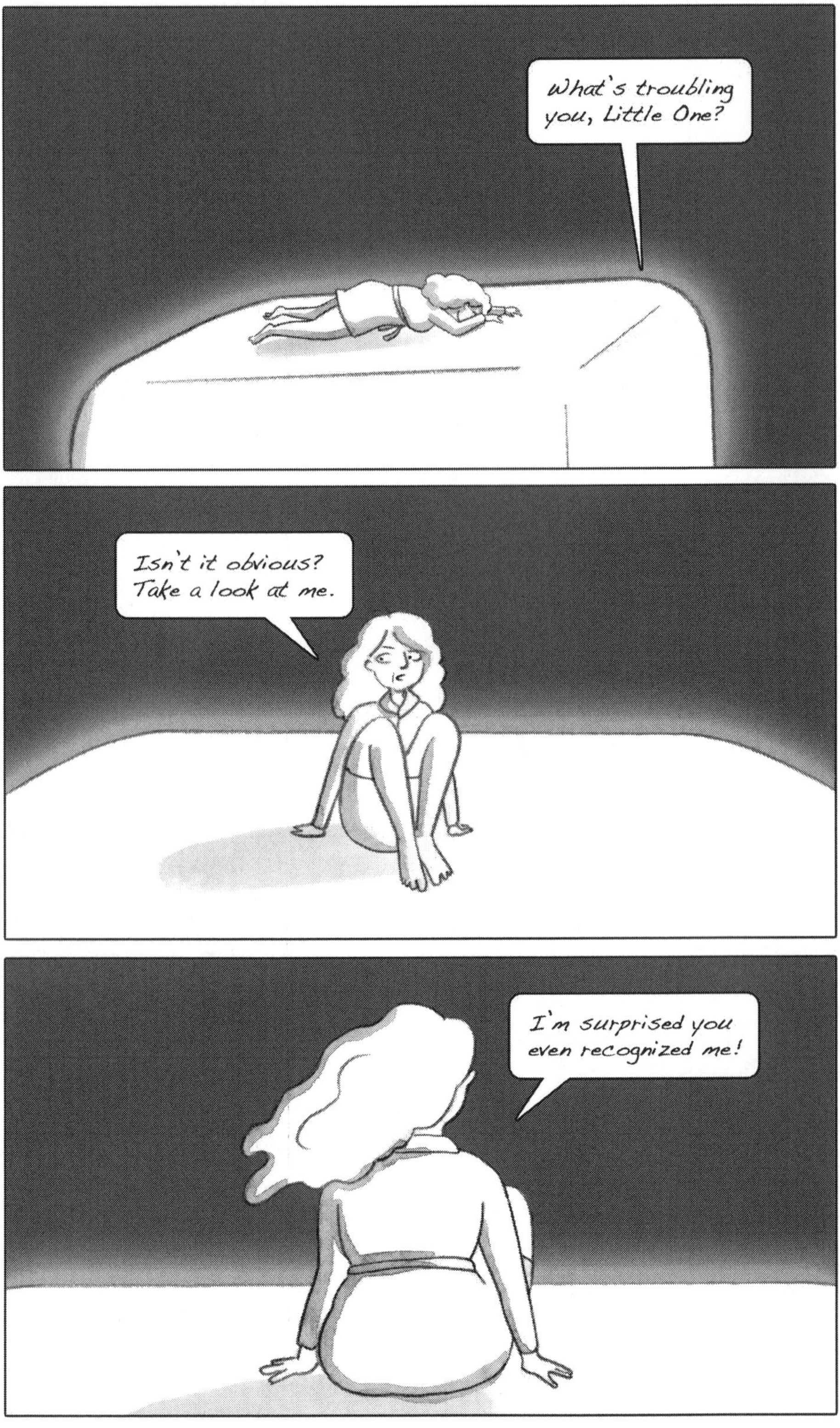
What's troubling you, Little One?
Isn't it obvious? Take a look at me.
I'm surprised you even recognized me!

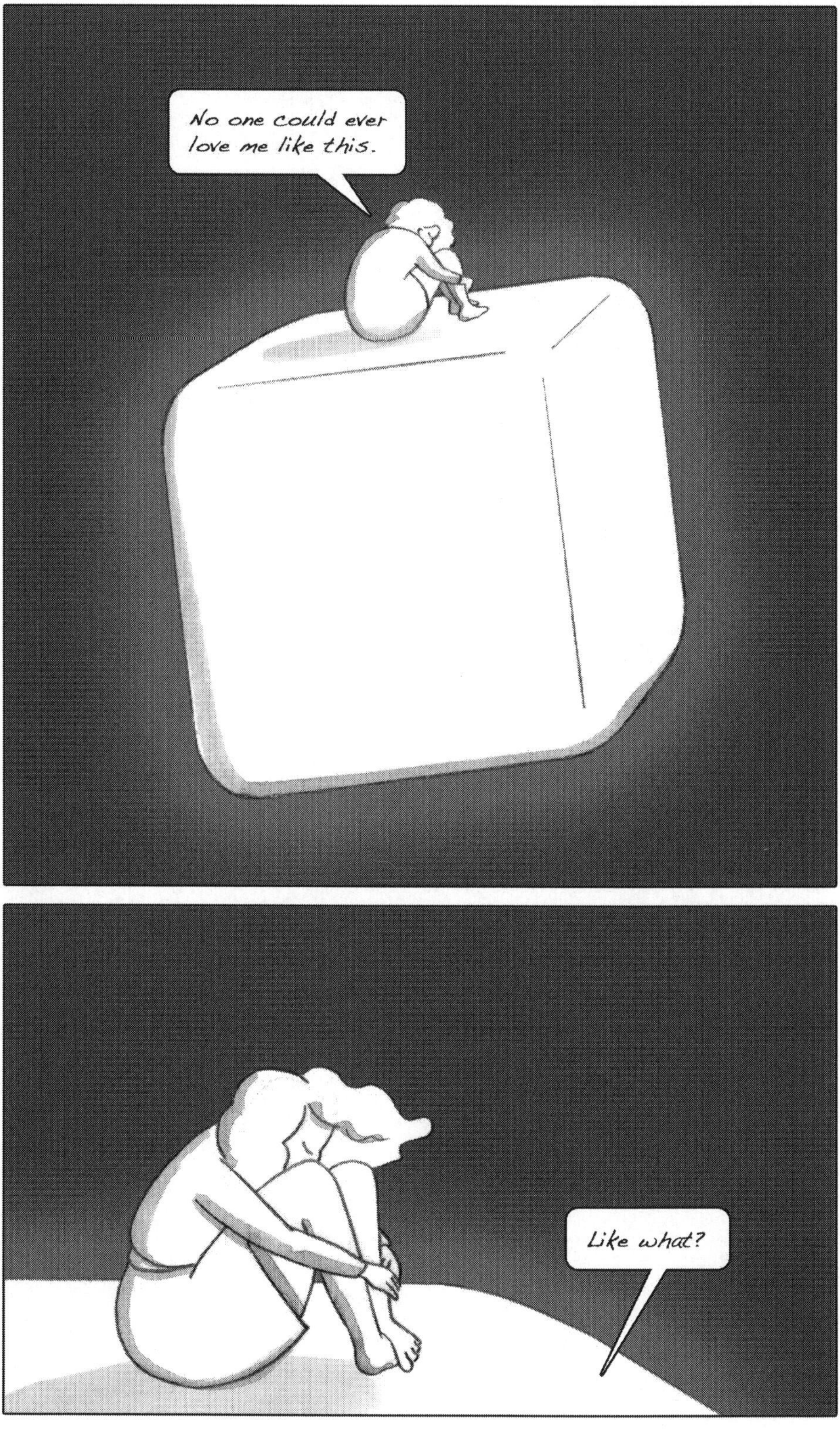
No one could ever love me like this.
Like what?

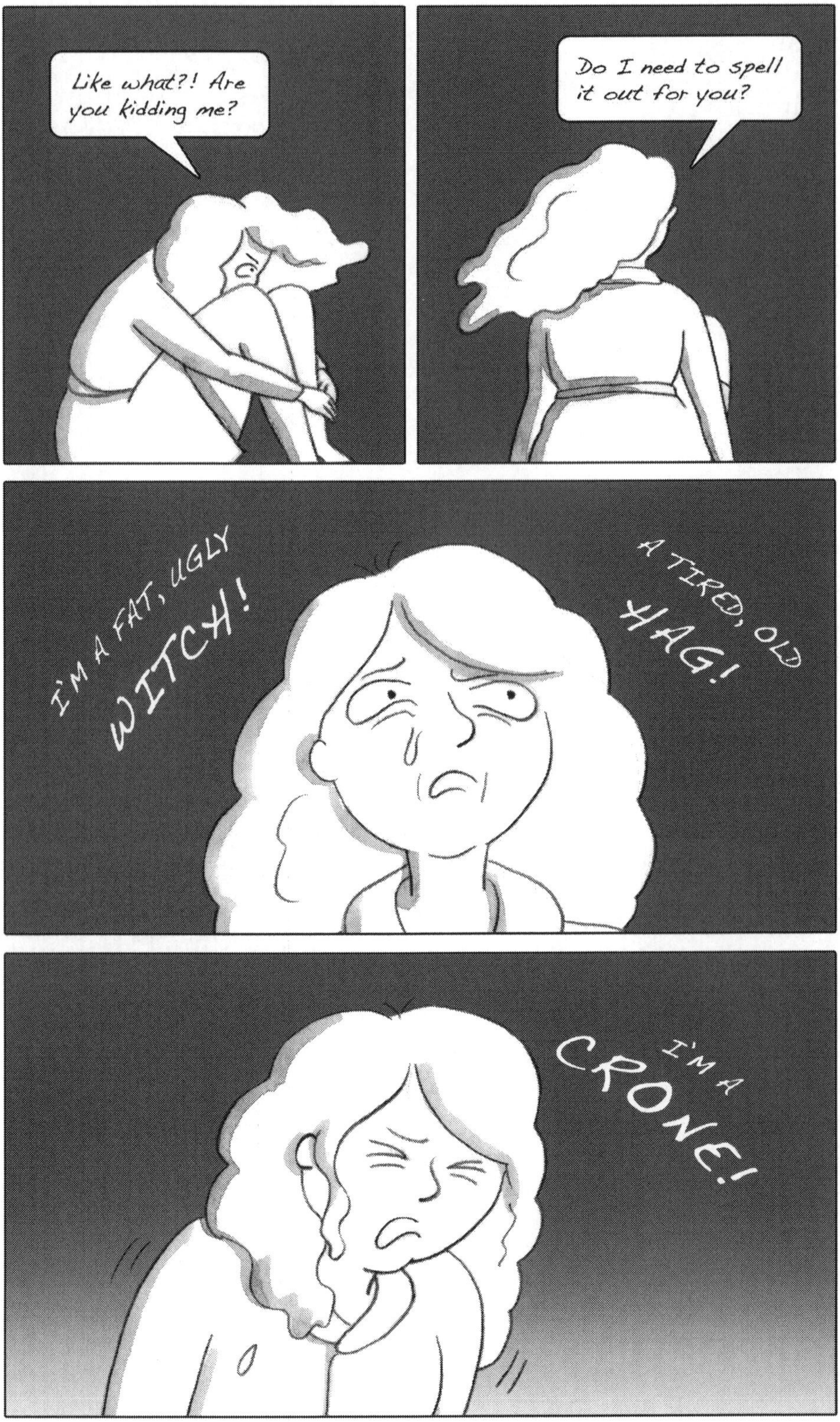
Like what?! Are you kidding me?
Do I need to spell it out for you?
I'M A FAT, UGLY WITCH!
A TIRED, OLD HAG!
I'M A CRONE!

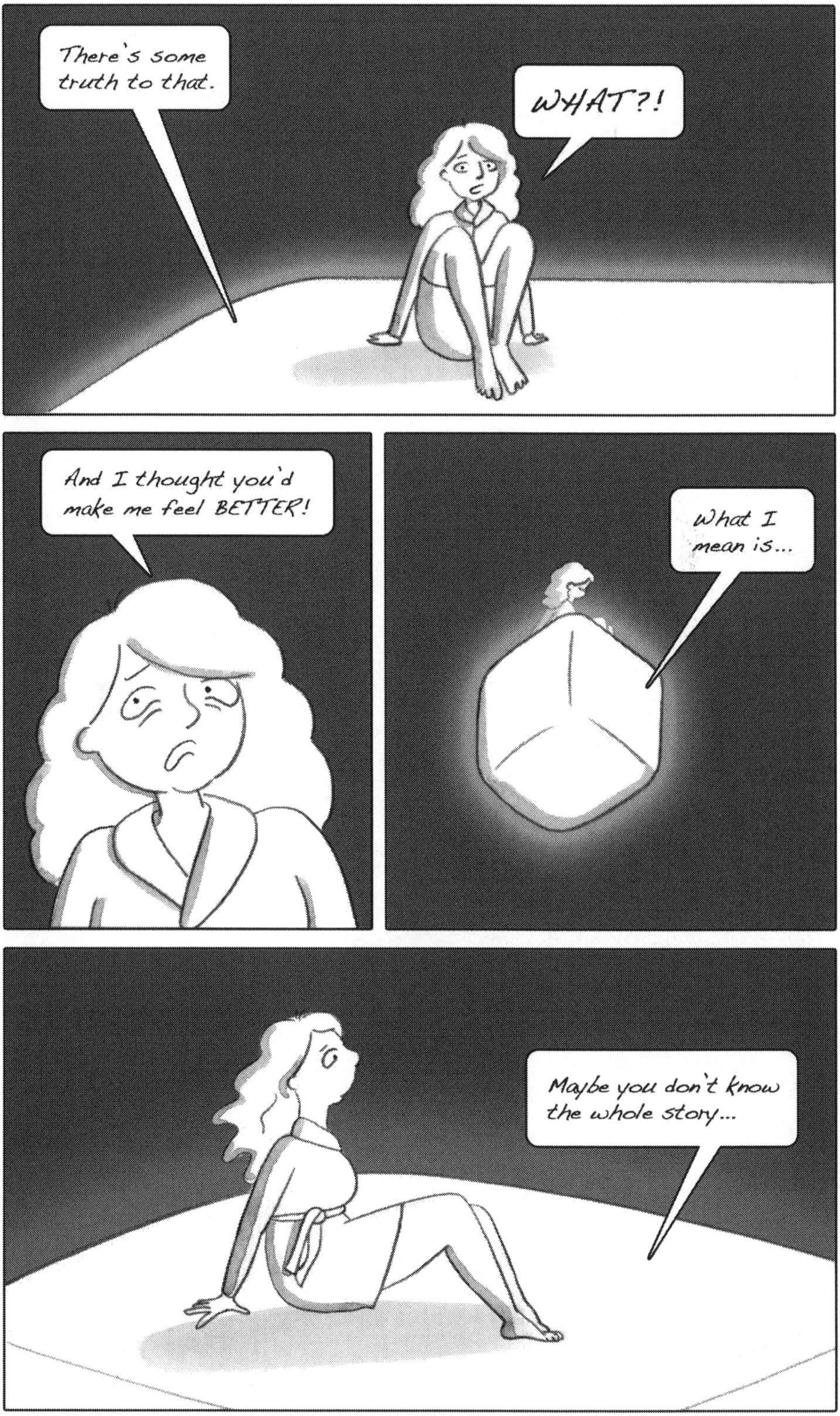
There's some truth to that.
WHAT?!
And I thought you'd make me feel BETTER!
What I mean is...
Maybe you don't know the whole story...

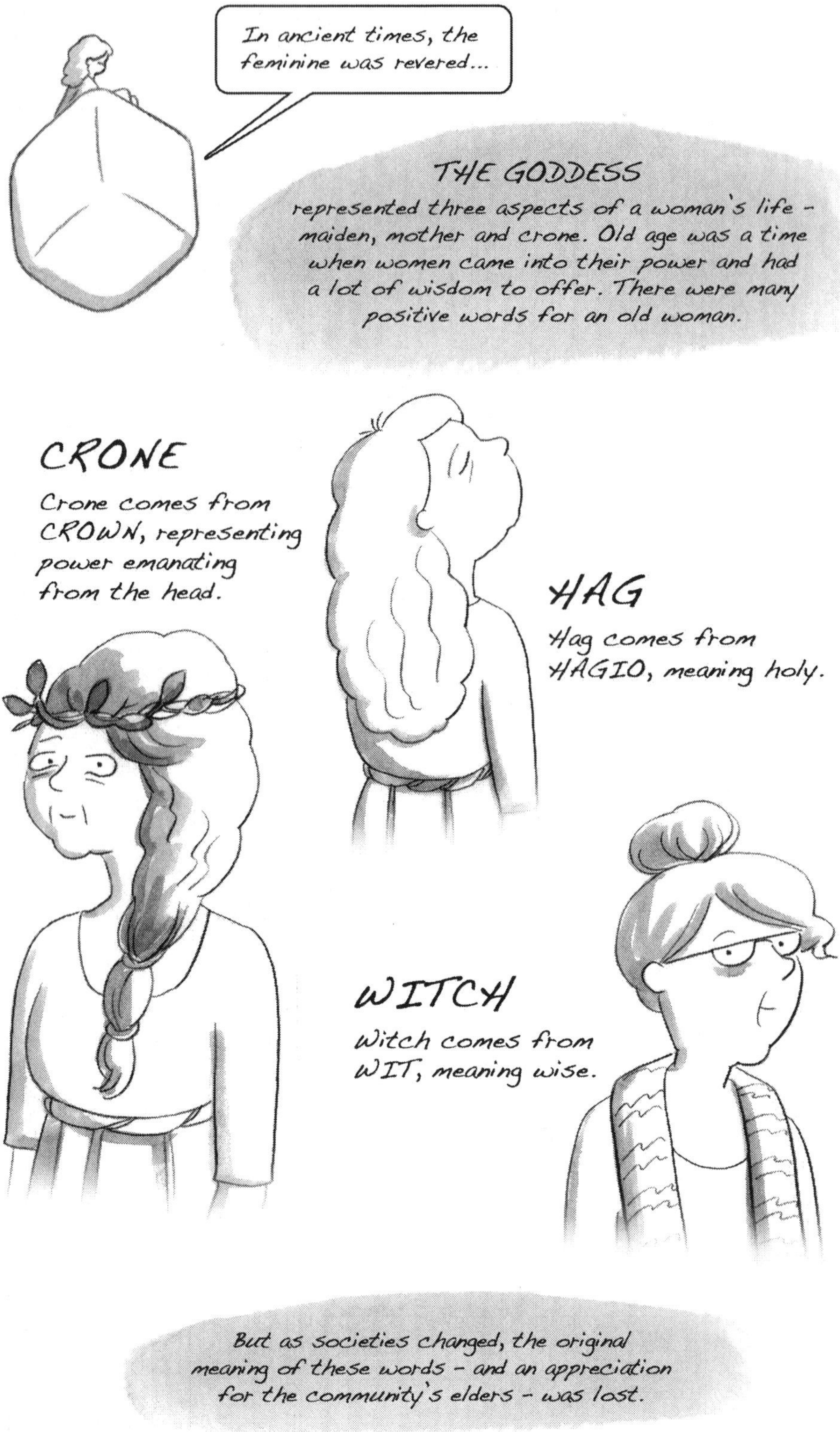
In ancient times, the feminine was revered...
THE GODDESS
represented three aspects of a woman's life - maiden, mother and crone. Old age was a time when women came into their power and had a lot of wisdom to offer. There were many positive words for an old woman.
CRONE
Crone comes from CROWN, representing power emanating from the head.
HAG
Hag comes from HAGIO, meaning holy.
WITCH
Witch comes from WIT, meaning wise.
But as societies changed, the original meaning of these words - and an appreciation for the community's elders - was lost.

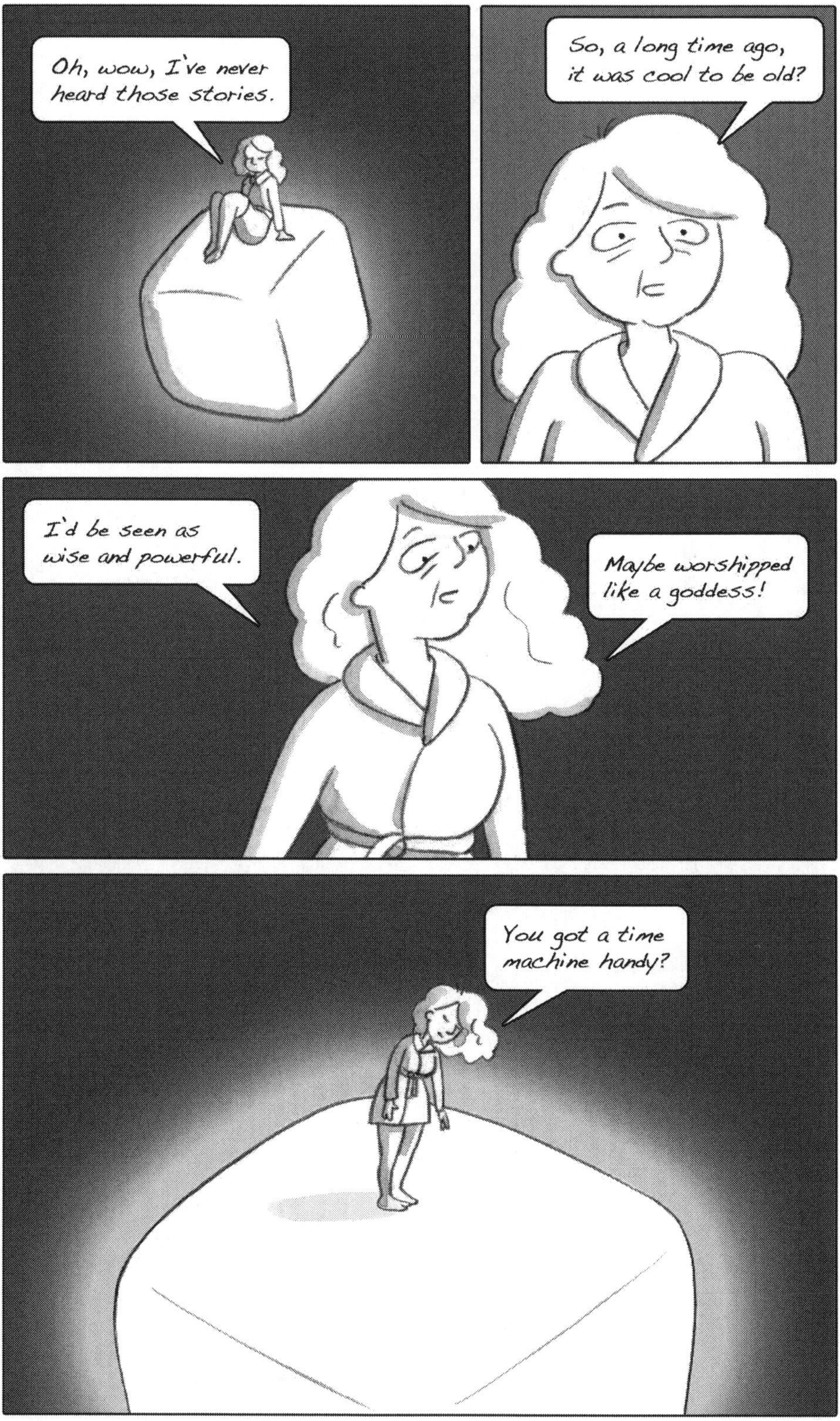
Oh, wow, I've never heard those stories.
So, a long time ago, it was cool to be old?
I'd be seen as wise and powerful.
Maybe worshipped like a goddess!
You got a time machine handy?

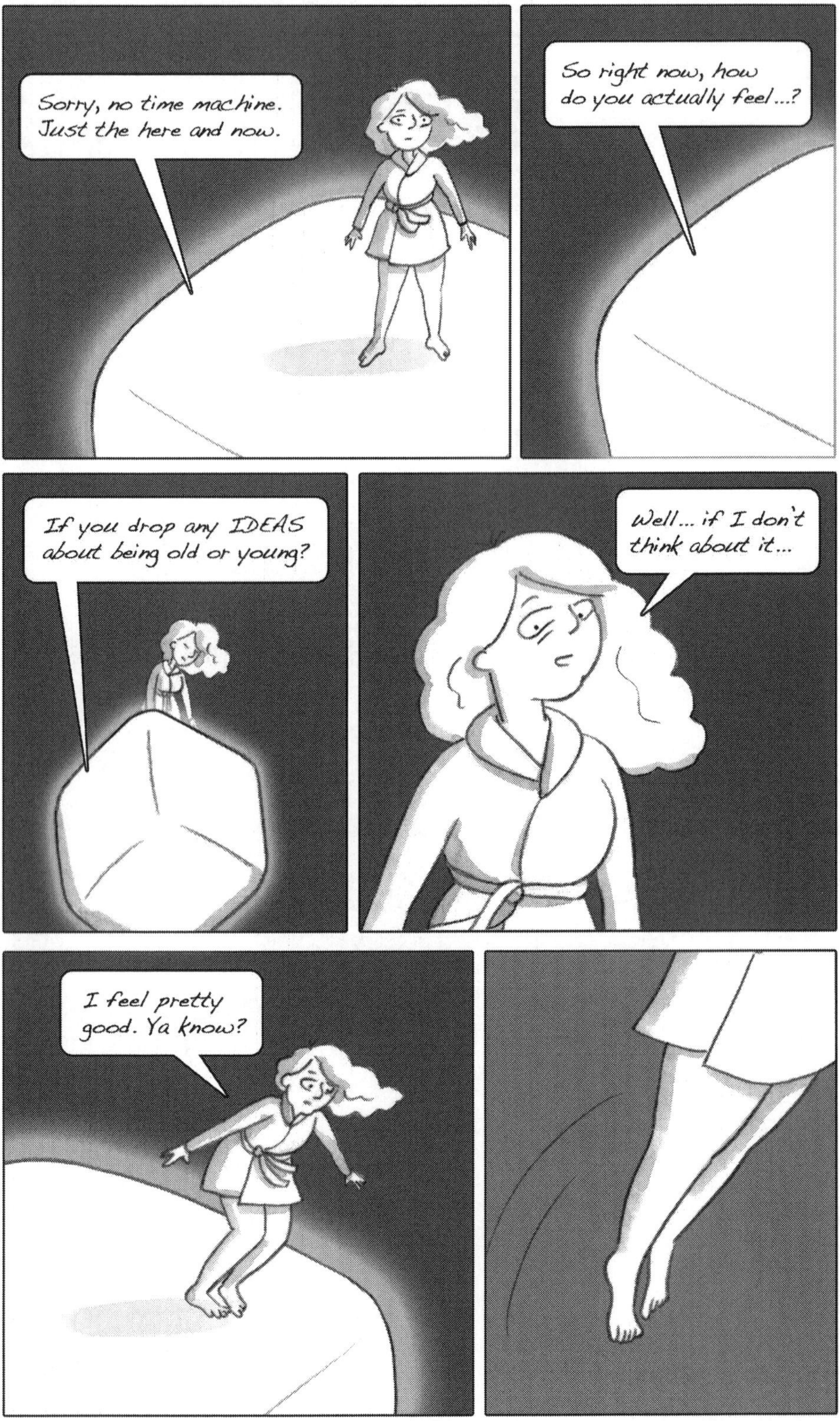
Sorry, no time machine. Just the here and now.
So right now, how do you actually feel...?
If you drop any IDEAS about being old or young?
Well... if I don't think about it...
I feel pretty good. Ya know?

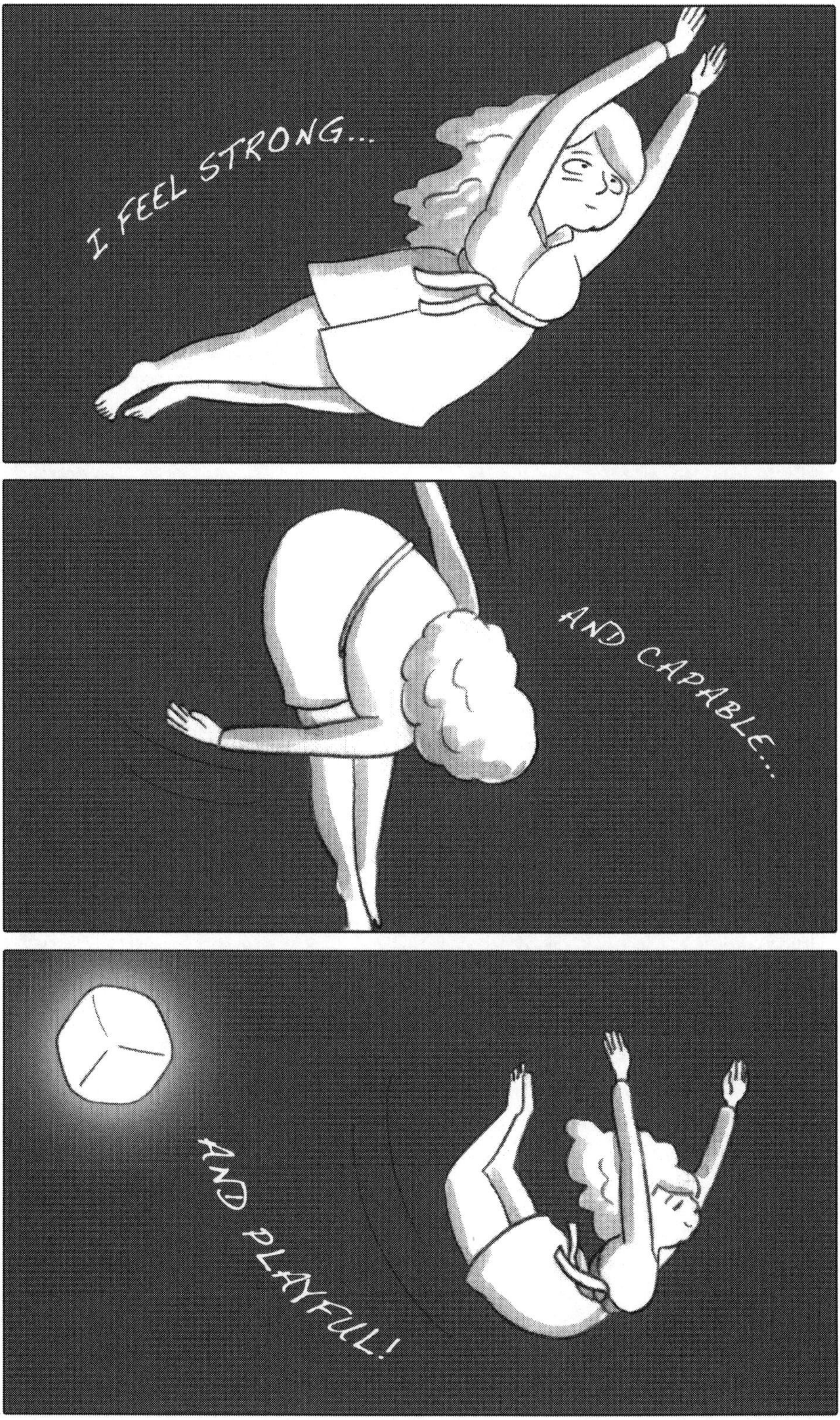
I FEEL STRONG...
AND CAPABLE...
AND PLAYFUL!

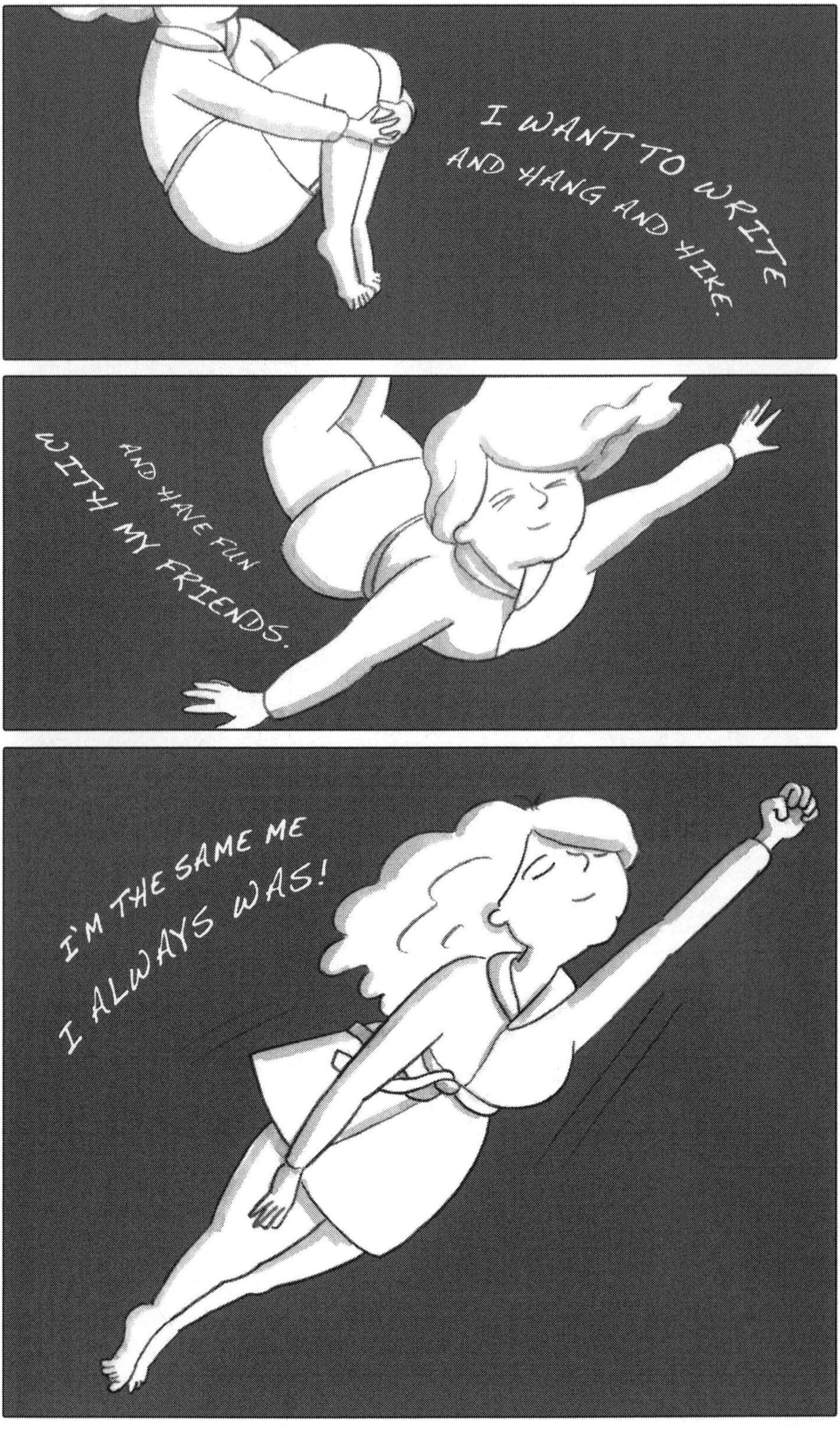
I WANT TO WRITE
AND HANG AND HIKE.
AND HAVE FUN
WITH MY FRIENDS.
I'M THE SAME ME
I ALWAYS WAS!

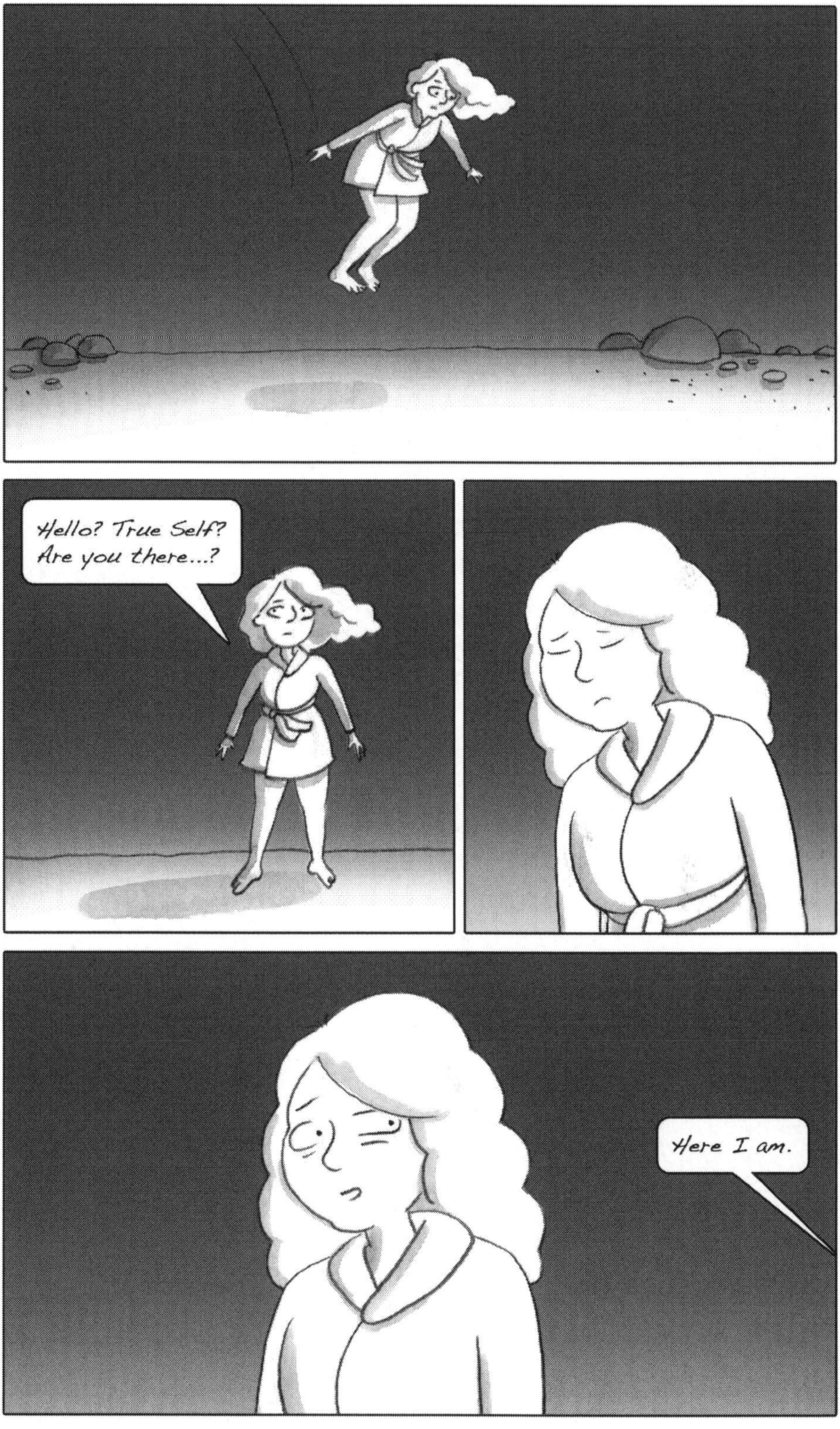
Hello? True Self?
Are you there...?
Here I am.

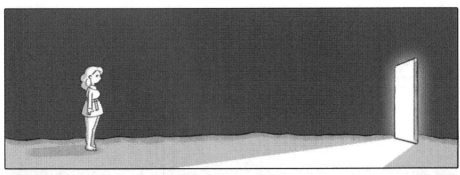

THE FIVE STAGES OF GRIEF

5) ACCEPTANCE

In the last stage, the inevitable future is embraced. The individual realizes there's no use fighting reality any longer.

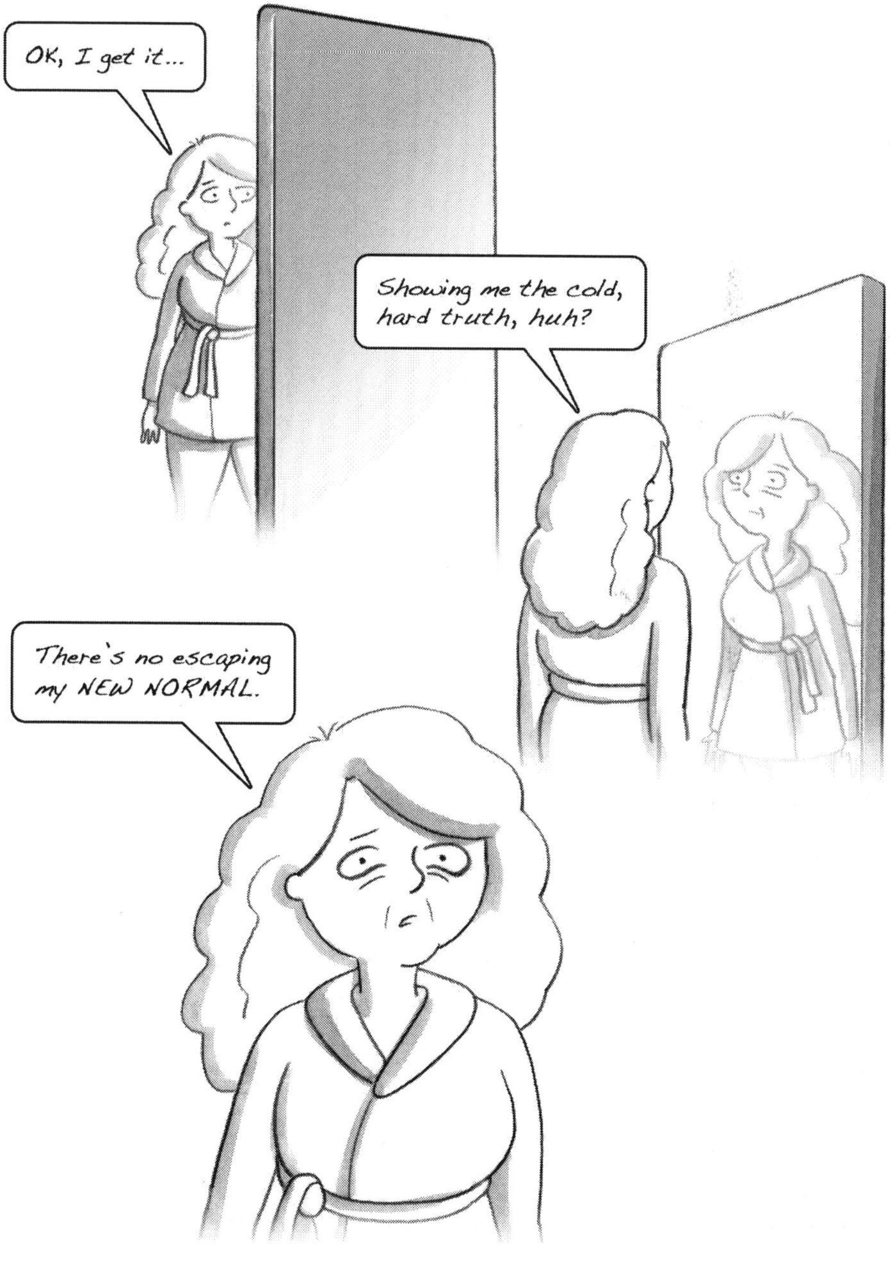
OK, I get it...
Showing me the cold, hard truth, huh?
There's no escaping my NEW NORMAL.

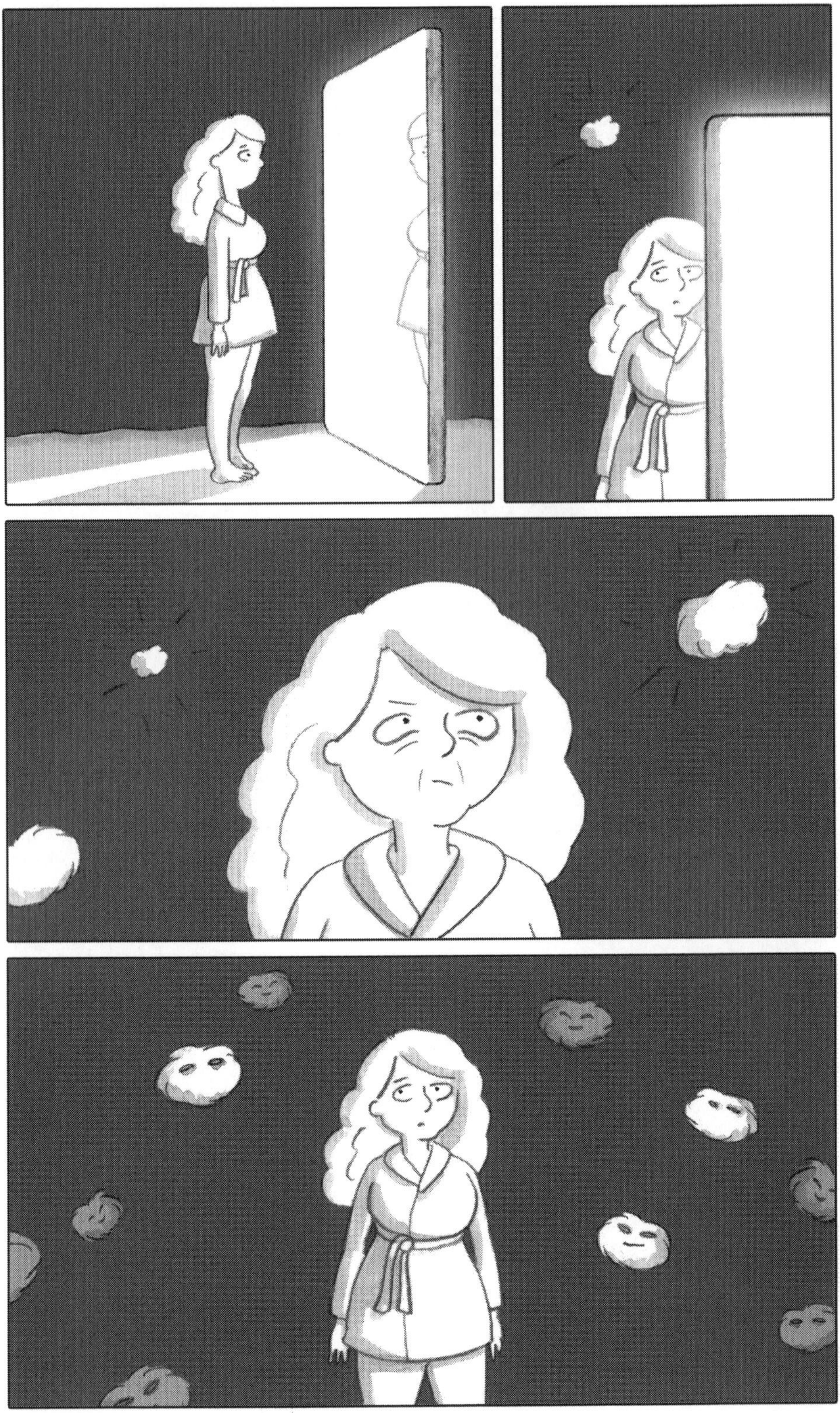

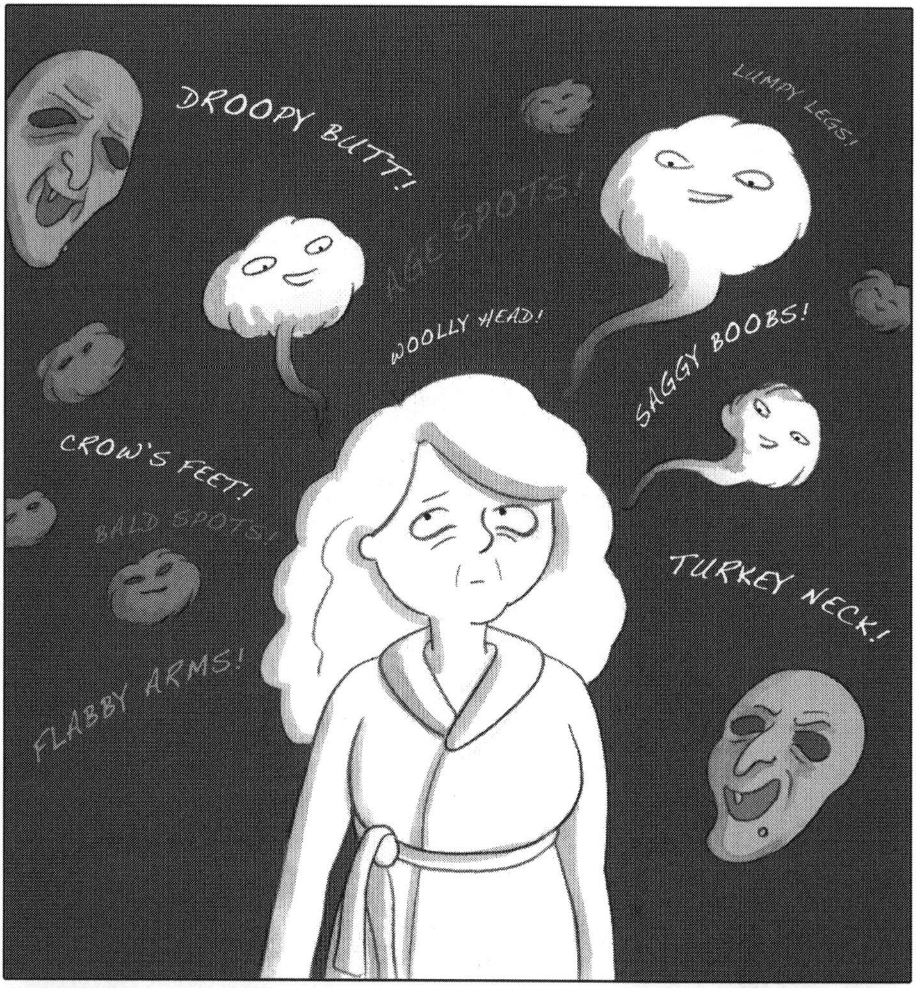
DROOPY BUTT!
LUMPY LEGS!
AGE SPOTS!
WOOLLY HEAD!
SAGGY BOOBS!
CROW'S FEET!
BALD SPOTS!
TURKEY NECK!
FLABBY ARMS!

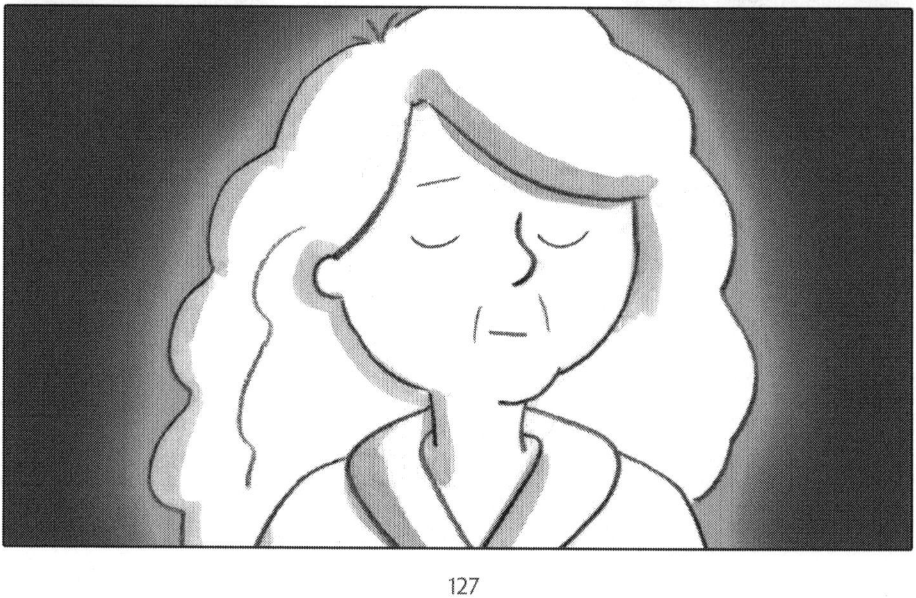

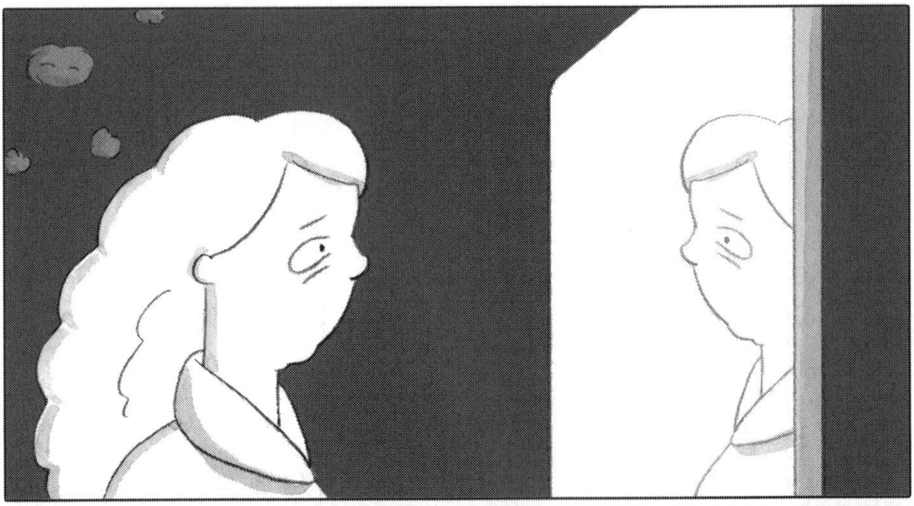

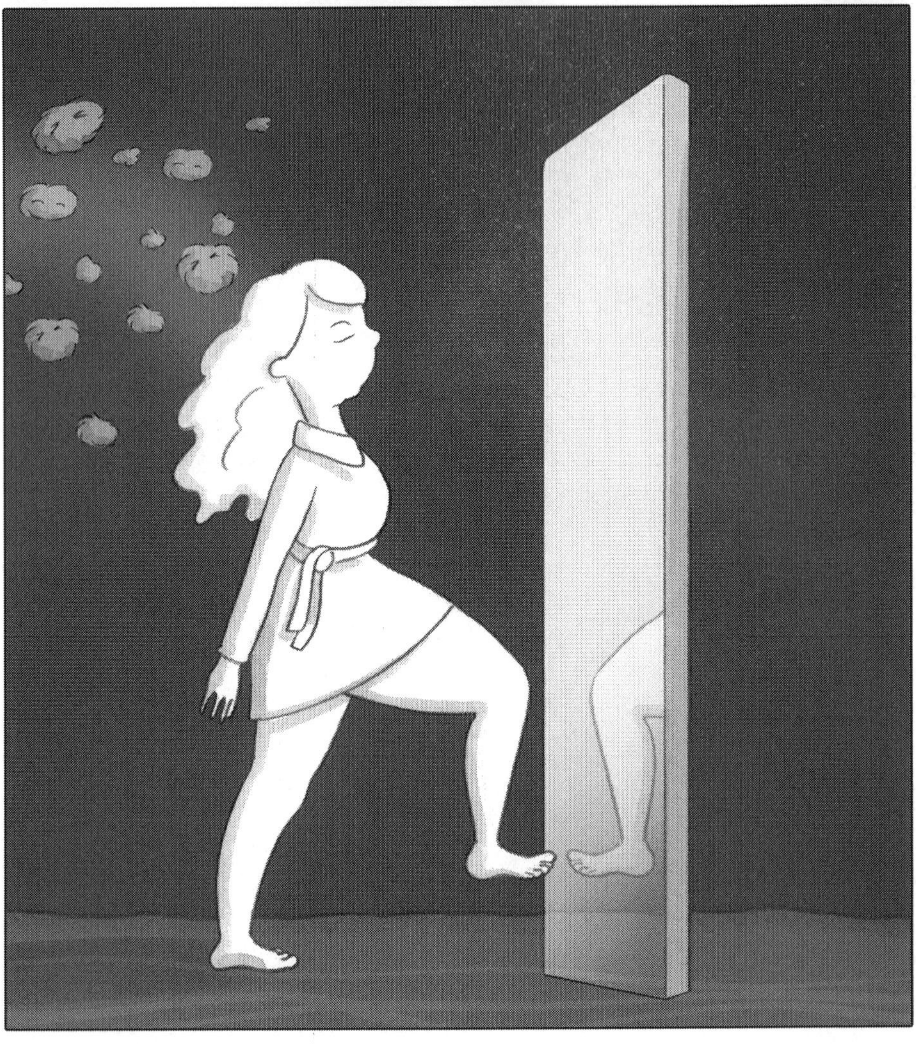

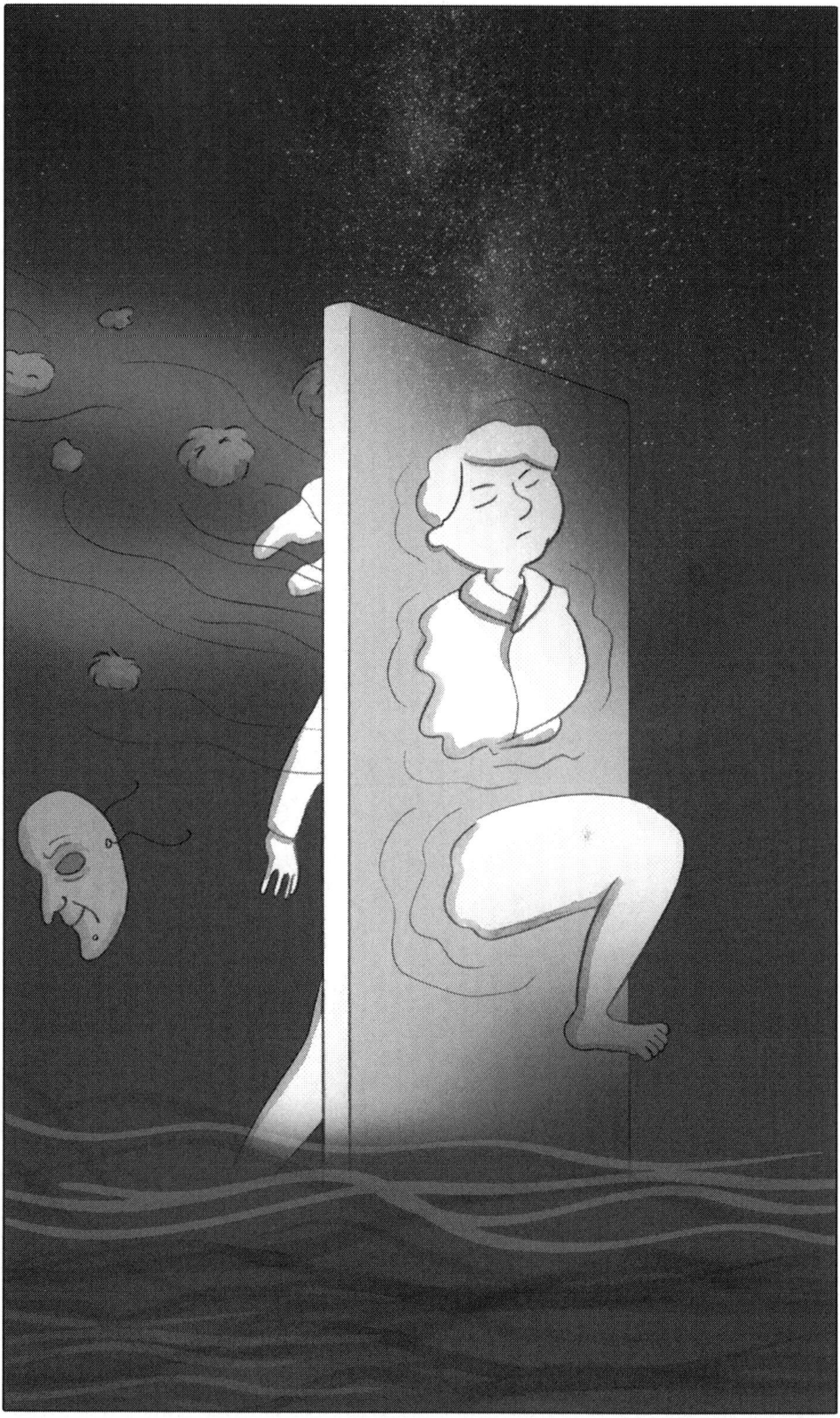

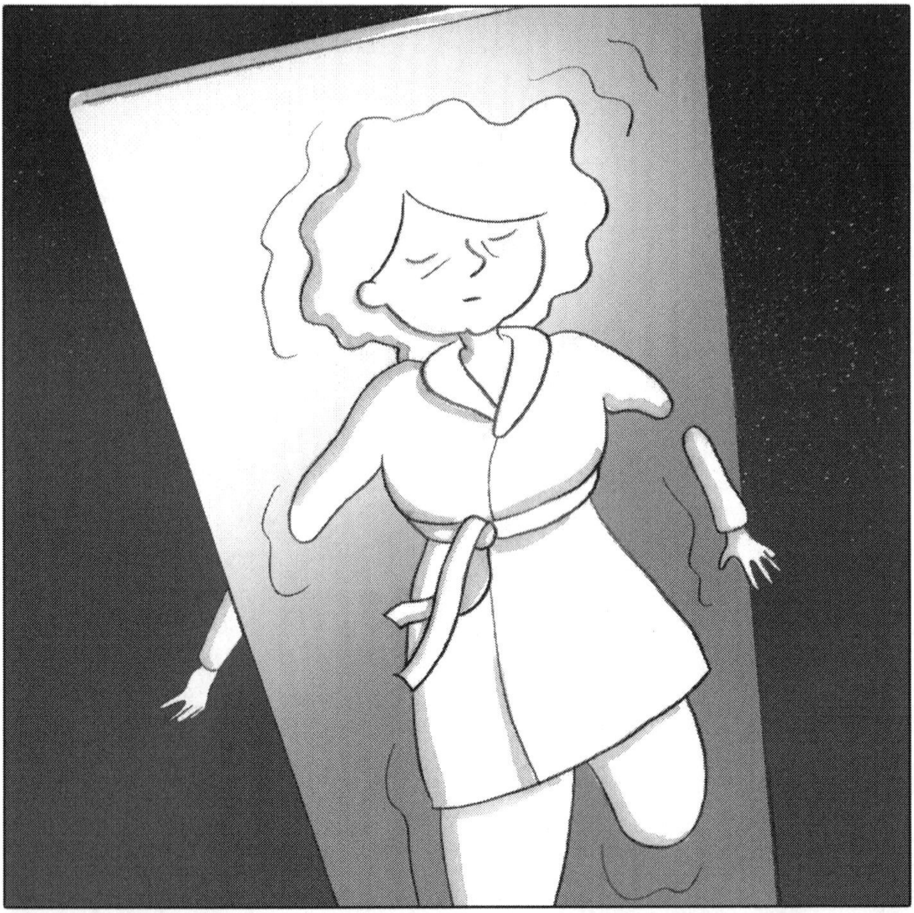

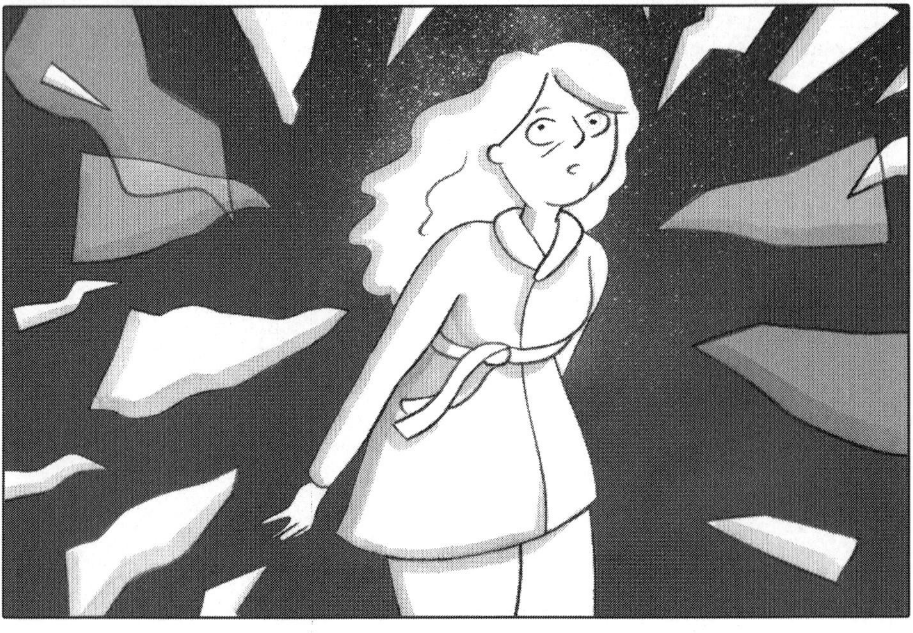

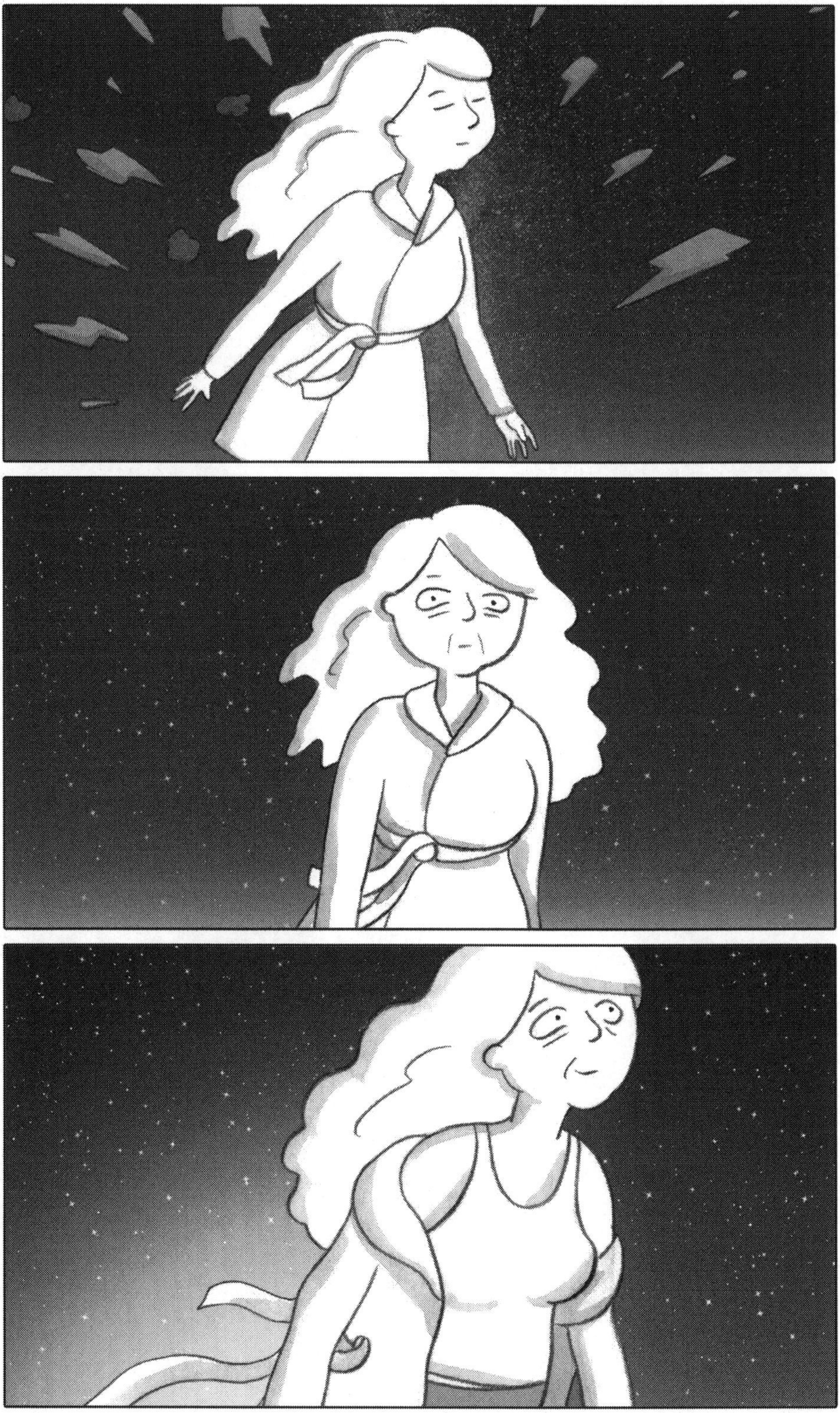

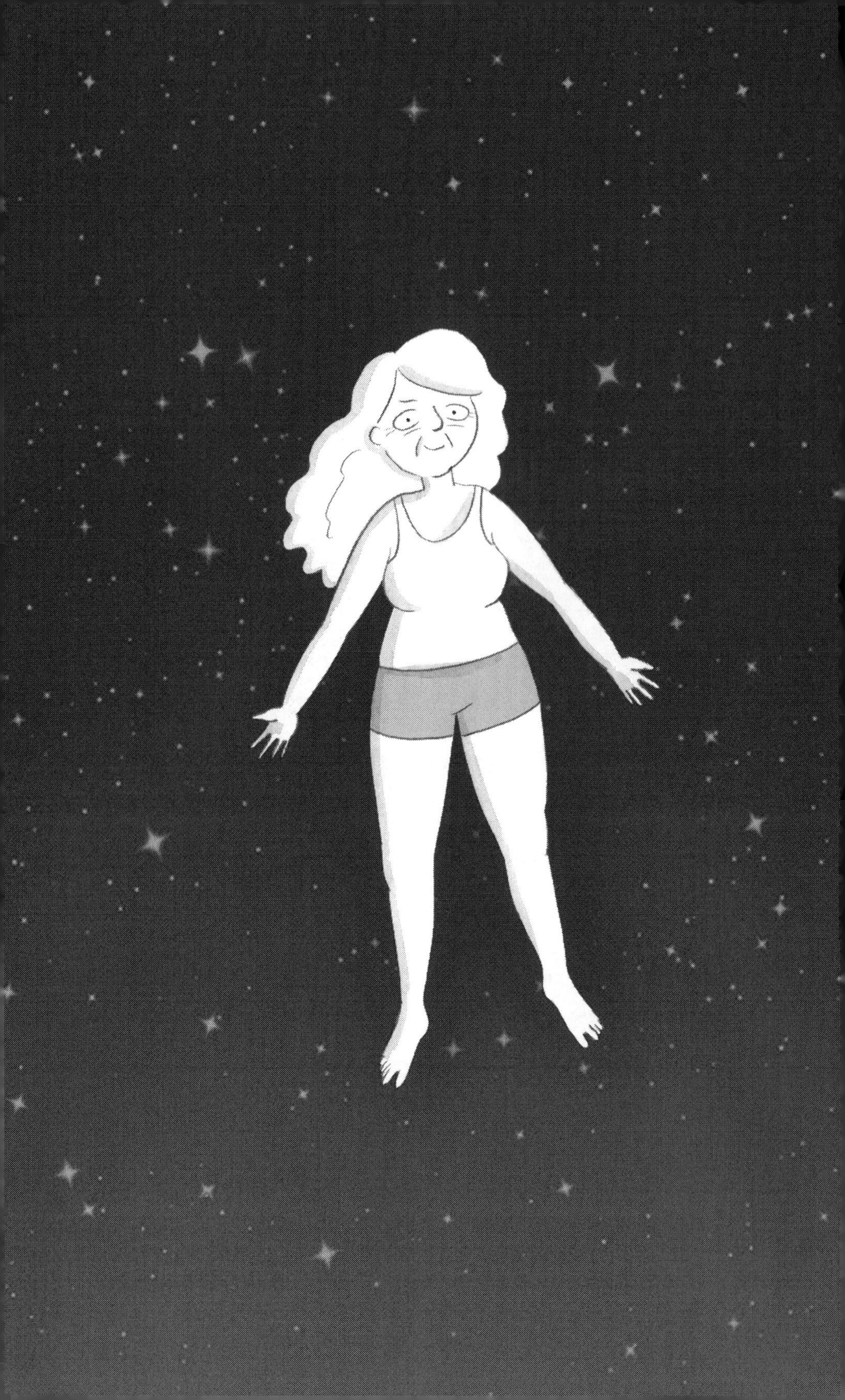

Who in the world am I?

Ah, that's the great puzzle.

ALICE IN WONDERLAND

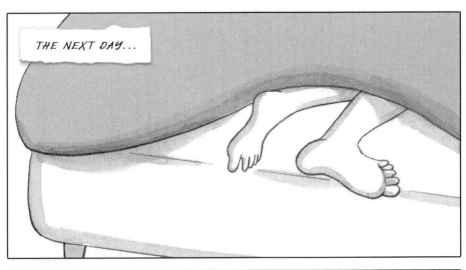

THE NEXT DAY...

BEEP! BEEP! BEEP!

CLUNK!

07:30

Well, this is it. Time for school.

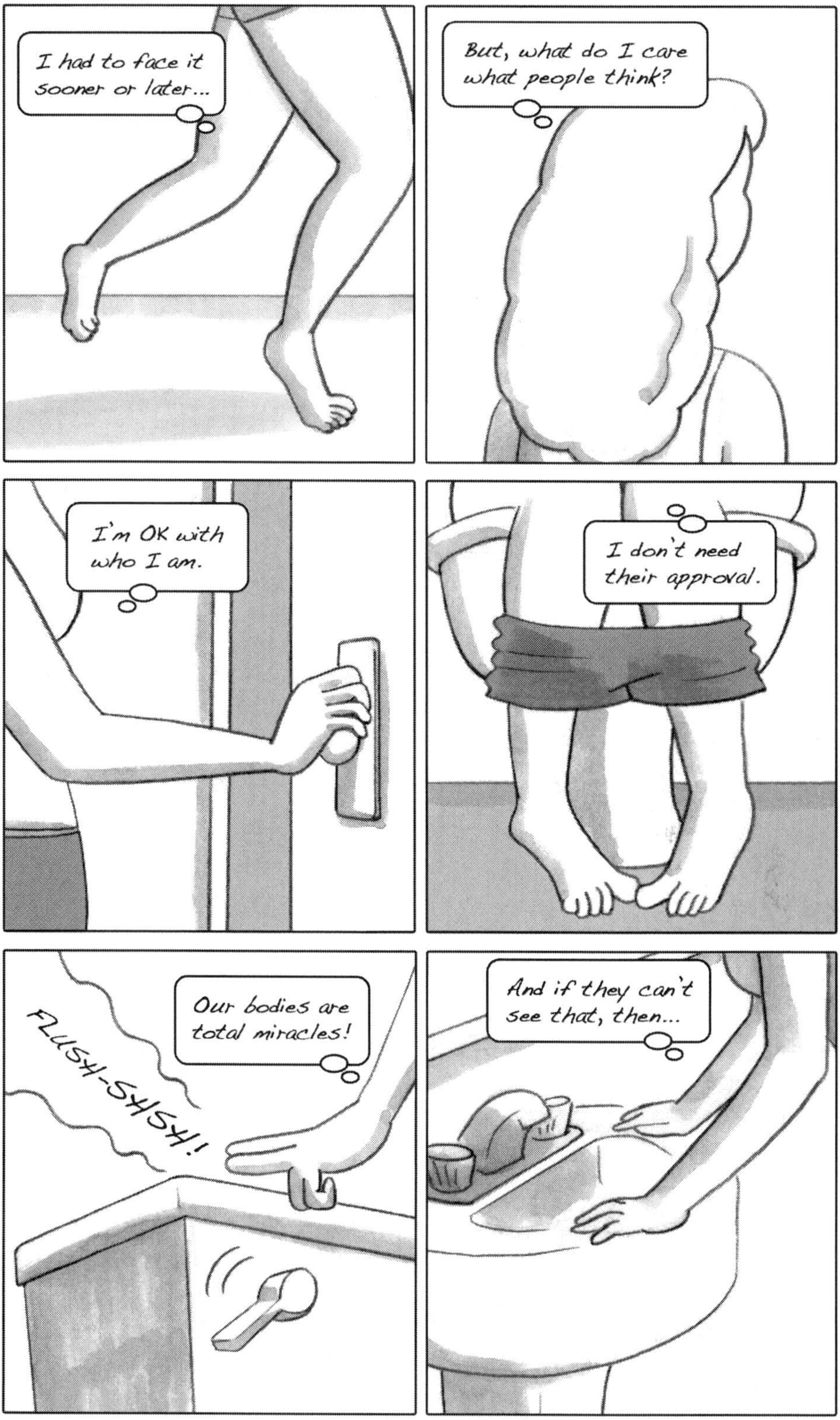
I had to face it sooner or later...
But, what do I care what people think?
I'm OK with who I am.
I don't need their approval.
Our bodies are total miracles!
FLUSH-SHSH!
And if they can't see that, then...

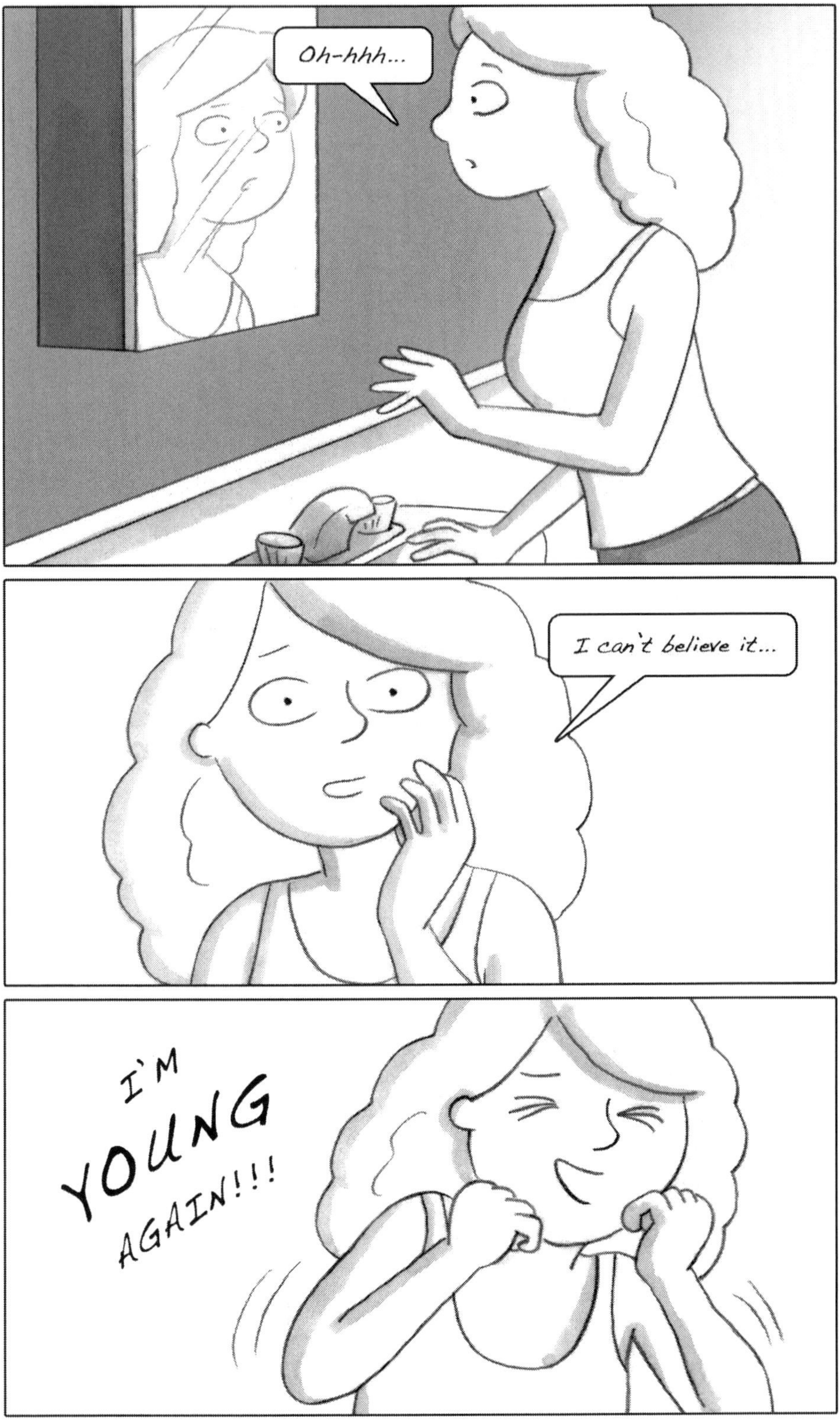
Oh-hhh...
I can't believe it...
I'M YOUNG AGAIN!!!

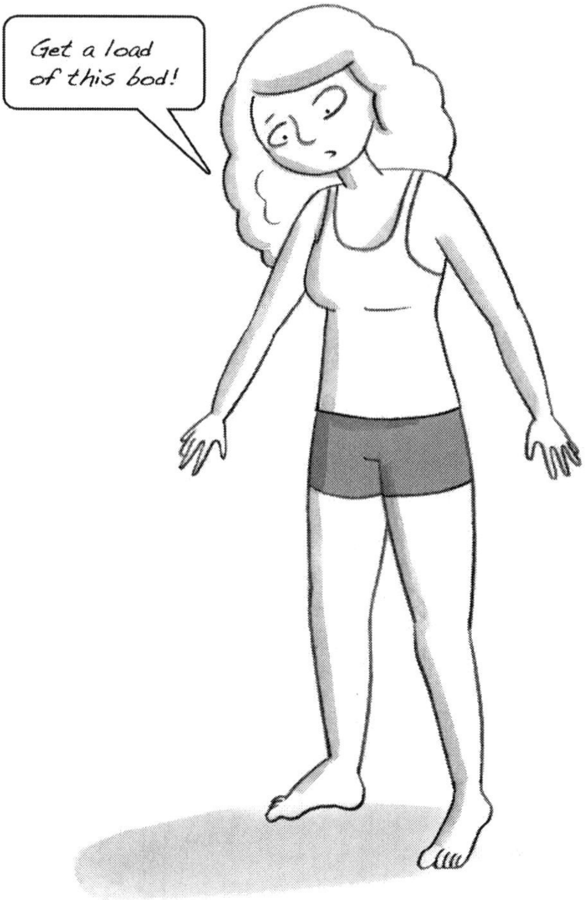
Get a load of this bod!

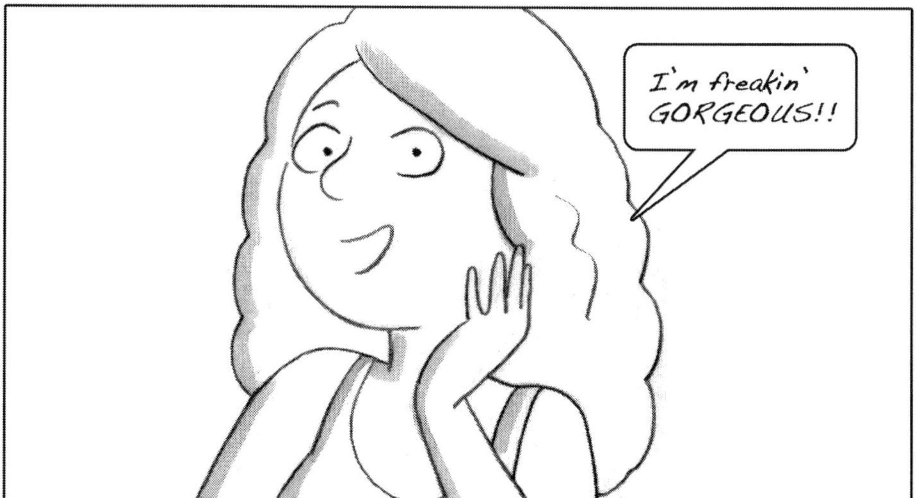
I'm freakin' GORGEOUS!!

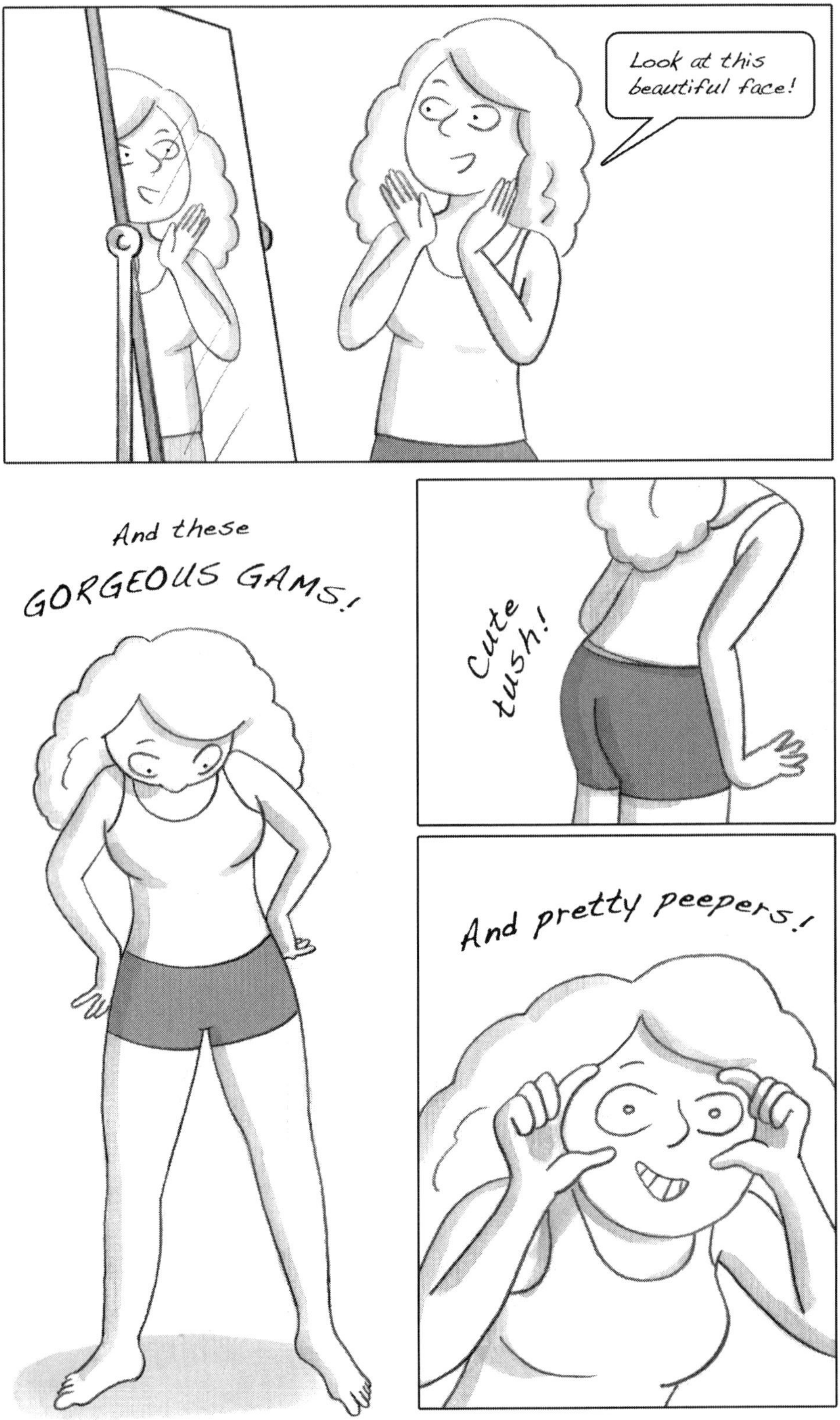
Look at this beautiful face!
And these GORGEOUS GAMS!
Cute tush!
And pretty peepers!

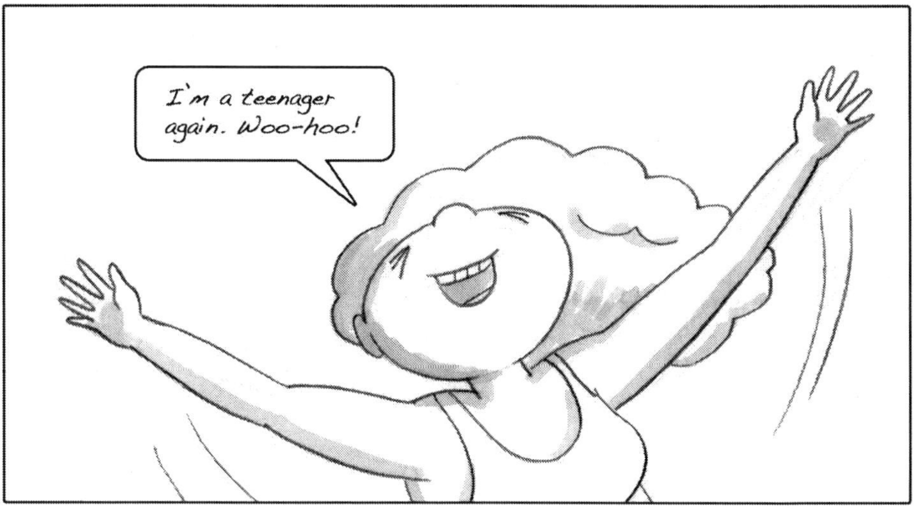
I'm a teenager again. Woo-hoo!

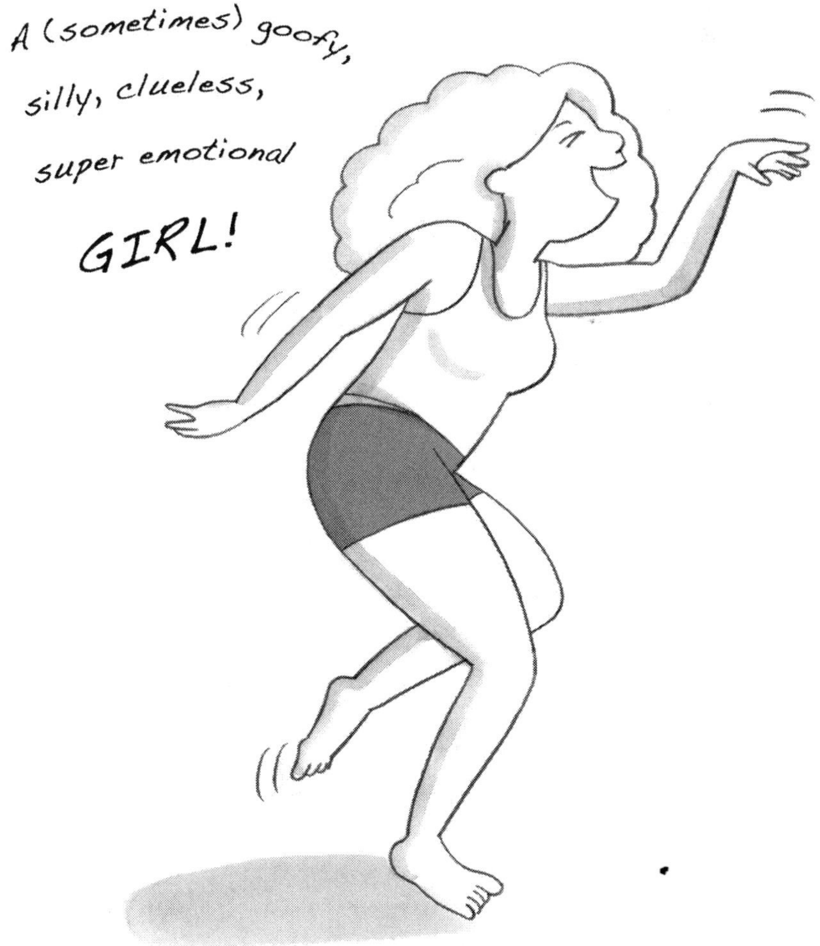
A (sometimes) goofy, silly, clueless, super emotional GIRL!

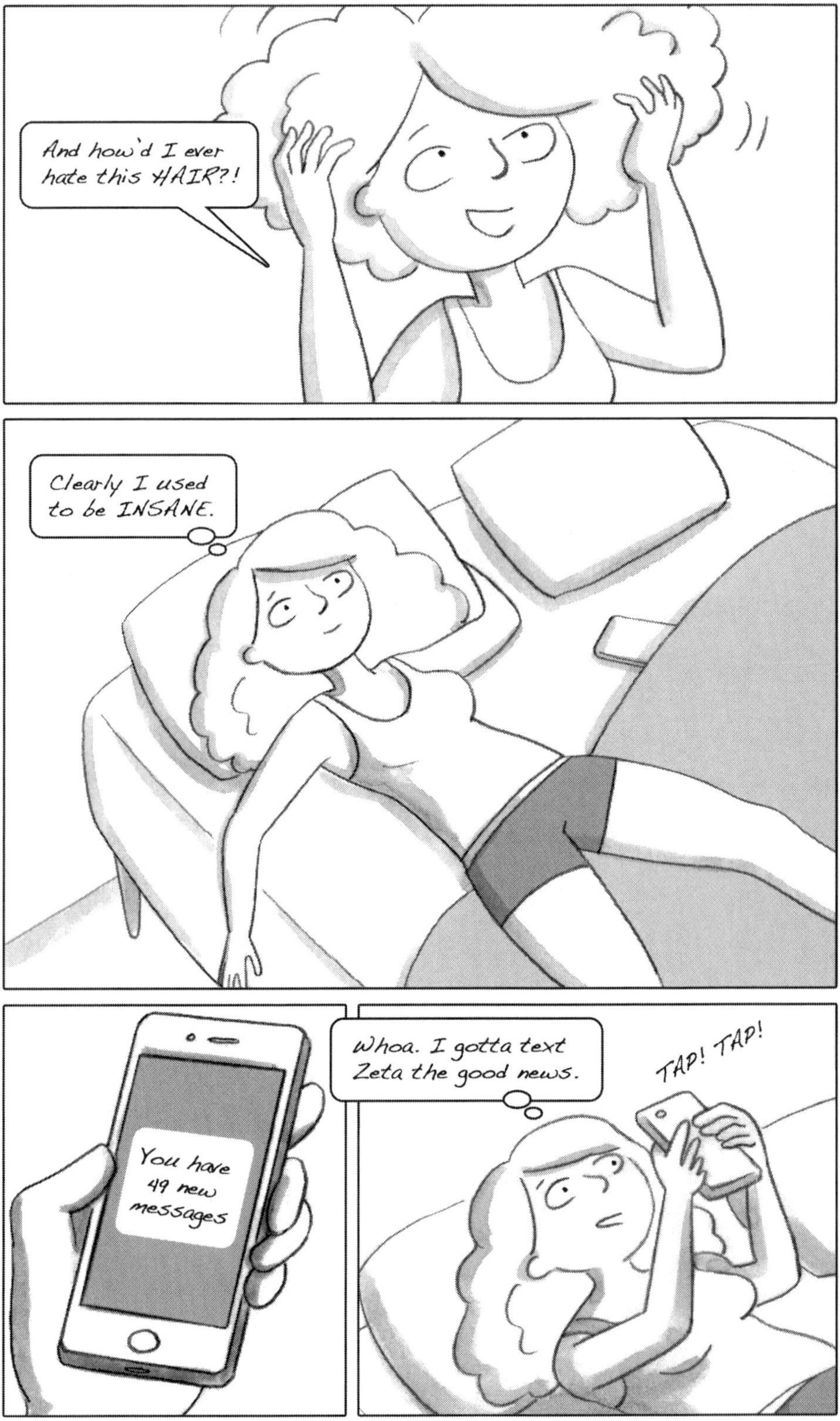
And how'd I ever hate this HAIR?!
Clearly I used to be INSANE.
You have 49 new messages
Whoa. I gotta text Zeta the good news.
TAP! TAP!

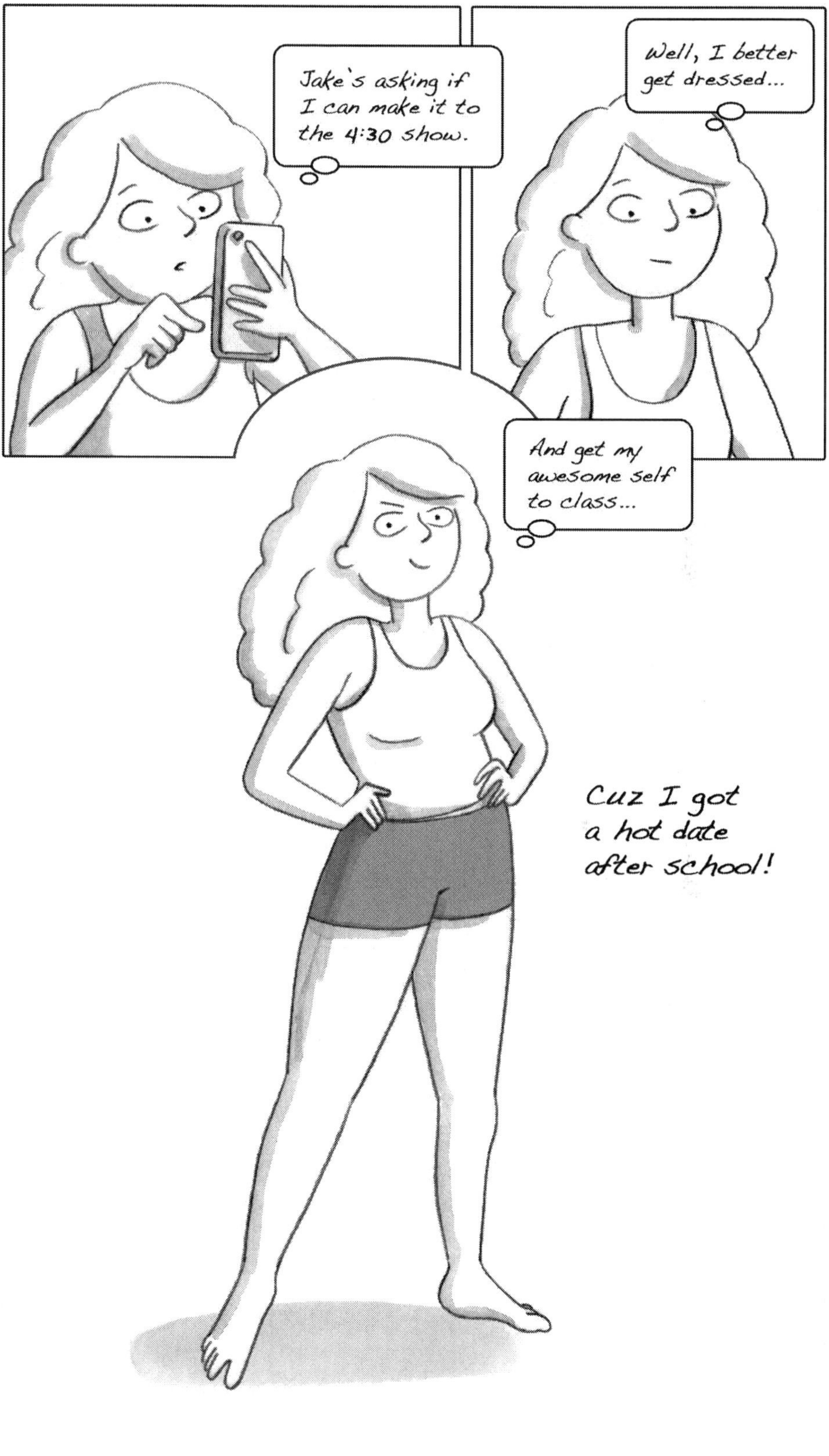
Jake's asking if I can make it to the 4:30 show.
Well, I better get dressed...
And get my awesome self to class...
Cuz I got a hot date after school!

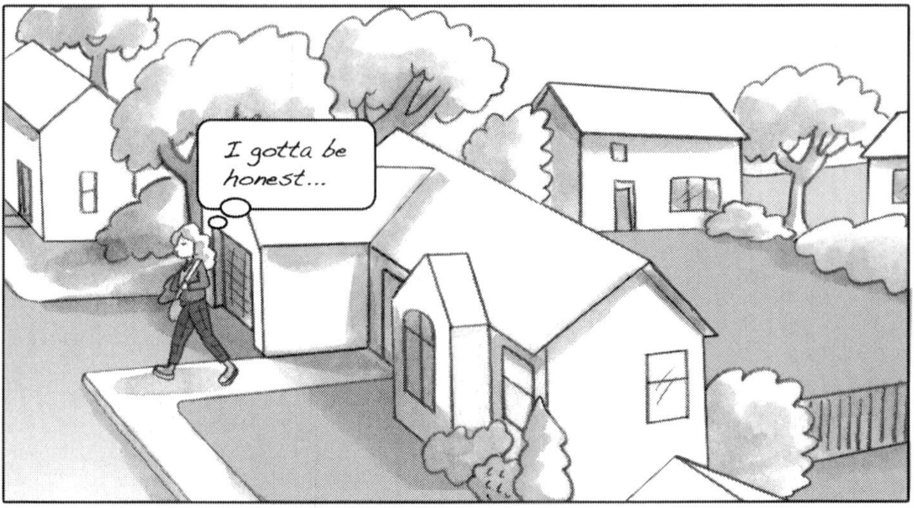
I gotta be honest...

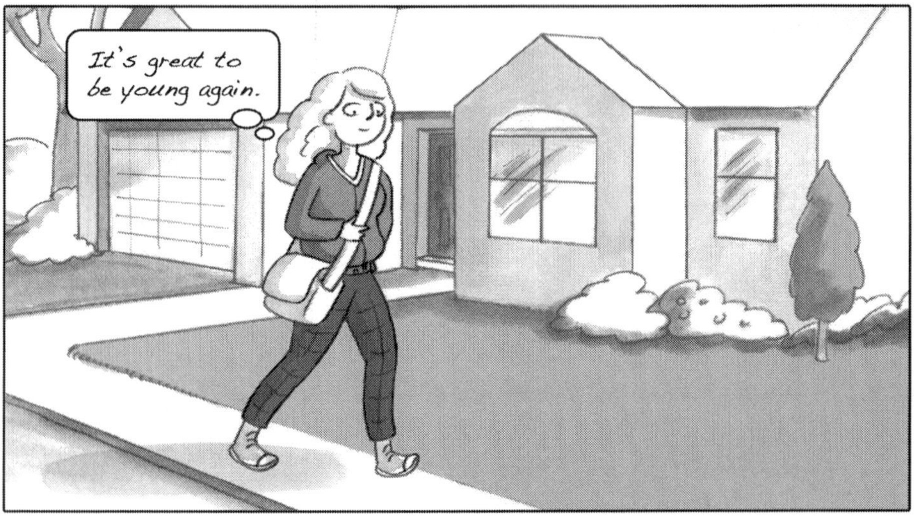
It's great to be young again.

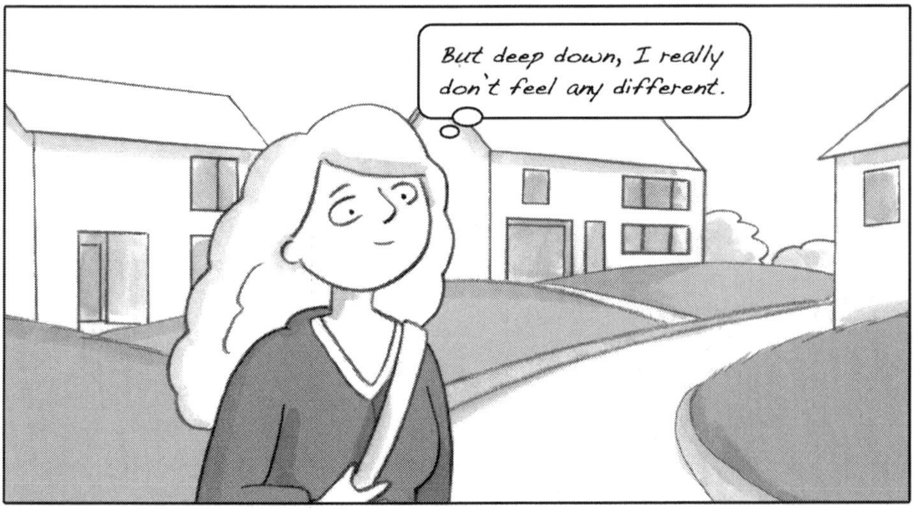
But deep down, I really don't feel any different.

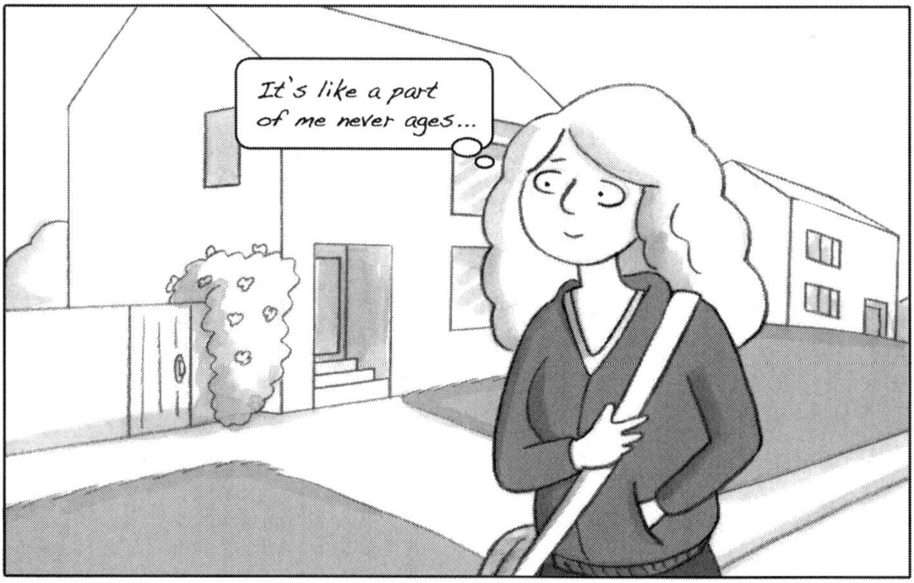
It's like a part of me never ages...

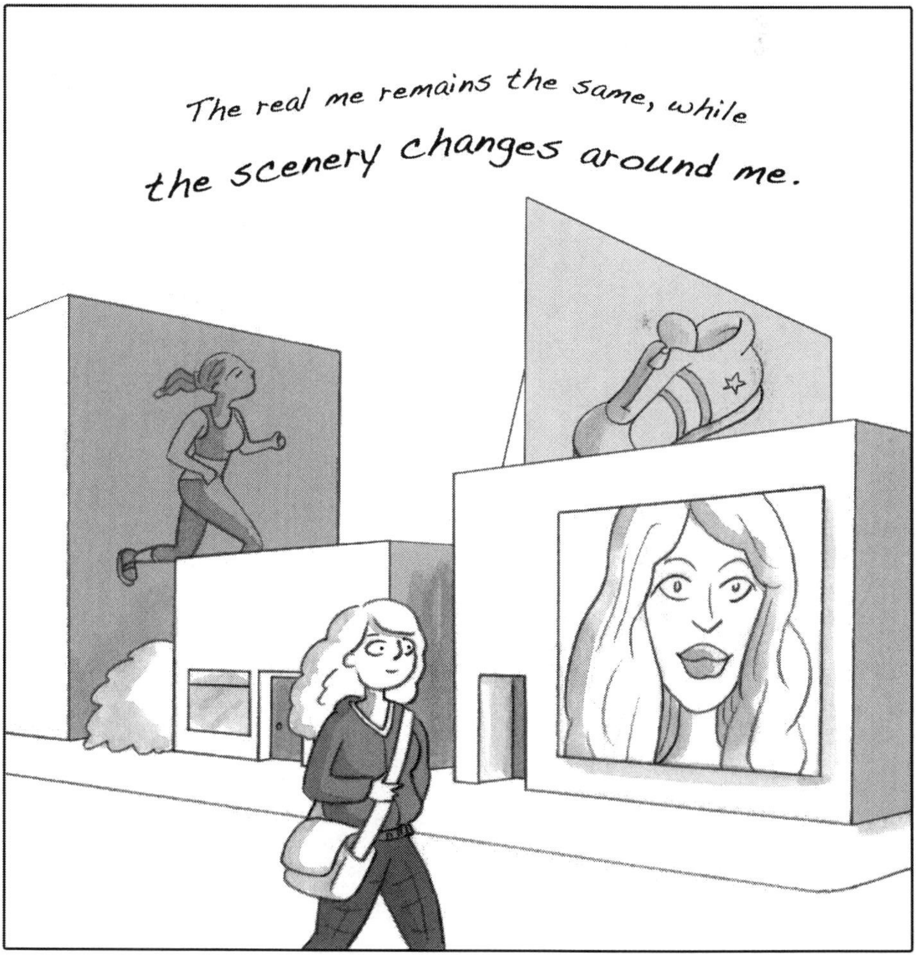
The real me remains the same, while the scenery changes around me.

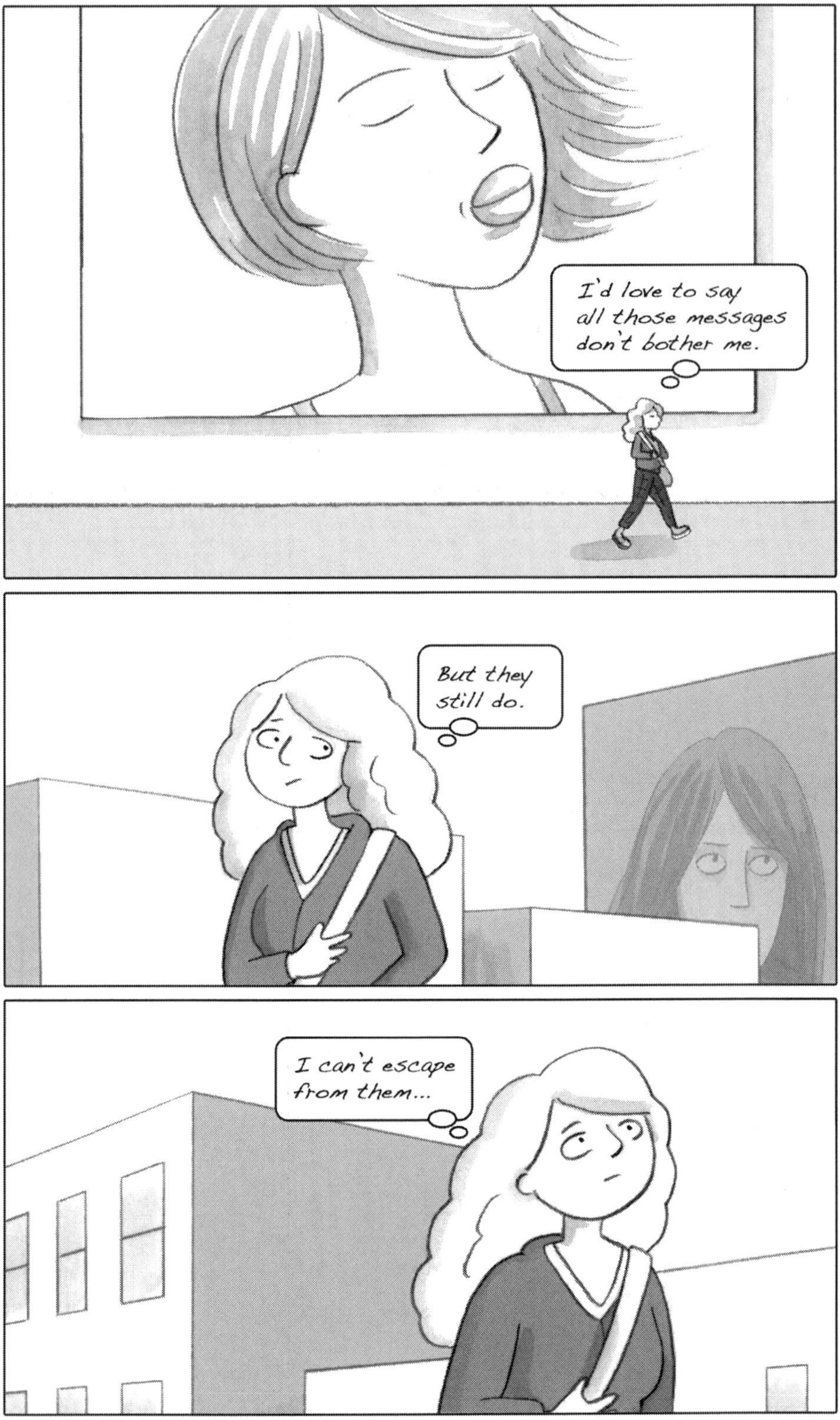
I'd love to say all those messages don't bother me.
But they still do.
I can't escape from them...

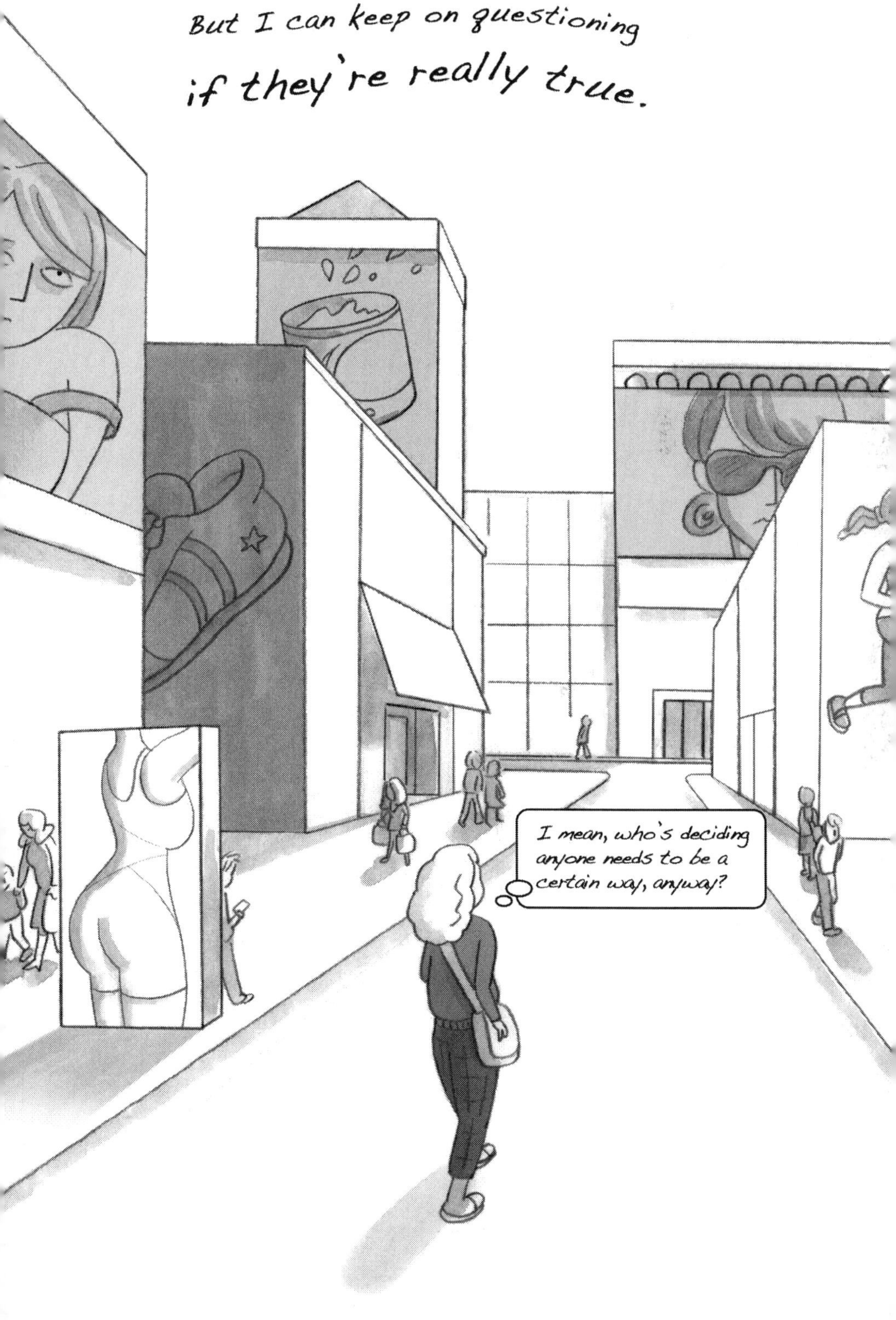
But I can keep on questioning
if they're really true.
I mean, who's deciding anyone needs to be a certain way, anyway?

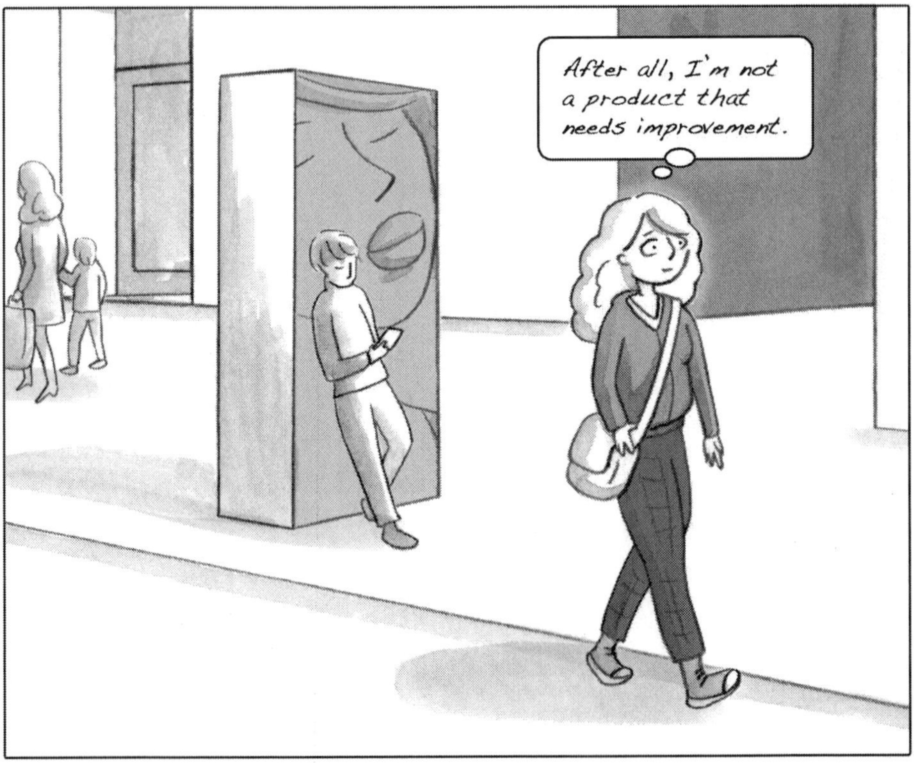
After all, I'm not a product that needs improvement.

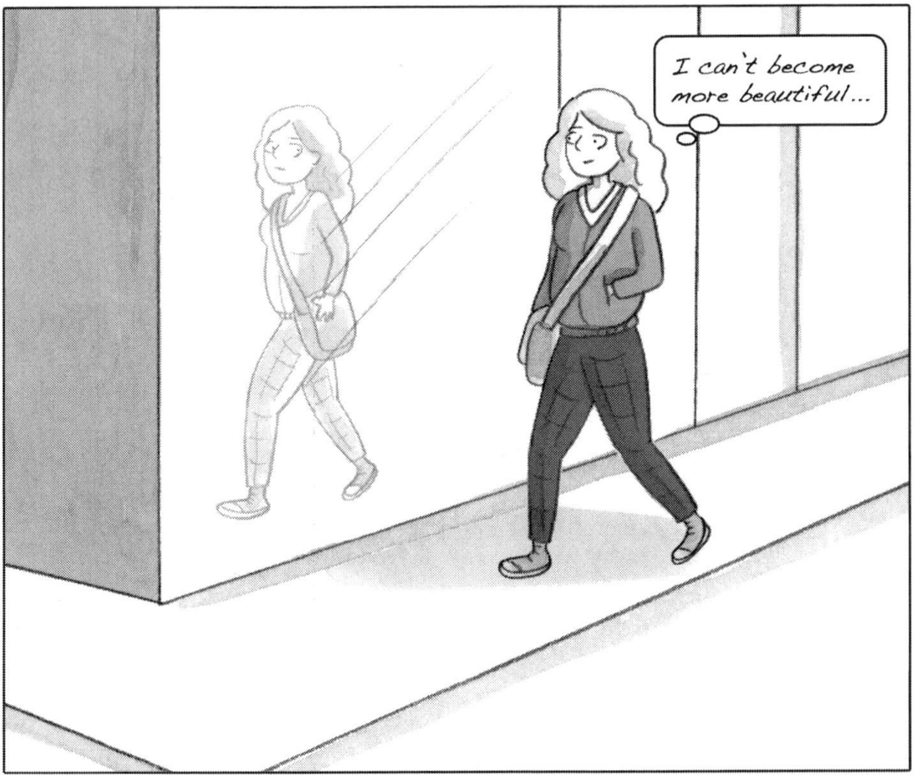
I can't become more beautiful...

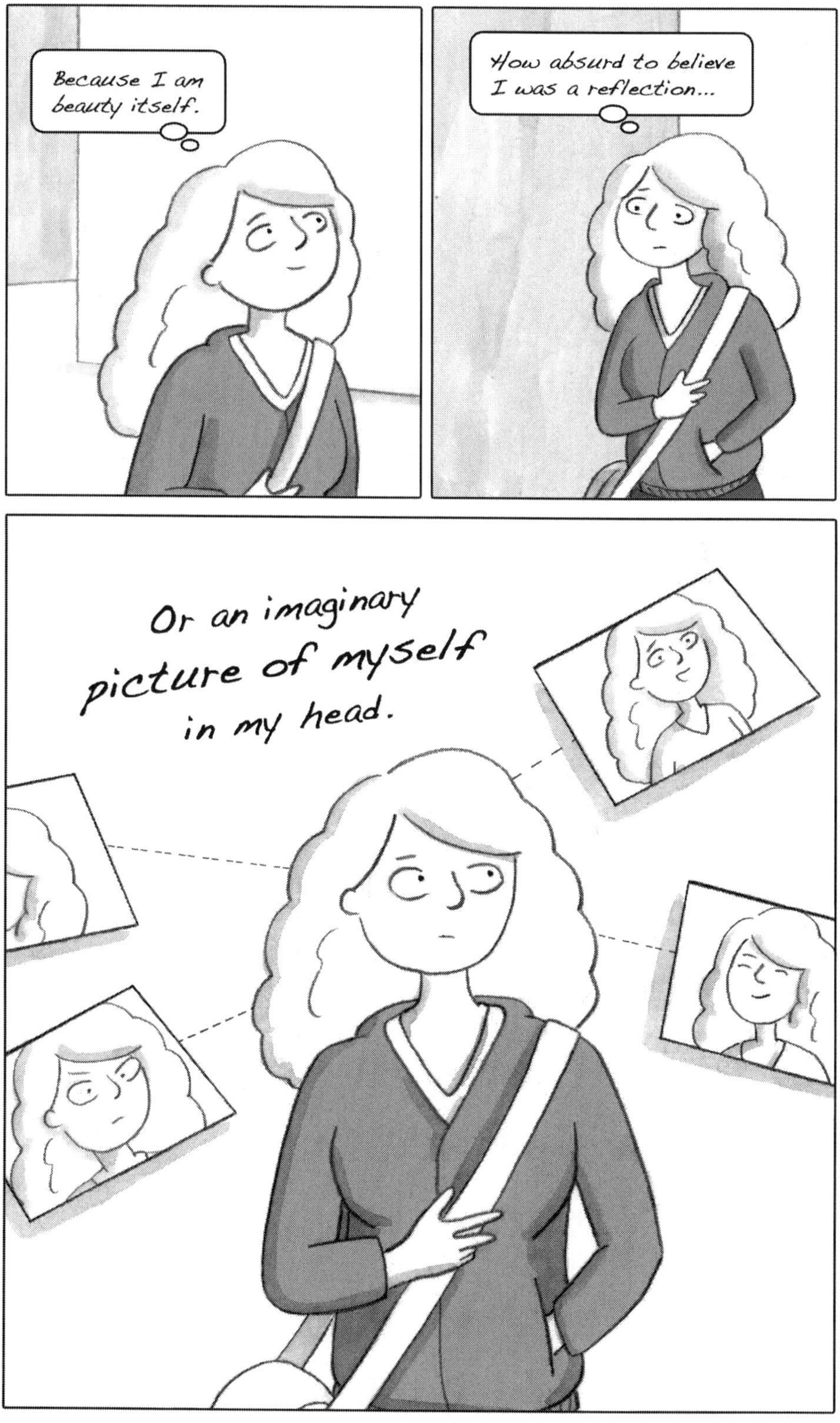
Because I am beauty itself.
How absurd to believe I was a reflection...
Or an imaginary picture of myself in my head.

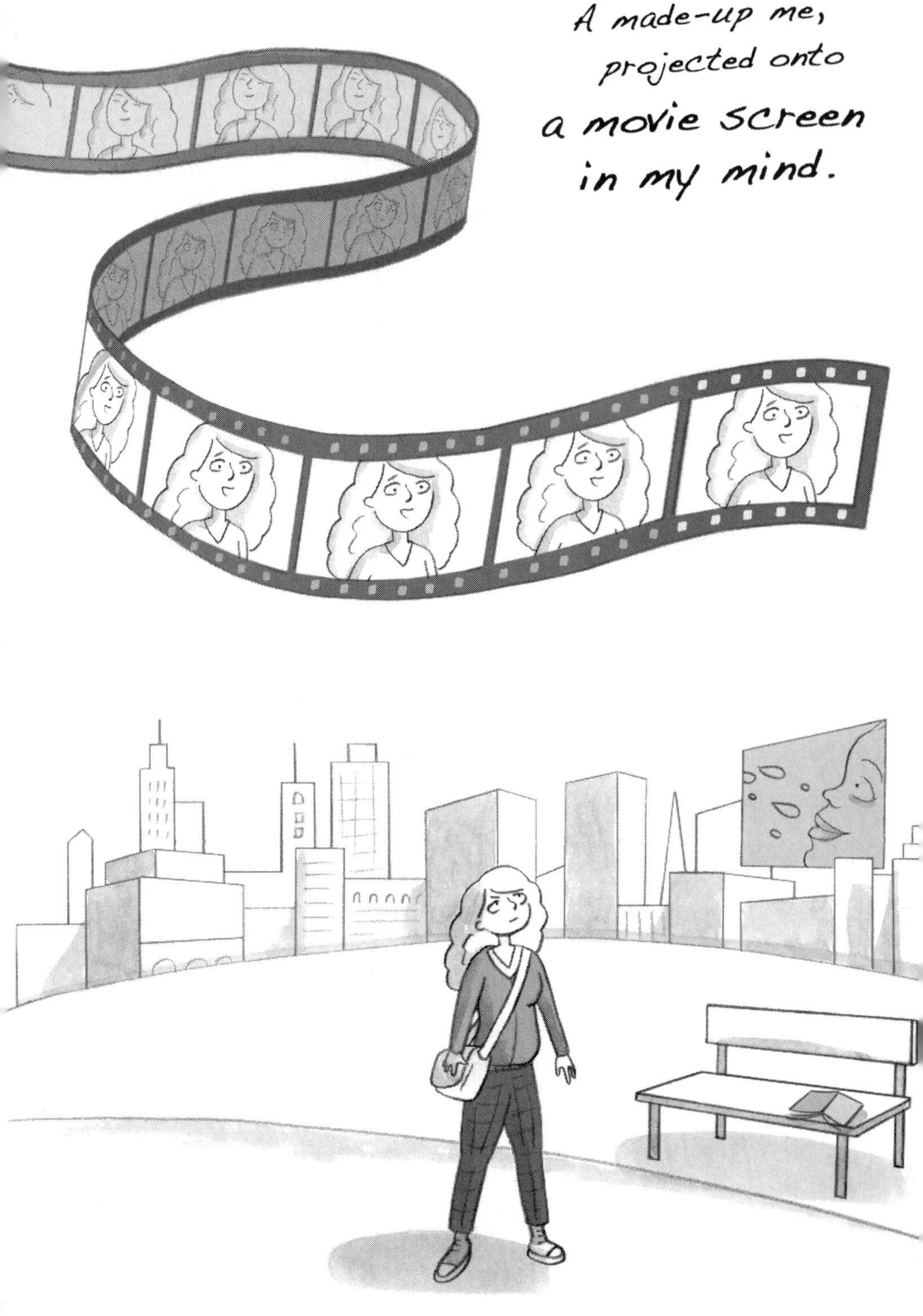
A made-up me,
projected onto
a movie screen
in my mind.

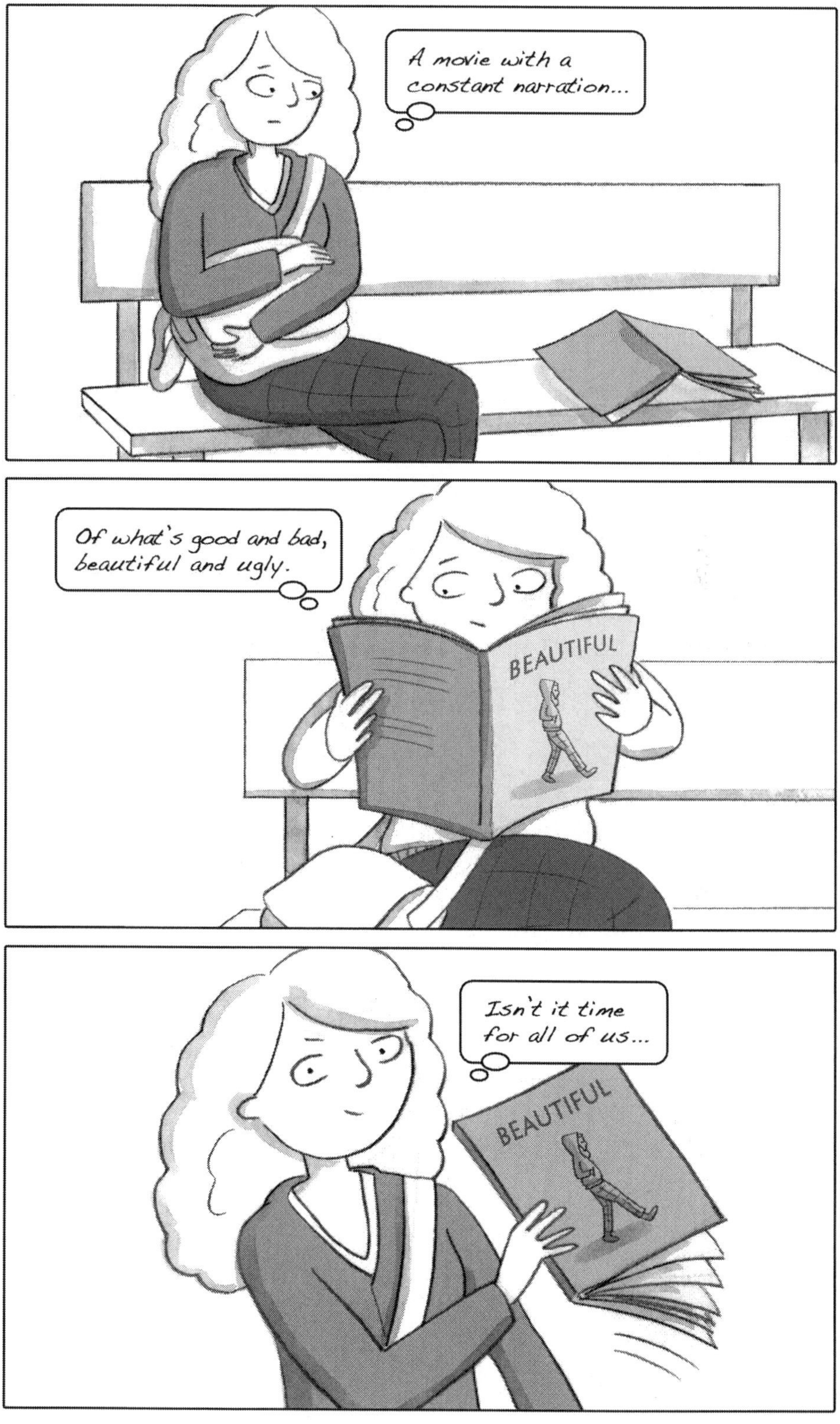
A movie with a constant narration...
Of what's good and bad, beautiful and ugly.
BEAUTIFUL
Isn't it time for all of us...
BEAUTIFUL

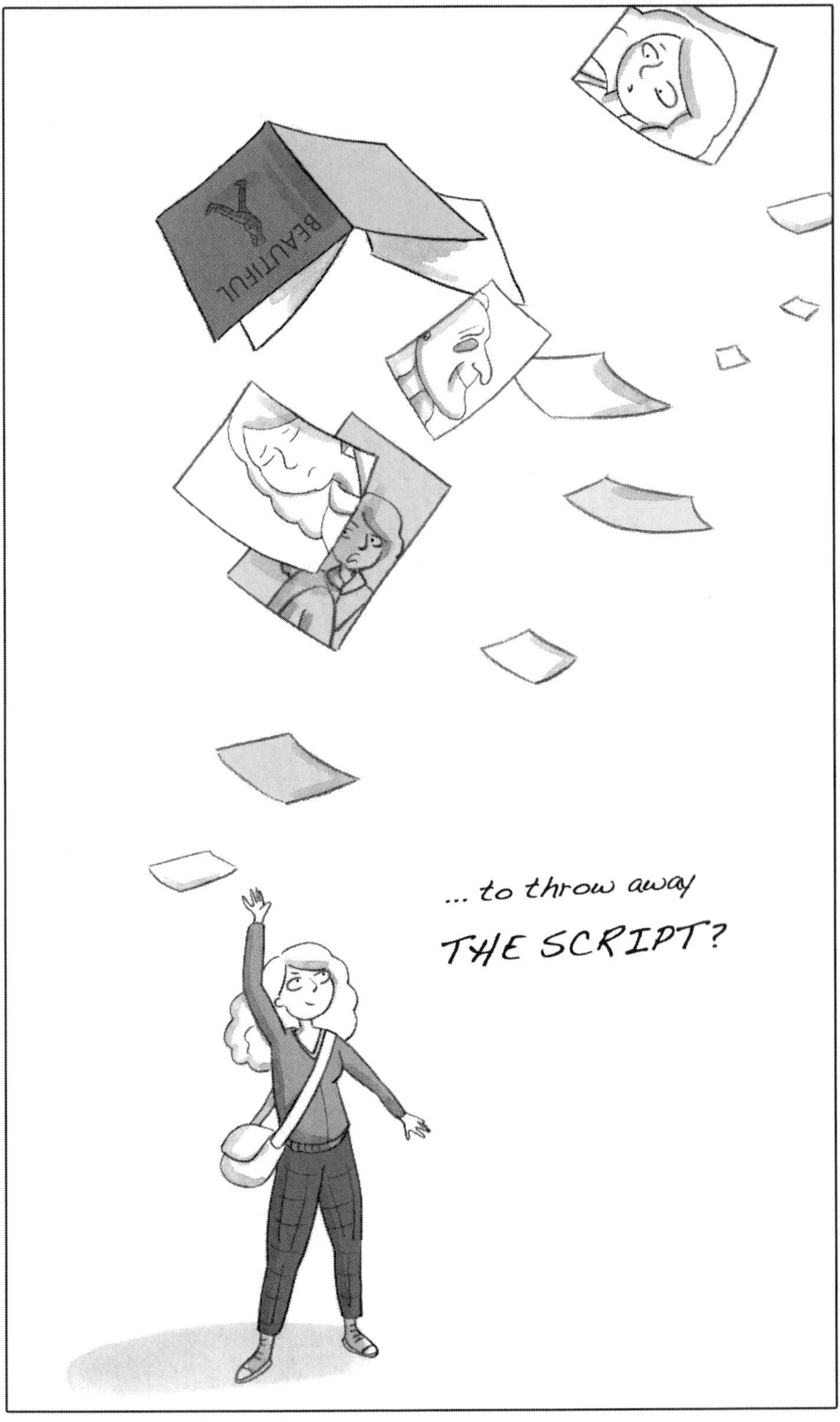
BEAUTIFUL
... to throw away
THE SCRIPT?

☆ ☆ ☆ ☆ ☆

DID YOU ENJOY THIS SERIES?
RATE IT ON AMAZON.COM

ABOUT THE AUTHOR

Marie D'Abreo likes to draw pictures, make up stories and sometimes even play a little music. She was born and raised in Sussex, England; studied art in Minneapolis; and now lives in San Francisco. She has a sticky-note on her mirror with a smiley face on it that says "Good Morning!"

THANKS

Thank you to my friends and colleagues who helped make the Beautiful Series a bit more beautiful. Libby for the round-the-clock calls. Karen for calling me her muse. Rhea for telling me I'm a feminist. Marcia for the dog therapy. Kristy, Renée, Lisa T, André, Chris O' and Nancy K for being fans. And Abigail, Lissa, Thorina, Mara, and Richard for the heartfelt encouragement. Their support and feedback along the way have been invaluable. And... a huge thank you to my family for always liking my drawings.

REFERENCES

The Stages of Grief segments, on pages 58, 70, 105, and 125, were adapted from the work of Elisabeth Kübler-Ross. The references to ancient history, on page 118, were inspired by the Crones Counsel.

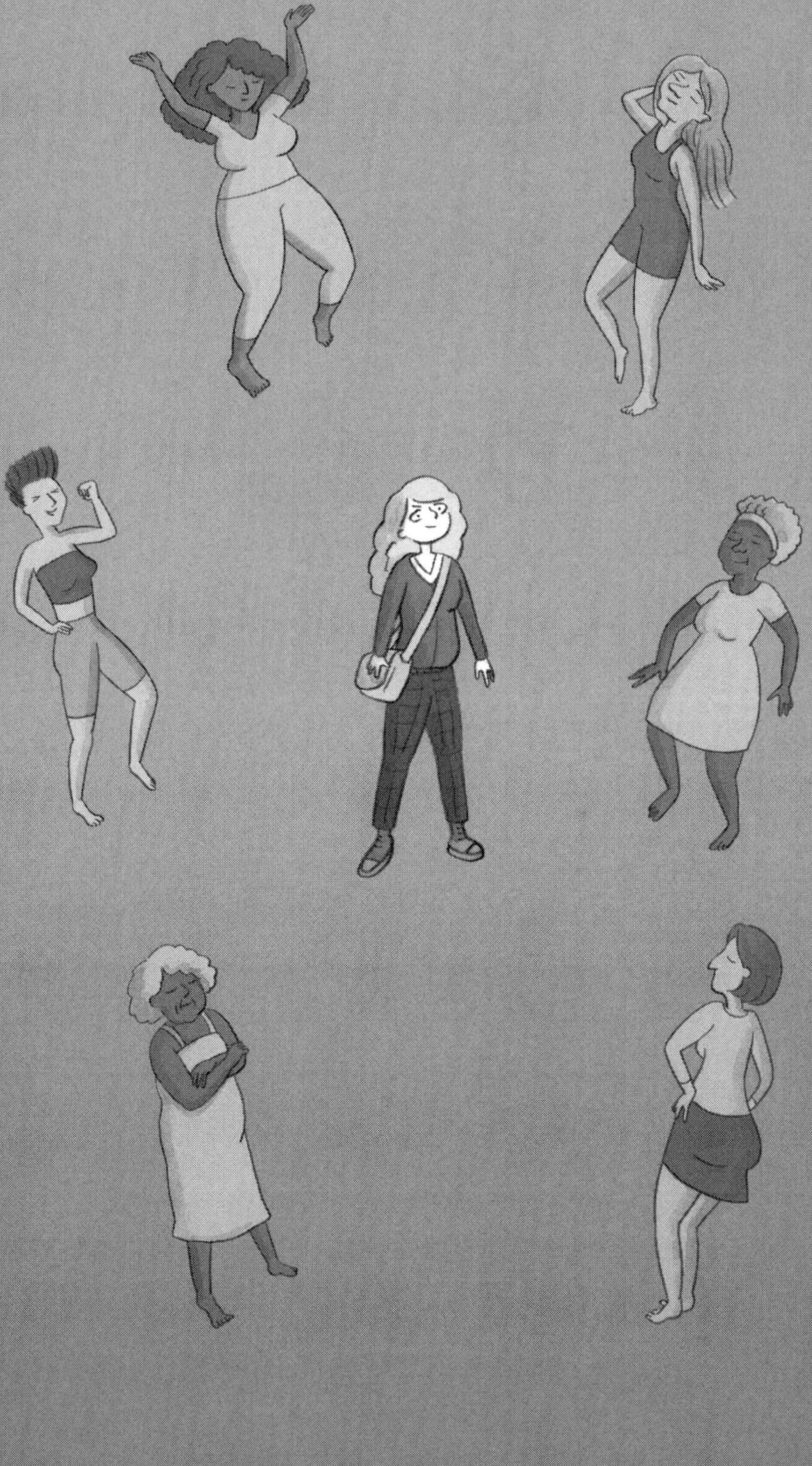

Made in the USA
San Bernardino, CA
19 February 2020